The Military History of Charles Xii. King of Sweden
by Gustavus Adlerfeld

Copyright © 2019 by HardPress

Address:
HardPress
8345 NW 66TH ST #2561
MIAMI FL 33166-2626
USA
Email: info@hardpress.net

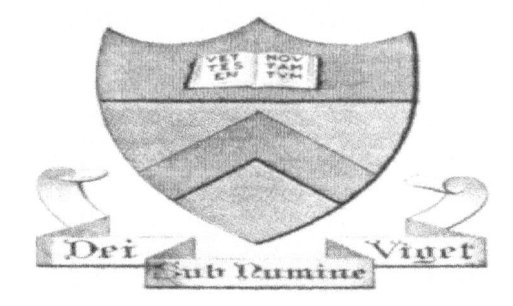

Library of
Princeton University.
In Memory of
Senator Frank O. Briggs
and Briggs Class of 1898

CHARLES XII King of S[weden]

Kraft pinxit Lundini Scanorum 1717.

THE
MILITARY HISTORY
OF
CHARLES XII.

King of SWEDEN,

Written by the expreſs Order of his Majeſty,

By M. *GUSTAVUS ADLERFELD*,

CHAMBERLAIN to the KING.

To which is added,

An exact Account of the Battle of *Pultowa*, with a JOURNAL of the KING's Retreat to *Bender*.

Illuſtrated with Plans of the Battles and Sieges.

Tranſlated into ENGLISH.

In THREE VOLUMES.

LONDON:

Printed for J. and P. KNAPTON in *Ludgate-ſtreet*; J. HODGES upon *London-Bridge*; A. MILLAR oppoſite to St. *Clement's* Church in the *Strand*; and J. NOURSE without *Temple-Bar*. 1740.

THE MILITARY HISTORY OF CHARLES XII.

King of SWEDEN.

Written by the express Order of his Majesty,

By M. *GUSTAVUS ADLERFELD*,

CHAMBERLAIN to the KING.

To which is added,

An exact Account of the Battle of *Pultowa*, with a JOURNAL of the KING's Retreat to *Bender*.

Illustrated with Plans of the Battles and Sieges.

Translated into ENGLISH.

VOL. I.

LONDON:

Printed for J. and P. KNAPTON in *Ludgate-Street*; J. HODGES upon *London-Bridge*; A. MILLAR opposite to St. *Clement*'s Church in the *Strand*; and J. NOURSE without *Temple-Bar*. 1740.

PREFACE,

From the FRENCH.

GUSTAVUS ADLERFELD, *the author of these Memoirs, and eldest child of* Charles Adlerfeld, *Treasurer or Controller of the Accounts to the Court of* Sweden, *was born in the year 1671, at a seat of his father's near* Stockholm: (*His grandfather had been Governor or Stadtholder of* Revel *in* Livonia:) *And, as he manifested an extraordinary genius in his earliest infancy, great care was taken to give it all the lustre of education.*

Nor did our young Gustavus *deceive the expectations that had been formed of him; but, on the contrary, made it appear they were perfectly well founded: the progress, which he made in learning, being so rapid, that he was soon qualified to be sent to the University of* Upsal; *where he applied himself with equal ardour and success to all the sciences that could adorn a Gentleman. History and Languages, both ancient and modern, were his chief delight, the last of which he learned with great assiduity. To these he joined the study of Heraldry and Genealogy, as thinking the knowledge of them absolutely necessary. He likewise judged, with great reason, that the Law of Nature and Nations was another principal accomplishment; and therefore*

PREFACE from the FRENCH.

therefore apply'd, with a very uncommon solicitude, to render himself a master of both: In all which elegant studies he became so early a proficient, that, in his twenty-second year, he gave the public the most convincing proofs of his great capacity, and the improvements it had received from letters, by a Latin *harangue* [a] *on the birth-day of* Charles XII. *then but heir apparent; which did him great honour, and was thought worthy of being printed* [b].

In the year 1693, *he likewise maintained, with abundance of applause, the Rational Theses on the Orders of Knighthood* [c], *according to the manner of the North; a little work, scarce, and much in request among the learned, because 'tis there only that a description of the ancient Military Orders of* Sweden *are to be found; it affords, beside, a grand Collection of Examples, to which is added the Plate, engraved by the famous antiquary* Elie Brenner.

Gustavus Adlerfeld, *having now finished his academic studies at home, began to think of extending his knowledge by travel; for which end he set out from* Stockholm, August 1. 1696, *and, after having seen the Court of* Denmark *at* Copenhagen, *and that of* Gottorp, *then residing at* Kiel, *he repaired to* Hamburgh, *from thence to the shining Court of* Berlin, *which he visited* en passant, *and proceeded on to* Hall in Saxony, *to study under the celebrated* Thomasius, *where having resided above a twelve-month, he set out for the* Hague, *towards the end of the year* 1697.

[a] In 1693.
[b] Which it was at *Upsal* the same year.
[c] *Equites, seu de Ordinibus* Equestribus disquisitio, præside Petro Lagerlof, *Historiograph. Regis & Prof. Ord.* Holmiæ, 1698. 4to. p. 67.

PREFACE from the FRENCH.

The treaty of Ryfwick *was then negotiating between the allies and* France, *under the mediation of* Sweden: *and our author waiting upon Mr. de* Lillieroth, *the Embaffador of that Crown, met with a moft gracious reception, and was afterwards employed by him, with fuccefs, in many fecret and delicate negotiations, as appears by the Memoirs left by Mr.* Adlerfeld, *now in the hands of his fon.*

Our author, having now vifited the principal cities in the Seven Provinces, and obferved every thing that could excite the curiofity of a traveller, fet out for Paris, *where he arrived* June 28, 1698, *and continued till the* 18th *of October, from which time he paffed through* Orleans, Blois, *and* Tours, *in his way to* Angers, *there to go through his exercifes; and from whence he did not return to* Paris *till the* 15th *of* February, 1699.

Being now defirous to make a vifit to England, *he left* Paris *a fecond time,* July 3, *to embark at* Havre, *and arrived at* London *the* 20th, *where having ftaid little more than a month, he returned, by the way of* Oftend, *to* Paris *the firft of* September *following; where he refided till* July *the* 12th, 1700, *and then took leave of that capital, in order to repair to* Aix la Chapelle.

Here having refolved on returning to his own country, he took the rout of Cologne, Hamburg, *and* Wifmar, *and arrived, at laft, at* Strahlfund, *where he embarked on board the fame yatcht with his late Serene Highnefs, then Duke-Regnant of* Schlefwig-Holftein, *brother-in-law of* Charles XII. *and Generaliffimo of the* Swedifh *armies in Germany,*

PREFACE from the FRENCH.

many, *and with whom he landed at* Tzelleborg *the 4th of* October.

The 10th, the Duke being arrived at Carlshaven, *when the King was on the point of marching through that place with his army into* Livonia, *Mr.* Adlerfeld *had leave to wait upon his Serene Highness, who introduced him himself to his Majesty. The King honoured him with a most gracious reception, declared him immediately to be his Gentleman, and ordered him, at the same time, to follow the Court: But, as he had many affairs to adjust, and the King's departure was too precipitate, he obtained his Majesty's permission to repair first to* Stockholm, *where he arrived the 26th, after an absence of four years and some months.*

It was easy to observe how greatly he was improved by his travels; which he had undertaken with no other view, but to enlarge his mind, and polish his manners, as well in the converse of the great world, as in the society of men of genius. In the Journal he has left of his Travels, he has not forgot to make mention of the favours he received at Paris *from the Marshal-Duke of* Berwick, *who, not content with inviting him frequently into his parties of pleasure, introduced him likewise to the most illustrious families both of the Court and City. He never spoke of that Nobleman, but with the highest praises and acknowledgments; who was, in truth, one of the most meritorious persons of his age. He set likewise a due value on the advantages he received from the company of Mess.* Despreaux, Cassini, Ozanam, Jaillot, Perrault, Bulteau, Hosier, Chevillard, *and* Sanson, *with the greatest part of whom he continued a correspondence by letter.*

These

PREFACE from the FRENCH.

These circumstances of his life do contribute greatly to the honour of his character: For to be intimate with persons of the first rank, both for merit and genius, argues the person so honoured to possess a large share of his own.

Having now adjusted his affairs, he prepared to follow the army, but was prevented by sickness till the following year 1701, *a little after the battle of* Duna. *In which interval, as he was, at all times, an enemy to sloth and idleness, he thought he could not employ himself better than in returning to his favourite studies, of History and Genealogies. It was then, likewise, that he formed his design of writing an exact Journal of the Campaigns of* Charles XII. *the first of which had been attended with such fortunate and illustrious success. This undertaking, though sufficiently laborious, did not, however, interfere with the researches he had already begun into the History of the antient and eminent Families of* Sweden; *of which his son has still preserved very ample collections, drawn from the originals themselves, and the most authentick authorities: and 'tis to be wish'd they may fall into the hands of some person, equally curious and capable, who would give himself the trouble of making a proper use of them, which would afford great lights into that part of the History of the* North, *hitherto very little known.*

In Courland, *our author joined the army of the King, who immediately received him into his good graces; and afterwards, when he was apprized of his design to compile the Journal above mentioned, and which he had already begun, his Majesty had the goodness not only to honour the plan of the work*

with

PREFACE from the FRENCH.

with his approbation, and encourage the author to proceed with it, but likewise to order his Council to furnish Mr. Adlerfeld with all the necessary Memoirs, State-Papers, &c. and his commanding Officers to communicate to him all their relations of Combats, Marches, Sieges, and Attacks by sea and land, that the series of his undertaking might be preserved, and the whole rendered as perfect as possible.

In return for all which signal instances of his Majesty's goodness, he endeavoured to distinguish, with the utmost exactness, whatever was worthy to be transmitted to posterity, either of his own knowledge, or of what could be selected from the most faithful and consistent accounts of others.

In the year 1704, the King, having for a while suspended the rapid progress of his victories, and being inclined to indulge his army with an interval of repose, gave leave to his Ministers and Generals to invite their Ladies to Hielsberg in Prussia; of which our author likewise took advantage, and, during his residence at that city, married Madamoiselle de Steben [a], who came there to meet him, and to whom he was contracted at Wismar in the year 1700.

During his Majesty's continuance in Saxony, Madam Adlerfeld repaired thither to visit her husband; and, as she was a Lady of great wit, and writ well in several languages, she undertook to make an Abridgment of his Journal, in German,

---

[a] She was the daughter of Mr. *de Steben*, descended from a noble family in *Franconia*, and then Commissary-General at War. He was Counsellor to the Regency of *Bremen* and *Verden* when he died, 1714.

PREFACE from the FRENCH.

to the King's Entrance into Saxony: *This she finished under the inspection of the author, and, at her return to* Wismar, *published it at her own expence. But, though that performance was greatly esteemed*, and was really worthy the approbation of the public, it met with the fate commonly attendant on works published by the author, which almost always meet with a bad sale, whatever their deserts may be: Beside, a great number of copies, that were destined for* Sweden, *were lost at sea, and contributed not a little to render it exceeding scarce in a very short time.*

When the King left Saxony, *in order to return into* Poland, *Mr.* Adlerfeld *never quitted his Majesty, whose favour he had now the honour to possess entirely; all which time he continued his Journal on the same plan he first began with; and with so rigid an exactness, that it appears from the manuscript he even worked upon it the very night before the fatal battle of* Pultowa, *where he was killed with a cannon-ball by the side of his Majesty's litter.*

As the illustrious family of our author was remarkably distinguished in the reign of Charles XII. *and still enjoys honourable employments, we believe the public will receive with pleasure certain circumstances regarding his brothers.*

---

* The learned Mr. *Seltmans*, in the Preface to the second tome of his History of *Charles* XII. published in *German* at *Hall* in *Saxony*, 1719 and 1720, in two volumes, *Octavo*, acknowledges the great use he made of it, and regretted exceedingly, that it came to his knowledge so late; a circumstance greatly in favour of the Journal we now publish entire, with all the circumstantial relations of the Generals themselves.

PREFACE from the FRENCH.

Charles Adlerfeld, *born in* 1676, *having first finished his studies, repaired to the army, where he was made Gentleman of the Court; after which he attached himself solely to the service of King* Stanislaus, *upon the coronation of that Prince at* Warsaw *in the year* 1705; *who first made him his Chamberlain, then Marshal, and lastly Grand-Marshal of his Court: in acknowledgment of which favours he rendered his Royal Master several important services, in sundry negotiations, in which he was employed, especially in* France, *till the year* 1720, *when he was recalled by the present King of* Sweden, *who had also honoured him with the office of Grand-Marshal of his Court. He died in* Sweden *in* December 1722, *greatly regretted by all those who were acquainted with his fine accomplishments. But no body was more sensible of his loss than King* Stanislaus, *who had ever given him such testimonies of his friendship and confidence, knowing how well he deserved them, as are alone sufficient to eternize his memory; though it had not been so notorious, that he possessed in a very eminent degree every advantage both of mind and body, and that, beyond all, he was well grounded in Religion, and had high notions of Honour and Probity.*

The second of our author's brothers was Peter Adlerfeld, *born in* 1680, *who, chusing a martial life, followed* Charles XII. *in all his battles from the year* 1700, *when the* Swedes *invaded* Zealand. *In the year* 1712 *he was made a Colonel, the night before the battle of* Gadebusch, *in which he behaved with so much bravery, at the head of his regiment, that even Count* Stenbock *himself acknowledged he contributed not a little to the obtaining the victory. After the death of* Charles XII. *the Queen of* Sweden, *now reigning, made him a*

Major-

PREFACE from the FRENCH.

Major-General and Baron, and sent him into Denmark, where the peace was concluded in 1721. *He was then ordered to* Strahlsund, *to take possession of* Pomerania, *which Mr.* de Wiche *ceded to him in behalf of his Danish Majesty. Being returned to* Copenhagen, *he resided there in quality of Envoy till the year* 1726, *when he took leave of the Court of* Denmark *to return to* Sweden. *As he was Governor of* Malmo, *he made it the place of his abode, together with his family, till the last Diet of* 1739, *when he was elevated to the dignity of a Senator of the Kingdom, and a Member of the Chancery-Royal.*

The third brother of our author called Charles-Albrecht Adlerfeld, *likewise took to arms, in which he appeared with distinction, having followed* Charles XII. *in all his campaigns, and even into* Turkey ; *who held him in great esteem, and ranked him among the bravest Foot-Officers in his service. He was killed in* 1715, *in the affair of* Stresau, *in the isle of* Rugen, *being then one of the oldest Captains of the Guards.*

We are here strongly tempted to do justice to the son of our author ; the obligation he has conferred upon the public, by the pains he has taken to translate this book of his father's, and render it fit for the press, deserves, at least, some acknowledgment : But, as his modesty will not permit us to expatiate on his merit and accomplishments, we shall content ourselves with inserting some circumstances of his life, which may one day be of service to those, who may be at liberty to undertake what we are forbid.

Charles

PREFACE from the FRENCH.

Charles Maximilian Emanuel Adlerfeld *was born at* Wismar *in* 1706, *and in* 1714 *was sent to* Deux-Ponts, *where King* Staniflaus *then made his residence. Here his uncle* Charles Adlerfeld *had him educated with abundance of care, and in* 1717 *took him along with him to* Paris: *After whose death, in* 1722, *he entered into the service of* Holstein. *In* 1725 *he repaired to* Vienna, *to officiate as Secretary to the Embassy; and for these eight years has waited on the Hereditary Prince, now Duke of* Holstein, *in quality of Gentleman of his Bedchamber*, &c.

Believing all these particulars deserved a place in this Preface, we could not excuse ourselves from making known to the reader, by some historical features, the illustrious family of Mr. Adlerfeld, *author of the work we are now to give an account of.*

Never work run a greater risque of being lost than this, it being preserved by little less than a miracle, in the manner following. In the month of March, 1703, *Prince* Maximilian Emanuel de Wirtemberg *repaired to* Charles XII. *at* Warsaw, *in order to enter into his service. He was accompanied by the Baron* de Voit, *Privy Counsellor to the Margrave of* Anspach, *and, after the departure of that Minister, the King conferred the care of the person and affairs of this young Hero on our author.*

Mr. Adlerfeld *was still in the service of the Prince of* Wirtemberg, *when he was killed at the battle of* Pultowa. *The Prince himself had the misfortune to be taken prisoner that fatal day; all his baggage likewise fell into the hands of the enemy,*

together

PREFACE from the FRENCH.

together with a part of Mr. Adlerfeld's; among which was this very manuscript, from that time believed to be lost; but, happily, the Prince of Wirtemberg was set at liberty by order of the Czar, and all his baggage restored, to which was added what belonged to our author. Upon the death of that Prince [f] *the manuscript was sent to Stutgard, and, some time after, put into the custody of Mr. Charles Adlerfeld, who dying in 1722, it was given to our author's only son.*

Nor could the work fall into better hands; Mr. Adlerfeld gladly undertaking to translate it into French *from the* Swedish *original; and it may be safely affirmed, he has acquitted himself with all possible fidelity and exactness. Without doubt he might have rendered it more entertaining to the reader, if he had contented himself with selecting the most curious and alarming passages, according to the example of Mr.* de Voltaire, *in the history of his Hero: But then he had forfeited his character of a Translator, and consequently omitted a great number of instructive narrations and interesting particulars, which abundance of persons will always read with pleasure.*

As to the style, the editor has made but a very few alterations, and those of very little importance,

---

[f] This Hero, worthy of a longer life, died of a burning fever in the flower of his age at *Dubno* in *Poland*, ann. 1709. upon his return from *Russia*. Mr. *Bardili*, who had followed that Prince through all his perils, and who is at present an eminent Prelate at *Herberstieg* in the Dutchy of *Wirtemberg*, has published his Memoirs at *Stutgard* in 1730. This work, which is written in *German*, and published in one volume 8-vo, contains many most curious and authentick particulars relating to the life of *Charles* XII.

PREFACE from the FRENCH.

as being persuaded, that a work of this nature, which is purely instructive, and wholly in the manner of a Journal, had no need of the usual ornaments bestowed on more florid discourses. It was at first proposed to retrench a great number of the terms and expressions; but, in consulting Mr. Adlerfeld, it was determined to follow his advice, and leave the translation in a manner as we found it; it being his desire, that even the word Valoches should be uniformly preserved instead of Valaques, which it was proposed to substitute in its stead; and for this he gave such convincing reasons, that we could not avoid coming over to his opinion.

We ought not to omit repeating here, that this work, abounding with anecdotes and curious particulars, was composed only from the authentick relations of Generals and other Officers; and that our author was himself an eye-witness of most of the events he recounts.

Of so many writers which have treated of the campaigns of Charles XII. and undertook to give us a history of that Hero of the North, there is none to be so much depended upon as this. Charles, who knew the great abilities of our author, and his zeal for his service, setting a very particular value upon it. How much is it to be regretted, that Mr. de Voltaire has not proceeded on such faithful and exact memoirs as these! His History of Charles XII. which is with great reason esteemed a master-piece, had then been complete. As to the Sieur de la Motraye, who busies himself to criticise on Mr. de Voltaire, his Memoirs only serve to confound the reader, and point out his own mistakes, which are to be met with in greater abundance, than those he attributes to his antagonist.

The

PREFACE from the FRENCH.

The work is divided into four Tomes, the three first of which contain the History of the Life and Military Exploits of Charles XII. *from the birth of that Prince to the battle of* Pultowa, *which happened in* 1709, *and in which our author was killed; and the fourth contains, first, a Narration of that Battle, which has a just title to be esteemed a most curious piece, as containing abundance of circumstances not to be met with any where else, and coming from the hand of an Officer of great merit, who chuses not to be known; and who has rendered it yet so much the more interesting, by inserting in it a series of Reflections on the true Motives which induced* Charles XII. *to attack* Russia *on the side of the* Ukrain. *The public is likewise obliged to the son of our author for the translation of this piece. A Journal of the King's retreat, after the loss of that battle, closes this last volume, which was sent from* Bender *by the first Courier that his Majesty dispatched: This little tract was circulated in manuscript, till such time as one* Samuel Heyl, *a bookseller of* Hamburgh, *thought proper to print it; and if he had kept strictly to the original, the public would have been obliged to him for it: But, finding it too short for a Pamphlet in* octavo, *he took it into his head to set a miserable Hackney-writer to eke it out with several circumstances of his own invention, and, that the Marvellous might not be wanting, threw in a fabulous description of a desart, through which his Majesty passed*[z]. *The*

---

[z] We read there, for example, that the King's retinue were forced to support themselves for some time with nutmegs, which they found there in abundance. All which did not hinder its being reprinted in 1730, as it at first appear'd, at the end of the Memoirs of the Duke of *Wirtemberg*, before mentioned.

translator

PREFACE from the FRENCH.

translator finding himself obliged last summer to consult Mr. le Baron de Neugebauer[h], on the subject of that retreat, he had the goodness to examine, together with him, the printed account, to strike out the falshoods, insert several interesting truths, and in fine reduce it from Romance to History; upon which alterations and corrections, that which we now present to the public is founded.

It remains for us to add a word or two, of the accurate portrait of Charles XII. and the several plans wherewith this work is enriched. In the year 1717, our Hero consented to sit for his picture, not being able to resist the pressing solicitations and tender prayers of Madam Royal his sister, now Queen of Sweden. At their interview at Wadstena in Ostrogothia, Kraft, a celebrated Painter, acquitted himself on this occasion like a master: But the King was so displeased with the exact resemblance, that he cut out the face with his pen-knife; notwithstanding which, Kraft immediately so well restored it to its place, that the seam was hardly discernible.

As the late Duke of Holstein was then at Lunden, he made it his business to procure a copy of this piece by the same hand, which is in no respect inferior to the original, still preserved in Sweden in the possession of his Excellency Count Charles Gyllenbourg, Senator, and President of the Chancery-Council. The Print before us is taken from that copied for the Duke of Holstein, and, to the

[h] This Minister is at present Chancellor to his *Swedish* Majesty at *Strahlsund* in *Pomerania*. He accompanied *Charles* XII. in his retreat into *Turkey*, and was the first Minister he sent to the *Porte* after he was arrived near *Oczakow*.

honour

PREFACE from the FRENCH.

honour of the Engraver it may be said, that 'tis not possible for any body to succeed better, either with regard to the beauties of the piece in itself, or its perfect likeness to the original.

This is sufficient for the History of the Portrait [1]; and as to the Plans of the Sieges and battles inserted in the work, the translator received them from Mr. Wolff, *Gentleman to the Duke of* Holstein, *and son of the late Major-General of that name, an accomplished Engineer, and some time Governor of* Tonningue, *who had made a noble and large collection of pieces of this nature, all designed by his own hand.*

[1] To which add the verses made by Mr. *Ronnow Dubler* on the Portrait of this Prince, which are to be found in Vol. III. p. 280, &c. *seq.*

Just Published,
By J. NOURSE *at the* Lamb *without* Temple-Bar,
(Price 2 *s.* 6 *d.*)

The FOURTH EDITION, *with Additions, of*

A Practical ENGLISH GRAMMAR, describing the Genius and Nature of the *English* Tongue, &c. To which is prefixed, An Account of the Rise and Progress of the *English* Language.

By JAMES GREENWOOD,
Late Sur-Master of St. *Paul*'s School.

N. B. The Author, in his Preface, acknowledges his Obligations to several eminent and learned Gentlemen; and particularly to the late Reverend and Learned Dr. *Samuel Clarke,* Rector of St. *James*'s; as also to the Reverend and Learned Dr. *Daniel Waterland*; who assisted him with their Corrections of the whole Work.

A Character of this Grammar by the Rev. Dr. Isaac Wats.

" Those who have a mind to inform themselves of the
" Genius and Composition of our Language, either in the
" original Derivation of it, or in the present Use and Prac-
" tice, must consult such Treatises as are written on pur-
" pose; among which I know none equal to that Essay to-
" wards a Practical *English* Grammar, by Mr. *James Green-*
" *wood*; wherein he has shewn the deep Knowledge, with-
" out the haughty Airs, of a Critick.

Where may be had, Price 1 s. 6 d.

The ROYAL ENGLISH GRAMMAR, by the same Author, design'd for the Use of Schools; being an Abstract of his larger Work. The Historical Preface and all the Critical Notes are left out.

THE LIFE and HISTORY OF CHARLES XII. KING of SWEDEN.

THERE have been few Princes, whose lives have abounded with more remarkable and more extraordinary events, than that of CHARLES XII. Every thing is striking in the history of this Hero; whether we consider his actions in private life, or those which he performed at the head of armies. Every particular in his expeditions is interesting, and capable of fixing the public attention.

We have here undertaken to give a representation of the Campaigns of this Prince, and with that view to enter into a very exact detail, omitting no circumstance of any consequence. There are two things which we imagine will recommend this work to the reader, namely, that it was writ by the order of his Majesty, and composed from the most authentick relations of the Generals who serv'd under him.

In order to give the world the most perfect comprehension of whatever concerns this Prince, we think ourselves obliged to go back to his birth, to say something of his education, and of what passed during his minority, together with the manner in which he first ascended the throne. These points will conduct us naturally to his first exploits in this bloody war wherein he engaged, and of which we shall lay open the original springs and causes.

Charles XI. King of *Sweden*, married, in 1680, *Ulric Eleonora*, daughter of *Frederick* III. King of *Denmark*. Of this marriage, on the [a] seventeenth of *June*, 1682, our Hero, to whom they gave the name of *Charles*, was born. He was immediately placed under the care of the Countess of *Bielke*, widow of the Treasurer of *Sweden*. When he was taken out of her hands, the Count of [b] *Lindshiold* was made his Governor, to whom succeeded the Count of *Gylenstolpe*. Mr. *de Nordenhielm* was fixed upon for his Preceptor. Baron *Stuart*, who was afterwards made a Lieutenant General, had the charge assigned him of teaching him the Mathematicks, particularly what belonged to Fortification. All these endeavour'd to emulate each other in improving the talents of their illustrious disciple. As soon as his age permitted him to follow his father, the King took him every year to those reviews of his troops, which he used to make in several places about his capital; and it was on these occasions, that the very extraordinary genius of this young Prince for war discover'd itself [c].

In

---

[a] The twenty seventh, according to Mr. *Voltaire*.

[b] Monf. *de Nordcopenter* was his first Governor. *Voltaire*.

[c] Mr. *Voltaire* gives us the following account: 'The first book he read was the work of *Samuel Puffendorff*, which was intended to give him an early insight into his own estates and those of his neighbours. He soon learnt

King Charles XII. of Sweden.

In 1693 he lost the Queen his mother, an

' learnt the *High Dutch*,
' which he spoke as perfect-
' ly as his mother-tongue.
' At seven years old he could
' manage his horse. The
' violent exercises in which
' he delighted, and which
' discover'd his martial in-
' clinations, form'd him ear-
' ly a vigorous constitution,
' capable of supporting the
' fatigues into which his dis-
' position hurried him. Tho'
' he was in his youth of a
' gentle temper, he had an
' invincible obstinacy. The
' only means to bend him,
' was, to nettle him with
' Honour: by the bare men-
' tion of Glory you might
' obtain any thing of him.
' He had an aversion for *La-*
' *tin*; but as soon as he was
' told, that the Kings of *Po-*
' *land* and *Denmark* under-
' stood it, he learnt it imme-
' diately, and retain'd enough
' to talk it all the rest of his
' life. The same methods
' were taken to bring him
' to the understanding the
' *French*; but he obstinately
' declined speaking it, even
' to those *French* Ambassa-
' dors who understood no
' other languages. As soon
' as he had attained some
' knowledge in the *Latin*, he
' was set to translate *Quintus*
' *Curtius*, a book for which
' he had a greater relish on
' account of the subject, than
' the style. His Preceptor,
' on explaining this author,

' asked him, *What he thought*
' *of* Alexander? *I think,* an-
' swer'd the Prince, *that I*
' *should be glad to resemble*
' *him.* But, replied the Pre-
' ceptor, *he lived no longer*
' *than to the age of thirty two.*
' *Ah!* said the Prince, *is not*
' *that sufficient, when one has*
' *conquered kingdoms?* When
' the King his father heard
' of these answers, he cried
' out, *This boy will not only*
' *exceed me, but the great* Gus-
' tavus *himself.* One day, as
' he was amusing himself in
' the King's apartment with
' the plan of a town of *Hun-*
' *gary,* taken by the *Turks*
' from the Emperor, and
' another of *Riga* the capital
' of *Livonia,* a province con-
' quered in the last age by
' the *Swedes,* he observed
' written at the bottom of
' the plan of the *Hungarian*
' town these words, taken
' from the book of *Job*; *The*
' *Lord gave, the Lord hath*
' *taken away, blessed be the*
' *name of the Lord.* The
' Prince having read these
' words, took a pencil, and
' wrote at the bottom of the
' plan of *Riga*, *God hath given*
' *it me, and the Devil shall*
' *not take it away from me.*
' Thus in the most indiffe-
' rent actions of his infancy
' several flashes of his invin-
' cible nature shone forth,
' denoting what he would
' one day be.

The LIFE *and* HISTORY *of*

incomparable Princess, whose memory is to this day dear to the whole nation. Mr. *de Nordenhielm* died soon after, whose place was filled up by Count *de Polus*, Counsellor of the Chancery, who was chosen with a view of forming in the young Prince a taste for State matters, not discontinuing at the same time his other studies.

The King dying the fifth of *April*, 1697, the Queen Dowager, grandmother of the young King, and widow to *Charles Gustavus*, was declared Regent of the kingdom during the Prince's minority, which disposition *Charles* XI. had made by his will. The Regent had five Senators to form her council, amongst whom the regulation of foreign affairs was allotted to Count *Benedict Oxenstierna*, first Minister and Chancellor; Count *Gyllenstierna* had the charge of the land army; the conduct of the marine affairs was given to Count *de Wreed*; the administration of justice to Count *Gyllenstolpe*; and Count *Wallenstedt* was made superintendant of the finances and of commerce.

The first cares of the Regency were employed about the making of a peace in *Europe*. At the beginning of the year all the contending powers had offered to make the late King mediator. After this Prince's death, *Denmark* would have stoln this honour from *Sweden*. It was apparently with this view, that *Christian* V. sent Messieurs *de Plessen* and *de Lente* to the *Hague* in quality of his Plenipotentiaries. This endeavour was ineffectual. The late King had already deputed thither Count *de Lillieroth* with the character of Ambassador, who knew so well how to conduct affairs, that these ministers only spent their money, without having any share in the important negotiation.

To

King CHARLES XII. *of* SWEDEN.

To aſſiſt Mr. *de Lillieroth*, the Regency thought proper to aſſociate with him the Count *de Bond*, Senator of the King, who was not able to ſet out till the end of *Auguſt*. At his arrival at *Hamburgh* he learnt, that the peace had been concluded at *Ryſwick* between *France*, *England*, and *Holland*, the 26th of *September*, 1697. The concluſion of this peace was owing to the induſtry of Mr. *de Lillieroth*.

The peace between the Emperor, *France*, and *Spain* was not yet perfected. As this was to be labour'd by the Count *de Bond*, he haſtened his journey, and at his arrival at the *Hague* ſet all his engines at work, in conjunction with Mr. *de Lillieroth*, to bring this affair to a concluſion. The peace was ſoon after made between theſe powers, but not to the ſatisfaction of the mediators; who, far from ſigning it, proteſted againſt all that had paſſed, aſſerting, that the King their maſter could not be guarantee of a peace ſo little conformable to that of *Weſtphalia*, which ſhould have been its baſis. Beſides which, other difficulties aroſe to obſtruct the ſigning it. The Imperial Miniſters diſputed the precedence with the mediators, who would not conſent to give up a right which they imagined to belong to them.

Whilſt *Sweden* was ſo warmly employed concerning the pacification of *Europe*, the King of *Denmark* was willing to take an advantage of the minority of *Charles* XII. to oppreſs *Frederick* Duke of *Schleſwich-Holſtein*, who had enter'd into ſtrict engagements with the crown of *Sweden*. As the differences which had ſo long continued between thoſe two branches of the houſe of *Oldenbourg*; the Royalty of *Denmark*, and the Dutchy of *Holſtein*, gave riſe to that war which we are going to treat of, it will not be foreign to our purpose to give the reader some small idea thereof; nor can we employ a little time better, than in disclosing the original of all those wars, which have produced such very extraordinary events.

It would be however very useless to enter here into a long detail of those things which are already known to the whole world, as well by history, as from a great number of writings published on this occasion: we will confine ourselves therefore to a few remarks, which have appeared to us of too important a nature to be passed over in silence. The eldest branch, or the family royal, have always disputed with the Dukes of *Holstein* [a] any acts of sovereignty in the Dutchy of *Schleswich*, which they imagined belonged to them, especially since the peace of *Roschild*, 1658, where that Dutchy was fully adjudged to them. This quarrel nevertheless was renewed in succeeding times with more animosity than ever; at last matters were carried so far, that after the battle of *Fehr-bellin* the Court of *Denmark* caused Duke *Christian Albertus* to be put under arrest at *Rendsbourg*, a *Danish* fortress.

This happened in 1675; they then obliged the Duke, by an act extorted from him, to renounce all the rights which he had ever enjoy'd;

---

[a] *Christian* III[d]. King of *Denmark*, out of a surprising affection for his brother *Adolphus*, divided with him the Dutchies of *Holstein-Gottorp* and *Schleswich*, and decreed that the descendants of *Adolphus* should govern *Holstein* jointly with the Kings of *Denmark*, which two Dutchies should belong to them in common; and that the King of *Denmark* should make no innovation in *Holstein* without the consent of the Duke, nor the Duke without that of the King. This was the source of those quarrels, which afterwards arose between the Royal and Ducal branches of that house; the former aiming at oppression, and the latter at independency.

they

they difarm'd his troops, and put *Danish* garrifons into all his towns and fortreffes. This magnanimous Prince chofe rather to abandon his country, than to lead a difguftful life at the difcretion of his enemies: he retired to *Hamborough*, where he remain'd till the peace of *Fountainbleau*, 1679, by which he was replaced in full poffeffion of his eftates, and all the rights of fovereignty, as before.

This apparent tranquillity was of fhort duration. New troubles arofe in 1684. *Sweden, England, Holland,* and the Dukes of *Lunenbourg* interefted themfelves in favour of the Duke. Negotiations were opened in 1687, and a peace concluded two years after at *Altena*. People flatter'd themfelves (of which indeed there was great appearance) that this peace would thenceforth have fettled all difficulties, and have put a final end to an unhappy difunion, which had fo long exifted between the two illuftrious branches of the houfe of *Oldenbourg*.

The Duke of *Holftein* obtained by that peace a perfect liberty of levying troops within a certain number, and of building places of force; on condition nevertheless, that he fhould raife none to the prejudice of *Denmark*. The confequences made it appear, that this court, ftung with the neceffity in which fhe faw herfelf reduced to give way to the times, hath always taken advantage of this claufe, when the fituation of affairs hath been favourable to her defigns, pretending, that the Duke took every occafion to give her new matters of complaint.

But this grew much worfe, when *Frederick* IV. Duke of *Holftein* fucceeded his father in 1694; the affair then began to blaze forth again more than ever. The powers, who had guaranteed the execution of the treaty of *Altena*, took the weaker part, and prevented the King of *Denmark* from coming to hostilities. They proposed to him the method of negotiation, to which this Prince consented with reluctance. *Pinnenberg*, a small town near *Hamborough*, was fixed on for the conference, whither repair'd on each part the Ministers of *Denmark* and of *Holstein*.

These conferences were held in 1696, and all that year passed without their bringing any thing to a conclusion. *Charles* XII. having succeeded the King his father the next year, furnished the Duke with some troops, which he wanted, to finish certain forts that he had caused to be built to cover his estates against an invasion, which sooner or later he expected.

Here was the foundation of this war. King *Christian* V. unwilling to suffer these barriers, ordered some troops to march and attack these forts, which were just perfected. He made himself master of them, and immediately rased them. All this passed during the conferences of *Pinnenberg*, which were however continued, tho' in a languishing manner. The Duke was too weak to oppose his enemy: he resolved therefore to dissemble his resentment, until *Sweden*, finding herself disencumber'd of the mediation, wherein she was engaged for the peace of *Ryswick*, was in a better condition to support his interests. As he was to marry the sister of *Charles* XII. he flatter'd himself, that this Prince would not fail to act in his favour.

During these transactions the Regency summoned the diet at *Stockholm*, as well to assist at the funeral of the late King, which was to be performed on the twenty fourth of *November*, as to deliberate on the affairs of the King. They
proposed

King CHARLES XII: *of* SWEDEN.

proposed immediately to declare the King of age, on which they were sufficiently divided in opinion. First, the King was not of the age prescribed by the * laws; secondly, the late King had ordained a longer Regency by his will; above all, great obstacles arose on the part of the Clergy, who were obstinate in denying their consent.

Notwithstanding all which, there was no time to lose; the situation of affairs demanded a quick resolution. They resolved accordingly to send Deputies to the Queen and the Counsellors of the Regency to communicate to them the design they had of advancing the King's age. After some deliberation, the Counsellors of the Regency gave their consent. The matter being thus settled, the Estates addressed the young Monarch by their Deputies to take into his hands the reins of the government, at a time when the storm which threatened at a distance demanded that he himself should govern his kingdom. This proposition was agreeable to the King; he answer'd, *that he was desirous to reign* ꜝ.

Affairs

* According to Mr. *Voltaire*'s account, by the laws of *Sweden* the King is of age at fifteen, but the will of *Charles* the eleventh had alter'd it to eighteen.

ꜝ Mr. *Voltaire* gives the honour of this to Count *Piper*, in the following manner: 'In the month of *November*, says he, the same year that his father died, as the young Prince was coming from a review of several regiments, Count *Piper*, observing the King sunk in a profound reverie, desired the liberty to ask his Majesty of what he thought so seriously. *I think*, answered the Prince, *that I am worthy to command these brave fellows; and am unwilling, that either they or myself should have recourse to the orders of a woman*. Piper presently laid hold of this opportunity to make his fortune: but as he had not sufficient credit to venture on so dangerous an enterprize, as the removal of the Regency from the Queen, and advancing the King's majority, he proposed

Affairs were in this situation, when the funeral pomp of the late King was ordained. This was performed the twenty fourth of *November*, with the usual ceremonies. We will not here amuse the reader with a detail of what passed at this funeral, nor will we say any thing of the medals which were struck on that occasion. The end which we propose in this work being only to make known the military exploits of this Hero, we will content ourselves with observing, that two days after the funeral of the late King, the Queen Dowager with the Counsellors of the Regency resigned the government to the young Prince; first in full Senate, and afterwards in the great hall of the royal palace, in the presence of the Estates of the kingdom. The King was crown'd at *Stockholm* with much solemnity, but without any magnificence [s]. An universal joy diffused itself through the whole kingdom, no person appearing disinterested in this affair.

The first step with which the King began his administration was a renewal of the alliances contracted with those powers, who were friends or allies with the Crown. He concluded three treaties; the first with *France*, the second with *England*, the third with *Holland*. The Count *de Bond*, who was then at the *Hague*, was dispatched to *London*, to restore to his *Britannick* Majesty the Order of the Garter, which the late King *Charles* his father had worn. The treaty with the *Dutch* concerned the tranquillity of the North, which was

'ed the matter to Count *Axel Sparre*, a bold man, and one who sought an opportunity to make himself considerable, by whose means the affair was soon completed.

[s] As the Archbishop of *Upsal* held the crown in his hands in order to put it on the King's head, he snatched it from him, and crown'd himself; an action much applauded by the populace.

King CHARLES XII. *of* SWEDEN.

was on the point of being disturbed by the affair of *Holstein*, in whose behalf his Majesty appeared to interest himself in a very singular manner. Care was taken to insert a separate article, with design to guarantee anew the treaty of *Altena*.

All these precautions were not unnecessary; the storm was forming on all sides, and war seem'd inevitable. There were no more hopes from the negotiations at *Pinnenberg*, which were just broke off: they endeavoured to renew them, but all that labour was in vain, it being now too late.

The Court of *Denmark* was resolved to pursue her point, and appeared determined to push matters to the last extremity. She had no reason to be pleased with the marriage of *Frederick* Duke of *Holstein-Gottorp* with the Princess Royal *Hedwige-Sophia*, eldest sister to the King of *Sweden*. The ceremony of this marriage was performed at *Carlberg*, a royal house near *Stockholm*. Mr. *Juel*, the *Danish* Ambassador, did all he could to obstruct it; he even offer'd a Princess of *Denmark* to the young Monarch in the name of the King his master. When he found all his stratagems ineffectual, he took leave of his *Swedish* Majesty, who received him very coldly.

The Duke of *Holstein* remained not long at *Stockholm* after his marriage, but soon departed with the Princess his spouse, after the King had made him General in chief of his armies in *Germany*. The King, with the Queen Dowager and all the Court, accompany'd them to *Carelscroon*. The Duke passed the sea under the escort of many men of war, commanded by the Count *de Wachtmeister*, Great Admiral, and landed safely in his own dominions.

Count *Guiscard* arrived this year at *Stockholm*, where he was to reside in the quality of Ambassador

bassador from the most Christian King. He came in the place of the Count *d'Avaux*, who was recalled into *France*, but did not make his entry till the close of the year. He knew immediately how to insinuate himself into the King's favour, who never failed to make him one of all his parties of pleasure: he had the secret of diverting the King by a thousand sallies of vivacity. This favour was however of no long duration; for having taken upon him to make remonstrances to the King, whose real character he was not perhaps sufficiently acquainted with, his Majesty was offended with him, and complained of him to the Court of *France*, who highly blamed the conduct of the Ambassador. He quitted *Sweden* some years after, not being able to obtain his audience of leave.

In the mean while the King of *Denmark* did not cease to work under hand to oppress the Duke of *Holstein*. Jealous of the alliance which the Duke had contracted with *Sweden*, and not doubting but that *Charles* XII. would take part with his brother-in-law, he being moreover guarantee of the treaty of *Altena*, he conspired at once the ruin of this young King, and sought all opportunities to raise him enemies. He addressed himself to *Augustus* King of *Poland*, who appeared disposed to enter into his measures.

Augustus [h] had brought his *Saxon* troops into *Poland*; and as they were become chargeable to the Republick, which would bear them no longer, he was charmed with finding an opportunity of employing them in the conquest of *Livonia*. The unfortunate *Patkul* first inspired him with the thought, which his Generals could not fail to approve.

[h] See the *Appendix*, N°. 1. and 2.

To

King CHARLES XII. *of* SWEDEN.

To incite *Augustus* to this enterprize, they represented to him the extreme youth of the King of *Sweden*, of which he might make an easy advantage. They shewed him at the same time, that a successful issue of this war would much contribute to reduce the *Polonese*, and dissipate for ever the several factions which had been formed against him. All these solicitations were well received by King *Augustus*, who was already allured by the hopes of a conquest which he thought so easy.

To thicken the storm which was to break on *Sweden*, they cast their eyes on the *Czar*, nor was any thing omitted to bring him into the league. This Prince hesitated at first, because he was then at war with the *Turks*; but presently having made peace with the *Porte*, he resolved to join his arms to those of the two allied Kings. This league was formed between the three Princes with all possible secrecy.

The King of *Sweden*, ignorant of all these preparations, sent an embassy into *Muscovy* to communicate to the *Czar* his accession to the throne, and to renew the ancient treaties of peace and alliance. This embassy was composed of Baron *de Bergenhielm*, Chancellor of the Court, of the Baron *de Lindhielm*, and Mr. *de Gothe*, brother of Count *de Lillieroth*. They did not arrive at *Moscow* till the month of *July*, where they met with many rubs on diverse occasions.

The *Czar* was yet employed in the war against the *Turks*, from whom he had taken the city of *Asoph*. He return'd not to *Moscow* till the month of *September*. The embassy from the King of *Sweden* gave him great perplexity; for being already in a manner engaged in the triple alliance, he knew not how to bring himself off with

with honour. He made the Ambaſſadors wait long for their audience. This he did as well to gain time, as to ſee what turn affairs would take in *Turkey*. At laſt the Ambaſſadors obtained an audience, and preſented the letter from the King their maſter. The *Czar*, who deſired to ſave appearances, gave them a moſt gracious reception; after which they were not a little ſurprized at the arrival of *Carlowitz*, Major-General to the King of *Poland*, at *Moſcow*. *Carlowitz* came poſt, tho' he was indiſpoſed; this gave the *Swediſh* Ambaſſadors room to believe, that he was charg'd with ſome commiſſion which required great haſte. *Patkul* came with him, but, to avoid ſuſpicion, did not appear in publick, but concealed himſelf in the houſe of the *Daniſh* Miniſter. He managed matters ſo well, that the Ambaſſadors of *Charles* were not informed of his arrival at *Moſcow* till after their departure from that city.

During their ſtay at *Moſcow*, they had many conferences with the Miniſters of that Court, without knowing what was then in agitation to the diſadvantage of their maſter. They brought back with them a letter from the *Czar*, by which that Prince promiſed King *Charles*, that he would inviolably obſerve the treaties between the two Crowns, and that he would ſhortly ſend a ſolemn embaſſy to *Sweden*. He refuſed however to take the oaths common on the like occaſion. All the inſtances which the Ambaſſadors uſed on this ſubject were uſeleſs: the *Czar* alledged for a reaſon, that he had already taken this oath at his coming to the Empire, before the death of *Charles* XI. and that it was very unneceſſary to have recourſe to this idle formality. This refuſal gave the Ambaſſadors reaſon to believe, that the

Czar had a design to break with the King their master. They resolved to return into *Sweden*, without being able to get any certain information on that head, tho' the storm was on the very point of bursting forth.

The proceedings of the King of *Poland* were not less secret than those of the *Czar*. To remove all suspicion from *Charles* XII. of what was hatching against him, he sent the Waiwode *Galeski*, a Senator, into *Sweden*, to assure that Prince of an inviolable friendship, as to a neighbour and near relation. The Ambassador, the better to conceal his play, pretended moreover, that he was charged on the part of his master, 1st, To confirm the peace of *Oliva*; 2dly, To desire the King to become mediator between his *Polish* Majesty and the Elector of *Brandenbourg*, to determine the differences which subsisted between these two Princes on the subject of the town of *Elbing*; 3dly, To demand a reimbursement to the town of *Thorn*, of the money which she had formerly advanced to *Sweden*. These propositions were well received by the Court of *Sweden*, which made no difficulty of ratifying all these articles, and of uniting herself to the King of *Poland* by a new alliance, from which that Crown might draw great advantages. As the instructions of King *Augustus*'s Ministers were not sufficiently ample, that Court offer'd to send that treaty ready drawn to Baron *Maurice Welling*, Lieutenant-General, and Ambassador of *Sweden* at the Court of *Warsaw*, who had orders to set the last hand to it.

This Nobleman, of well-known ability and a most delicate understanding, had been sent to congratulate *Augustus* immediately on his accession to the throne. This Prince received him in the most

most gracious manner, at the same time affecting to distinguish him from all other Ministers. Baron *Flemming*, who hath since made such a figure in the world, and who feared the penetration of Mr. *Welling*, bound himself to him in a strict friendship; and to carry on the deceit with the greater *finesse*, they affected on both sides to keep the affair very secret, and to carry on the negotiations only by night: at last, when every thing was regulated and adjusted, the King of *Poland* signed the treaty with *Sweden*; and Mr. *Welling*, ravish'd at the imagined success of his negotiation, immediately dispatched it to the King his master at *Stockholm*. As to Mr. *Galeski*, he set out for *Denmark* with a view of settling the articles and conditions on the triple alliance.

The preparations for war were carried on in the midst of all these negotiations. The armament, which the King of *Denmark* was fitting out by sea, at last began to alarm the Duke of *Holstein*; who, seeing himself threaten'd on all sides, and having no more to hope from the method of negotiation, set himself to work to put his affairs in a condition of resisting force. The fortifications of the town of *Tonningue*, situated on the *Eyder*, three leagues from the ocean, were carried on with the utmost diligence. As the garrison of this place was not strong enough to defend it, they drew about a thousand *Swedish* troops out of *Wismar*, who enter'd safely into the town without the *Danes* being able to hinder them.

No one could blame the Duke of *Holstein* for putting himself in a posture of defence, in a time when his dominions were in immediate danger of an invasion. The King of *Denmark* however complained highly of this Prince's conduct.
He

King Charles XII. *of* Sweden.

He sent the Count of *Reventlau* to the Court of *Vienna* with his complaints against the Duke. The Count passed through *Dresden*, under the pretence of paying his compliments to *Augustus* on the part of the King his master, where he remained some days, and employed that time in putting the last hand to all the secret articles of the triple alliance ; which treaty was at length concluded, and executed with all the formalities requisite. In the night the conferences were carried on with *Flemming*, and in the day they endeavoured to amuse Baron *Welling*, who was so much the dupe of these two Ministers, that he had not the least suspicion of what pass'd. Things were in this situation when the King of *Denmark* order'd his troops to advance, threatening to attack the Duke, if he did not disarm himself. The mediators in vain tried a last effort to allay the storm. All the measures were already taken on the part of the allies, who had resolved to decide this quarrel with the sword.

Frederick IV. who succeeded his father *Christian* V. push'd on the affair very briskly, and entered on more vigorous measures than had hitherto been taken. He sent in *August* a squadron of twelve ships, under the command of Admiral *Stoeken*, who were to cover the passage of four regiments of foot into *Pomerania*. *Stoeken* made a feint of attacking the *Swedish* fleet commanded by Admiral *Ankarstierna*, which however he did not attempt ; but having seen the convoy pass and repass, he set sail for *Copenhagen*. The King of *Sweden*, on the other side, seeing his brother-in-law in danger of being crush'd, was not forgetful of bringing the guarantees of the treaty of *Altena* into his interest ; to which purpose he employed the Count *de Lillieroth* as his

The LIFE *and* HISTORY *of*

his Ambaſſador to the States General of the *United Provinces*, and the Baron *de Friſendorff* as his Envoy to the three branches of the houſe *de Lunenbourg*. The negotiations of theſe two Miniſters ſucceeded very happily.

As for the Duke of *Holſtein*, he ſet out with the Dutcheſs his ſpouſe for *Sweden*, after having publiſhed a manifeſto explaining the reaſons of his conduct. The arrival of this Prince at *Stockholm* caus'd exceeding great joy; and he was received there with all the tenderneſs imaginable. He remained there the reſt of the year, during which the King gave him all ſorts of diverſions and magnificent entertainments, which were managed by Baron *Teſſin*, who had ſent for a very good company of Comedians from *France* for that purpoſe. What perſon, who had ſeen this young Monarch ſo violent in the purſuit of ſuch pleaſures, would have believed him capable of ſo ſudden a change of his ſentiments?

We were now informed of the reſolution of the guarantees of the treaty of *Altena*. They declared expreſsly to the King of *Denmark*, who haughtily rejected all propoſitions of an accommodation, that if he ordered his troops to enter into the Dutchy of *Holſtein*, they would look on this ſtep as a manifeſt infringement of the peace of *Altena*, and conſequently would treat him as a common enemy. Theſe menaces produced no effect; his *Daniſh* Majeſty, far from having any regard to theſe repreſentations, recall'd his Miniſters from *Hamborough*, and cauſed ſome troops to enter into the ducal territories. This was an open ſignal of the war, and all hopes of avoiding it were henceforth loſt.

The Court of *Sweden* began the year 1700 with very ſuperb entertainments and diverſions.

No

No one would have imagined in the midſt of all theſe pleaſures, that any thought was had of thoſe preparations of war which were making in the neighbourhood. We did not however neglect to hold ourſelves ready againſt all events, nor to take neceſſary meaſures in order to aſſiſt the Duke. But what drew moſt the attention of the King of *Sweden*, was the ſtep taken by *Auguſtus* King of *Poland*. This Prince had ſo well diſſembled his true ſentiments, that the Court of *Sweden* thought ſhe had nothing to fear from him. But on the contrary Mr. *de Welling* had been ſcarce ſooner aſſured of the reſolution which he had taken to make a more ſtrict alliance with the King his maſter, than we were informed of *Flemming*'s expedition, whereof *Patkul* had formed the project. His deſign was to ſurprize *Riga*, the capital of *Livonia*. In order to this enterprize, he had marched from *Polangen* in *Samogitia* (having put ſome *Saxon* troops into winter quarters in the neighbourhood) towards *Janiſki*, a little town in the confines of *Courland*. The Count of *Dalberg*, Velt-Marſhal and Governor of *Livonia*, fail'd not to get an early information. On the firſt news which he received, he writ to the Court to adviſe them of what had paſſed; and to prevent all ſurprize, he reinforced the garriſon of *Riga*, mounted the ramparts with cannon, and armed the frontiers with advanced guards. In the mean time *Flemming*, to juſtify the conduct of King *Auguſtus*, ſent letters of protection from *Janiſki* to all the ſubjects of *Livonia*, in which he ſuppoſed that the *Swedes* had attempted to ſurprize the *Poliſh* troops in *Lithuania*, which the King his maſter was under a neceſſity of preventing, and of entring *Livonia* with an

C 2 armed

armed force. After this declaration he marched directly to *Riga*. As the *Duna* was frozen over, and the works on the banks of the river not yet in a complete posture of defence, he flattered himself to be able to take the town at the first onset, or at least without much difficulty; the better to conceal his march, he surprised an advanced guard of 30 men, some of which nevertheless found means to escape, and give notice of the approach of the enemy. At this news Count *Dalberg* immediately set fire to the suburbs, and to spread the alarm throughout, ordered a double discharge of all the cannon from the ramparts.

The enemy appeared before the town the 11th of *February*, with about 4000 men. *Flemming*, much surprized to find the place in a condition to make a vigorous resistance, and being moreover unable to advance or retreat without loss of his honour, resolved to attack fort *Cobrun*, opposite to *Riga*, in order to be master of the *Duna*, he commanded 2000 men to attack it, who carried it sword in hand, and made Captain *Bildstein* the Governor prisoner, with fifty men. After *Flemming* had taken this fort, he gave it the name of *Oranienbaum*, instead of *Cobrun*, by which it had been formerly known. He then writ to the King of *Poland* to inform him of this first conquest.

While this was doing, *Augustus* had forbid Baron *Welling* the Court, and given orders at the same time to fresh troops to march and join the body under *Flemming*, having obtained from the Elector of *Brandenburg* permission for these troops to pass through his territories.

The King of *Sweden* was diverting himself 1700. with hunting bears at *Kongsobr* [h], when he heard the news of the irruption of the *Saxon* troops into *Livonia*. He was not at all moved at this, but said smiling to Count *Guiscard* the *French* Ambassador, *We shall soon oblige them to return back the same way they came.* This Prince did not leave off his hunting, which he performed in a very uncommon manner, exposing himself every moment to the danger of his life. Instead of pursuing the bears and killing them with a fusee, as was the ordinary manner, he endeavoured to take them alive. Every one followed his example, and armed themselves with forked sticks, by the assistance of which they pushed the bears on all sides, till those animals were so spent, that they were to be taken and bound. The King feared not to attack one of a prodigious size with only a stick in his hand: he found himself exposed to the most imminent danger; the bear had already torn off his [i] peruke, and was going to trample on him, when he found means to escape from his clutches, and convey himself out of danger; he did not however abandon his purpose, but with the help of the hunters, who accompanied him, he overcame the bear, and himself assisted at binding him. They took fourteen alive in this manner, which were all transported to *Kongsobr*, all fast bound upon sledges to the sound of hunting-horns. The King diverted himself with this dangerous exer-

[h] A place so called, fourteen leagues from *Stockholm*.

[i] It appears by the first coin which was struck at the beginning of this Prince's reign, that he always wore a peruke, till he came into *Seeland*, where he left off that fashion, and never afterwards resumed it.

The LIFE and HISTORY of

cife during the month of *February*, being the depth of winter.

This party of pleasure did not hinder his Majesty from providing every thing which was necessary for *Livonia*. Baron *Otto Welling*, General of horse and Governor of *Narva*, received orders to cause all the troops which were in *Livonia* and *Finland* to march. They presently formed a body of 10,000 men, to act in opposition to the *Saxons*. They made likewise other preparations in *Sweden*, with the view of supporting a long war, which they foresaw would become extremely bloody.

The King of *Denmark* having received advice of *Flemming*'s irruption, and knowing that the *Czar* was preparing to follow his example, began to talk in a higher tone. He rejected all the propositions of accommodation made him by the mediators, and pretended to give laws to the Duke, into whose estates he ordered *Charles Rudolph* Duke of *Wurtenberg-Newstadt* his General in Chief, to enter at the head of 16,000 men, and after having spread abroad a manifesto, by which he endeavoured to justify his proceedings, he made himself master of all the flat country, seizing all the demesns and revenues of his Highness, and exacting great contributions of the Dutchies of *Schleswich* and *Holstein*.

On the first motions of the King of *Denmark*, the mediators made new remonstrances at the court of *Copenhagen*, with a view of hindering the progress of a war, which was becoming general. All their instances producing no effect, they renewed their alliance and the guarantee of the treaty of *Altena*, promising to give the Duke all the succours which his affairs should require.

require. On the other side, the King of *Poland*, who saw the affair of *Holstein* very happily begun, caused a large manifesto to be spread abroad, to justify his enterprize on *Livonia*. He alledged I know not how many pretended infringements of the peace of *Oliva*, committed on the part of *Sweden*. He said, he could not dispense with the oath which he had taken at his accession to the throne, to regain *Livonia* for the Republick, to which it had formerly belonged. He pretended at last, that he was bound to assist the King of *Denmark* against the Duke of *Holstein*, whom *Sweden* determined to support against all reason and justice [k].

It was not difficult for the Court of *Sweden* to refute such weak reasons, nor did she fail to answer them, and to demonstrate in an evident manner, that interest, envy, and the right of conveniency had had a greater share in this violence, than all the other motives which were alledged without any foundation [l].

That we might be able to oppose the enemy, all the dispositions which were thought necessary were continued to be carried on on the *Duna*. *Patkul* had taken all measures to gain the Nobility, and bring them over to a revolt. All that he did to this purpose was without success. The Nobility themselves presented a writing to the King on this occasion, by which they assured his Majesty of an inviolable fidelity.

Flemming undertook to make new conquests: He formed a design of attacking fort *Dunamund*, which is situated on the mouth of the *Duna*, and surrounded on one side by the *Bulderaa*, which renders the access difficult enough. He contented himself at first with cannonading it

[k] See the Appendix No. 3.   [l] See the Appendix No. 4.

briskly,

briskly, and throwing some bombs into it, to intimidate the garrison. This first attempt produced not the expected effect. As Colonel *Budberg*, who commanded in that fortress, did not appear disposed to surrender it so soon, *Flemming* judged, that he had nothing to do but to give an assault. Every thing appeared favourable to the execution of this design; the *Bulderaa* was frozen over, and there was a courtin intirely destroyed and very weakly covered with pallisades, for they were on the point of building cazerns. Major General *Carlowitz* (the same as had been so much employed in the negotiations) commanded the attack on the night of the 12th of *March*, having under his command a body of 2000 men: He was repulsed, after a brisk and bloody fight, which lasted some hours.

This attack cost the enemy dear, whose loss was very considerable: General *Carlowitz* himself lost his life therein. The garrison, tho' not numerous, and tho' it had six bastions to defend, made a very vigorous resistance. The women distinguished themselves in fighting on this occasion, one of whom was wounded in her shoulder. As the fire on both sides ceased all at once, it was believed at *Riga* that the enemy had carried the fort. Old General *Dalberg*, who continued on the ramparts of the town during the attack, caused a signal to be given by the discharge of two cannons, to inform the Governor of the success of the enterprize, which *Budberg* answered by a return of the same number, and thereby spread an universal joy through that city.

This joy was of no long duration. In effect, *Flemming* having two days afterwards shewn Colonel *Budberg*, that the darkness of the night occasioned their missing the weaker part of that place,

place, (a mistake which they would not commit for the future) this Commandant, who wanted both men and provisions, saw himself under a necessity of capitulating. They allowed him four field-pieces, and he marched out with all the honours of war, taking his rout to *Reval*. Lieutenant-General *Flemming*, who was very desirous of making his court to the King of *Poland*, gave the name of *August-burgh* to the fort which he had conquered.

In *Holstein* the *Danes*, who were masters of the country, endeavoured to seize on all the towns and fortresses. Major-General *Carmaillon* took the town of *Slefwick*; the town of *Husum* and the fort of *Holmer*, with that likewise of *Husum*, which was not yet quite finished, surrendered themselves without delay; and *Frederickstadt* was carried sword in hand. The fort of *Ramstedt* had the same fate; so that there remained only the fortress of *Tonningen*, which was soon invested by an army of 8,000 men, under the command of the Duke of *Wurtenberg*. The castle of *Gottorp* surrendered at the same time, by composition, to Colonel *Baligni*.

Baron *Bannier* threw himself into *Tonningen* with 4000 men, and defended it with great valour and conduct. The Duke of *Wurtenberg* summoned it in vain to surrender, to save the blood which would be spilt on both sides. The Baron rejected this proposition with scorn, and made at the same time all the necessary dispositions to sustain a vigorous siege. The enemy threw more than 5000 bombs into the place in eight days, and still continued to bombard it; till a resolution was taken of besieging it in form. The trenches were opened, and they attacked the counter-scarp with much vigour, which the garrison

rison defended very gallantly, and repulsed the *Danes*, who, without being dismayed, renewed the attack the second time, and carried it.

Affairs were in this situation, when the guarantees of the treaty of *Altena* began to set about executing their promises. *England* and *Holland* equipt out fleets, which were to enter the *Sound*. 12000 men held themselves ready to march at his Majesty's first orders. Two camps were formed on the side of *Norway*, in order to enter it in case of necessity: The one was commanded by Major-General *Fagerskiold*, the other by Monsieur *Schaar*, who was likewise a Major-General and Governour of the province of *Jempterland*. They drew together likewise another body near *Gothenburg* under General *Rehbinder*, which was ordered to join the others in case of need.

In the midst of all these preparations, the King of *Sweden* went with the Duke of *Holstein* from [m] *Stockholm* to *Carlscroon*, to press the equipment of the fleet. He left the management of affairs to the Senators, and formed a Council of Defence [n], which was to have the care of the militia during his absence. He took with him only two Senators, Count *Piper* and Count *Polus*; the latter was intrusted with foreign affairs, those of the kingdom being committed to the care of the former.

The King of *Sweden*, after a stay of some days at *Carlscroon*, proceeded to *Malmoe*, where was the rendezvous of the body of 12000 men. From *Malmoe* the King went to *Gothenburg*, accompanied by the Duke of *Holstein*, who embarked

---

[m] He never returned to *Stockolm* any more.

[n] This extraordinary council was to provide for the safety and defence of the kingdom during the King's absence.

King CHARLES XII. *of* SWEDEN.

there to join the army of his allies, which were ready to enter into his estates in order to drive out the enemy. Baron *Gyllenstern*, a *Swedish* General, was already arrived with several regiments of the country of *Bremen*. General *Lieven*, who was then at *Wismar*, had also taken care to send some troops; these troops joined those of *Lunenburg* near *Tollenspicker*, some leagues from *Hamborough*, where they were all to join. The Elector of *Hanover*, who commanded in chief, was there in person with the old Duke of *Zell*.

Before they passed the *Elb*, they sent the King of *Denmark* new propositions of peace, which were all rejected. He flattered himself that he should carry *Tonningen* in a few days. He arrived in the camp before it, and was often present at the approaches, in order to encourage the soldiers; all which, far from intimidating the besieged, animated them the more, and drove them to make a vigorous resistance: but nothing raised their courage more than the news which they received at this time of the birth of the hereditary Prince *Charles-Frederick*, of whom the Dutchess of *Holstein* was now delivered at *Stockholm* the 30th of *April*. The besieged celebrated the birth-day with a general discharge of the cannon from their ramparts.

Every thing appeared disposed to produce some action of importance. The King of *Denmark* having refused to hearken to those propositions that had been made him of peace, the army of the allies passed the *Elb* in order to raise the siege of *Tonningen*, and deliver the Duke of *Holstein* from an enemy, who was so obstinately bent to oppress him. The army advanced towards *Rheinbeck*, a Ducal castle, where the enemy had posted 1500 *Danish* dragoons, who undertook

dertook to dispute this pass, but were soon repulsed by two *Swedish* battalions under Lieutenant-Colonel *Beyor*, and some horse of *Zell* commanded by Monsieur *de Bois-David*. The army advanced from *Rheinbeck* towards *Vansbeck* and *Altena*. All the royal country of *Holstein* was laid under contribution. General *Dopp*, at the head of the troops of the States-General, join'd the army of the allies near *Pinnenberg*; after which conjunction the army was 14,000 strong. The Duke of *Wurtenberg* then judged it proper to raise the siege, which had lasted six weeks, and marched directly to the allies.

As a bloody battle, which might draw on very mischievous consequences, seemed now just ready to be fought, the allies were desirous to renew the negotiations. The Elector of *Hanover* wished nothing so much as a speedy end of this war. The Elector of *Brandenburg*, who was of the same sentiments, offered to enter into the affair in the quality of a mediator. This Prince neglected no means to persuade the allies to return home; and to give more weight to his propositions, he caused an army to advance to the frontiers. As to the Duke of *Holstein*, he was inflamed with the desire of coming to blows with the enemy, and at last obtained a promise from the allies, that they would determine the quarrel, at what price soever it might cost.

As the presence of the army of the allies might contribute to bring the enemy to reason, they advanced towards *Oldeslobe* to follow the *Danes*. At the same time Major-General *Dompré* was detached with 700 horse on the side of *Segeberg*, to levy contributions. These meeting with a body of 300 *Danish* horse under the command of Major-General *Labatt*, attacked them,

over-

overthrew them, and took 712 prisoners. The army of the allies encamped at *Segeberg*, in the sight of that of *Denmark*; yet, tho' there was only a little rivulet between them, they nevertheless remained quiet enough, and contented themselves with disputing the forage and the ground, till the peace was at length concluded at *Travendab*, as we shall see a little afterwards.

To force the King of *Denmark* into more pacifick measures, the King of *Sweden* at his return from *Gothenberg* to *Carlscroon*, had so prest the equipment of the fleet, that it was ready to sail about the month of *June*. His Majesty immediately embarked the two regiments of *Ulpland* and *Calmar*, and then on the next day the fleet sailed out of the port, after having first celebrated divine service on board the ships. This fleet consisted of 38 men of war, without reckoning the frigats, five fire-ships, and a bomb-ketch. They sailed the 16th, not being able before, on account of contrary winds.

The King was on board this fleet, with Count *Guiscard*, Count *Piper*, and Lieutenant-General *Rhenschild*: there were likewise a great many men of quality and officers of the first rank. It was generally expected, that the King would attack the *Danish* fleet, which would have effectually happened, if the wind had favoured.

After the *Swedish* fleet, by means of traverse sailing, was arrived in the latitude of *Ystedt*, the King went on shore, and took the road of *Malmoe*. He now heard of the arrival of the *English* and *Dutch* fleets in the *Sound*; these consisted of 30 ships, commanded by the Admirals *Rook* and *Almond*, who waited only the orders of his Majesty to act. This Prince presently sent the Count *de Wreed*, his Chamberlain, to compliment them,

them, and defire them to advance towards *Helfingburg*. The *Danish* fleet, which then anchor'd under the cannon of *Cronenberg*, thought itfelf not fecure; fcarce were thofe of *England* and *Holland* feen, when the fleet retired to the paffage of *Rendela*, between the iflands of *Amack* and *Saltholmen*. To hinder the conjunction of the two fleets of their enemies, the *Danes* took away all the marks ufed by the pilots to pafs in fafety that dangerous coaft. Here they ranged themfelves in order of battle, to wait for the *Swedes*, having firft planted feveral batteries of cannon on the iflands on both fides.

The King, not knowing what ftep to take, fent for Admiral *Taube* and Rear-Admiral *Sparre* to *Malmoe* to afk their opinions, and to know of them in what manner the fleet might pafs, to go and join thofe of the allies: He expreffed to them at the fame time a very eager defire to attack the *Danes*; but thefe being fo advantageoufly pofted, it was thought a matter of too much rifk; and happily another paffage was difcovered, named *Flint-renan*, hitherto little ufed.

Count *Wachtmeifter*, Great Admiral, thought this paffage too dangerous for the fhips to attempt; however, the contrary advice having prevailed, the fleet hazarded the paffage, which they very happily executed the 4th of *July*.

This fleet confifted of forty fail, without reckoning fome large veffels which returned to *Carlfcroon*. The King immediately fent Meffieurs *Taube* and *Sparre* to the Admirals of the allies, who had approached the ifland of *Ween*, between *Helfingburg* and *Landfcron*, to inform them of what had happened. Thefe Gentlemen returned with the news, that the King of *Denmark* had requefted a fufpenfion of arms for fix days, to
which

which the King would not consent; and as he wished for the conjunction of the two fleets, it was resolved to attack that of *Denmark*, if this durst oppose itself to them.

At this time four *Saxon* regiments took the road of *Holstein* to join the *Danes*: Count *d'Ablefeld*, whom the King of *Denmark* had made Stadtholder, or Governor of the Dutchy of *Schlefwick*, went to meet them, to conduct them to his master's army. As they committed some waste in the Dutchy of *Zell*, through which they passed, that Duke marched some troops against them under the command of Lieutenant-General *Goor*, who obliged them to return back. Nor were they better received in the territories of *Brunswick*, where the militia of the country pursued them so briskly, that they dispersed themselves, and were obliged to abandon their baggage, and their Major-General *Neitsch* and many other Officers, who were made prisoners.

The conjunction of the *Swedish* fleet with that of *England* and *Holland* was happily accomplished on the 7th of *July*; that of *Sweden* took the right; they remained together two days at anchor, and sailed on the 10th to go and look after the *Danes*. These also weighed anchor at the approach of the fleet of the allies, and were retired to the road of *Copenhagen*. The *Danish* Admiral then demanded by an Officer of the *English*, *If he came thither as a friend, or whether they were to regard him as an enemy?* All the answer which he received from Admiral *Rook* was, *That he should know very shortly*; and at the same time threw four bombs into the *Danish* fleet, which would not expose itself any farther, and took immediate measures to shut itself up within its ports.

This

This motion having taken from the allies all hope of drawing them to a battle, they resolved to bombard the enemy. This resolution was executed the same evening, the *Danes* returning the compliment from sixteen mortars, with very little damage on either side. The fires which appeared from time to time at *Copenhagen*, and on the vessels, were immediately extinguish'd; however, the bombardment was continued reciprocally for some days.

This manner of making war did not suit with the King's taste; his Majesty being desirous of conveying a letter to Mr. *Leyonclo*, the *Swedish* Ambassador at *Copenhagen*, found a pretence to send a Captain thither with it. This Captain was attended with a sea-officer disguised in a sailor's dress, and was charged to observe the disposition of the enemy, by which means his Majesty was informed, that he tormented himself to no purpose, and that it was impossible to attack the enemy with any advantage: this news changed the King's resolution, he then thought of making a descent into *Seland*; and to hinder the King of *Denmark* from repairing thither, they shut up his passage with many vessels which were then in the *Baltick*.

Whilst *Charles* XII. was busy in the execution of this project, and the taking necessary measures to push the war with vigour, King *Augustus* at length obtained of the Republick of *Poland*, that she would defray the expence of the war in *Livonia*, to carry on which he had drawn together 15,000 men on the frontiers of that province; the conquest of which appeared to him infallible, a great number of *Poles* and *Lithuanians* had already betaken themselves thither with all their equipages.

We

t was made into SEELAND *in the*

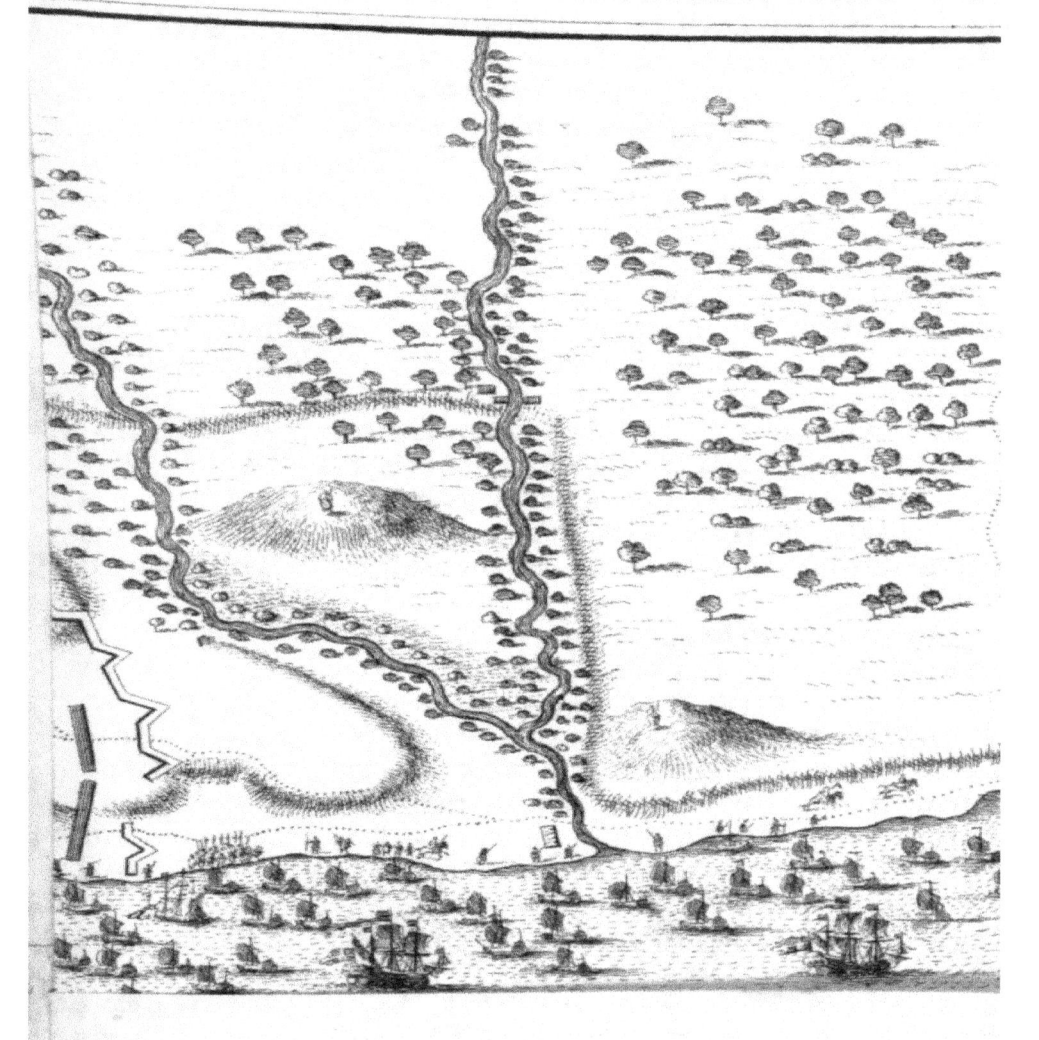

King CHARLES XII. of SWEDEN.

We have seen above, that General *Otto Welling* had received orders to oppose *Flemming* with all the troops which he could gather together: He acquitted himself very handsomly of this commission, and repulsed likewise some *Saxon* troops which would have passed the *Duna*, but was nevertheless obliged in the end to yield to numbers, and could not hinder the enemy from executing the design which he had formed.

On the 20th of *July*, *Augustus* advanced with all his army and a great train of artillery to attempt the passage, with which view he fixed on a place near *Riga*, called *Probestinghoff*. Here was some hilly ground, commodious for planting his cannon; Mr. *Welling* hastened hither, but could not hinder a great part of the enemy's foot, which had already taken the post, from intrenching themselves in a manner impossible to be forced.

King *Augustus*, who had in great haste made a bridge of boats, passed the river with the rest of his army, and made a feint of attacking Mr. *Welling*, who, after amusing the enemy with some skirmishes, made a very fine retreat, and posted himself under the cannon of *Riga*, into which town he pushed all his foot, and retired with his horse farther into the country, to cover it against the *Saxon* parties.

Augustus thought not proper to pursue Mr. *Welling*; he invested *Riga*, which he contented himself with blocking up, not having a sufficient force to attack it in form; for the garrison was very numerous, and commanded by old Count *Dalberg*, a very able Engineer, and one of the most experienced Generals of his age. *Augustus* threw some bombs into it with little effect, and put all the country round under contribution.

The LIFE *and* HISTORY *of*

Colonel *Braus* was detached with 600 *Saxon* horse to inveſt *Kokenbuſen* on the *Duna*, two leagues above *Riga*. The enemy took theſe meaſures to ſhut up the town on all ſides, and conſequently to prevent its receiving any proviſions or troops for its defence.

This firſt progreſs of the King of *Poland* rendered the King of *Denmark* yet leſs tractable than he was before. This Prince was ſo far from hearkening to any mention of peace, or negotiation, that he haughtily rejected the propoſition of the allies, of a ſhort ſuſpenſion of arms. The King of *Sweden* therefore found himſelf under a neceſſity of executing the project he had form'd to make a deſcent on *Seeland*.

This Prince cauſed 12000 men, which were in *Scania*, to march without delay towards *Landſcroon*, and himſelf took the poſt of *Malmoe*. At the ſame time he embarked his foot upon a great number of ſhallops and other ſmall veſſels. As the paſſage was ſhort, his Majeſty order'd it to be cover'd by a ſquadron under the command of Admiral *Anckerſtierna*. As ſoon as the neceſſary preparations were made, Baron *Stuart*, Camp-Marſhal, and the King's chief Engineer, ſailed before with a yacht to *reconnoitre* the moſt proper place for a deſcent. He ſoon returned, and on the advice which he brought they weighed anchor at four in the afternoon, and ſtood for *Humblebeck*, the place deſigned for the diſembarkation, being ſituated between *Copenhagen* and *Helſingobr*.

They obſerved the following order in their paſſage. Seventy one ſhallops, in which were embarked 254 Grenadiers, took the Van; between every ſhallop there was one filled with *Chevaux de Frize*. They were followed by thirty-four

boats

To face page. 35.

The SWEDISH ARMY drawn up in Order of BATTEL at their Camp near RUNSTA KROGH in SEELAND An. 1700.

Horse.	Troops	Men.	Squad	Horses
The Kings Drabans Commanded by Major Gen. Arvid Horn.	2	200	1	200
The Regiment of Horse Guards, Com. by Maj. Gen. Speres.	12	1600	6	266
The Westrogoths.	8	1000	4	250
The Regimt. of Smoland Com. by Major Gen. Nieroth.	8	1000	4	250
The Ostrogoths Com. by Maj. Gen. Morner.	8	1000	4	250
Foot.	Com.ⁿ	Men.	Bat.	Men.
The Foot Guards Commanded by Major General Posse.	12	1800	3	600
The Regiment of Upland Com. by Col. Lowen.	8	1200	2	600
The Regimt of Dahl Carlia Com. by Count Stenbock.	8	1200	2	600
The Regimt. of Wesmonland Com. by Col. Axel Sparre.	8	1200	2	600
One Batallion of Col. Faleburgs Regiment.	4	500	1	500

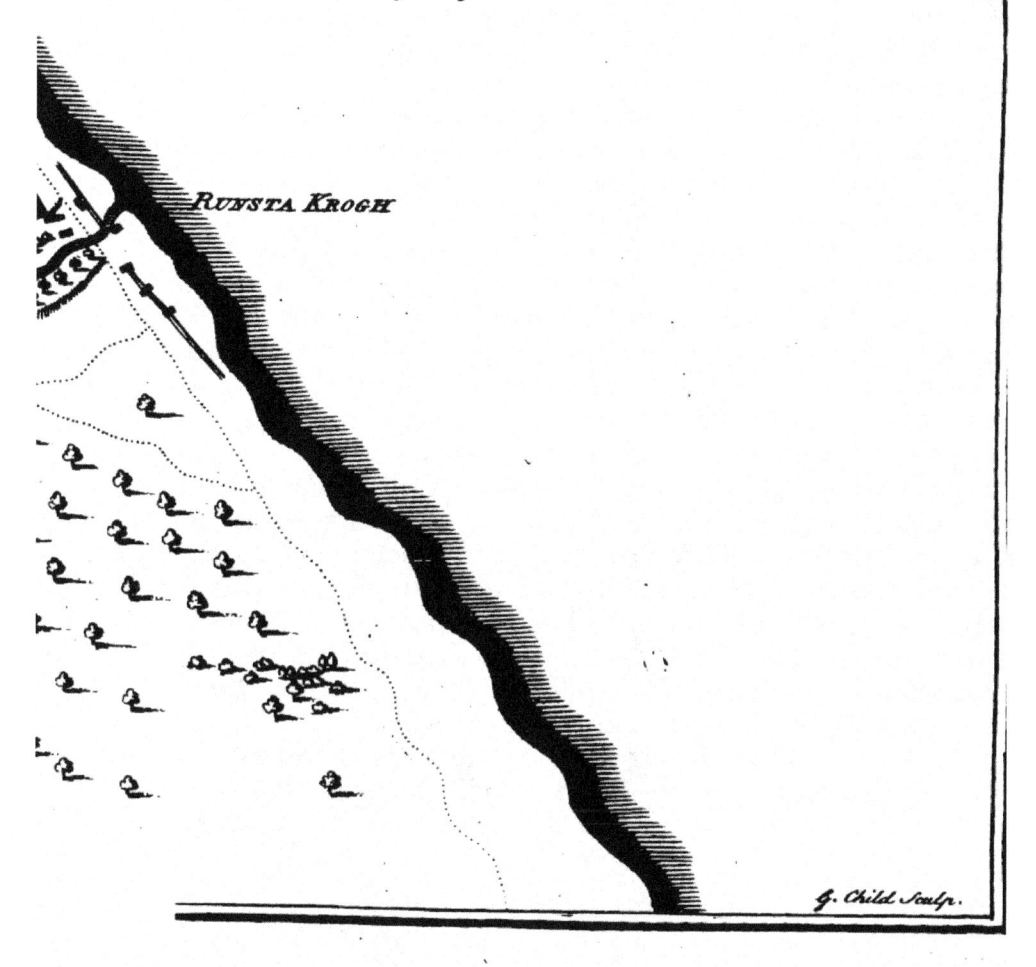

(in each Squadron.) (in each Batallion.)

RUNSTA KROGH

G. Child Sculp.

boats laden with shovels and fascines. Next followed forty-four small vessels, in which were 500 men, to support the Van-guard. These were again followed by many other ships, containing the corps of battle. The King was on the right, with Count *Wachtmeister* Great Admiral, Baron *Knut Posse* Major-General, Baron *Stuart*, Count *Charles Wrangle* Lieutenant of Drabans, Chamberlain *Hord*, and several persons of distinction.

General *Rhenschild* commanded on the left: He had with him the Prince Palatine of *Stegeborg*, Baron *Arwid Horn*, Captain-Lieutenant of Drabans, and Major-General and Colonel *Otto Wrangle*, Lieutenant of Drabans. Ten men of war full of foot covered the attack, which was to be made in the following manner.

A battalion of guards, commanded by Lieutenant-Colonel *Palmquist*, was on the extent of the right wing, with orders to attack a wind-mill which stood on a rising ground. The second battalion of guards, commanded by Major *Hamers*, formed the extent of the left wing, and were to attack the intrenchment of the enemy in flank. The third battalion of guards, under the command of Captain *Ebrenstein*, were to hold themselves near the first, on the right wing, to support the attack of the mill, and then to make themselves masters of a house which stood on another piece of rising ground. A battalion of the regiment of *Faltsbourg*, commanded by Lieutenant-Colonel *Buchwaldt*, joined the second battalion on the left wing. In this manner the Vanguard and the four battalions immediately disembarked, while the rest of the troops held themselves on board the men of war.

As soon as the King had made this disposition, the signal was given by the discharge of eight cannon,

cannon, and by hoisting a red flag on the mainmast head of the Great Admiral's ship. It was now six in the evening. The men of war immediately saluted the *Danes* with a broad-side, who were ranged in order of battel behind their intrenchments on the shore. The *Danes* return'd a very weak fire from some field-pieces. As the water was very low, the shallops were aground an hundred paces from the shore.

The King threw himself first into the water up to his arm-pits, with his sword in his hand [k]. All the troops followed his example. The *Danes* then came out of their intrenchments, and approached the banks of the sea, whence they charged the *Swedes* very vigorously; but these having insensibly gained ground, after a short fight obliged the *Danes* to retire, which they did with precipitation, abandoning their intrenchments and cannon, of which the *Swedes* took instant possession.

The King had also caused the regiment of *Upland*, commanded by Baron *Lowen*, and that of *Calmar*, under the command of Colonel *Diurklo*, to disembark during the action. After it was over, all the troops began to intrench themselves, which work they carried on till the arrival of the horse. As to the *Danes*, they retreated under the cannon of *Copenhagen*, and abandoned the flat country, which was now ex-

---

[k] The King, who had never before heard the discharge of small arms charg'd with ball, asked Major *Stuart*, who was near him, *What that whistling was, which he heard in his ears? It is the noise of the musket-balls, which they fire at you,* answer'd the Major. *Very well,* says the King; *this shall be my musick henceforward.* At the same instant the Major received a shot in his shoulder, and a Lieutenant fell dead on the other side of the King.

posed to the incursions of the *English* and *Dutch* sailors, who committed great destruction there.

The *Swedes* lost very few men in this action. Baron *Stuart* was wounded in the thigh, and obliged to repass the sea. The next day the King order'd the horse, with the rest of the foot which were in *Scania*, to march: he likewise brought up the artillery, designing to lay siege to *Copenhagen*. All the country was put under contribution.

The *Swedish* camp was soon provided with every thing necessary for the troops; the inhabitants of *Seeland* brought in provisions from all parts, which they sold to the soldiers. Those of *Helsingohr* having desired the same liberty, the King granted it them on condition that they would pay certain contributions. This Prince at the same time spread his letters all through *Seeland*, by which he promised his protection to the inhabitants. To hinder any disorder, he made his troops observe an exact discipline[1]; he only permitted them to hunt stags in the King of *Denmark*'s parks. No one had any reason to complain of the conduct of this Prince; his enemies were themselves in the number of his admirers, and praised his clemency and justice. The day after the publication of those letters, by which his Majesty took these people under his protection, others appeared on the part of the King of *Denmark*, forbidding his subjects on

---

[1] His camp was under so exact a regulation, that the peasants chose rather to sell their provisions to the *Swedes* their enemies, than to the *Danes*, who did not pay them so well. The citizens of *Copenhagen* were obliged more than once to come to the King of *Sweden*'s camp to buy provisions, of which, for the foregoing reason, there was great scarcity in their own markets.

1700. the pain of death from any commerce with the *Swedes*. These menaces made little impression on the people's minds, seeing that the *Swedes* were every where masters, and could force them to deliver whatever they wanted.

The *Swedish* troops, as well horse as foot, had then pass'd the sea, and form'd a body of about 12000 men. While they were gathering together, Admiral *Rook* arrived at the beginning of *August* at the King's camp, to congratulate him on the success of his enterprize. All the Ministers of the foreign Powers, who had followed his Majesty in this expedition, emulated each other in testifying to this Prince the pleasure they had in his good fortune.

The news of this expedition of the King of *Sweden* entirely changed the face of affairs in *Holstein*. The *Danish* Ministers, who till then had formed a thousand difficulties on the preliminaries of the peace, became more tractable, and desired themselves, by order of the King their master, to enter into negotiation with those of the Duke at *Travendahl* in *Holstein*. They instantly desired, on the behalf of his *Danish* Majesty, that above all things there might be a suspension of arms in *Seeland*. The mediators immediately dispatched a courier to the King of *Sweden* to advise him of this, assuring him, that his *Danish* Majesty had engaged to give the Duke of *Holstein* all suitable satisfaction.

This news was not agreeable to the King; he fear'd, that these propositions were only made to him with a design of gaining time: so, that he might obtain more advantageous conditions, he marched at the head of his army from *Humblebeck* to *Runstad*, about a league and half from *Copenhagen*, fully resolved to lay siege to that town,

town, as soon as his artillery was arrived. In the mean time the peace was concluded at *Travendahl* *, in a very advantageous manner to the Duke of *Holstein*. Twelve conferences had been held for this purpose, in which the treaty of *Altena* was confirmed in all its points: they assured to this Prince the sovereignty of his estates, the liberty to build fortresses, and to keep on foot a certain number of troops.

Charles, who knew nothing of the conclusion of this peace, was then employed in making the necessary preparations for the siege of *Copenhagen*. The fleets already blockt up the town towards the sea, and he was upon the point of approaching it nearer, when the news arrived of the peace concluded at *Holstein*. This news was brought him on the 11th of *August* by a *Danish* Captain, who arrived in his Majesty's camp with a *Swedish* Ensign, and several prisoners of war, who had been taken by the *Danes*.

The Count of *Reventlau*, a *Danish* Major-General, arrived likewise the day following: He was charged on the behalf of the King his master, to desire his *Swedish* Majesty to cause a cessation of hostilities, not to advance farther into the country, and to re-establish the antient friendship and good understanding, which had reigned between the two courts, the Duke of *Holstein* having had all the satisfaction he required. The same was farther confirmed the same day by Messieurs *de Blohm* and *Dahldorff*, who came to his *Swedish* Majesty on the part of the Duke of *Holstein*. The King received Count *Reventlau* very graciously, giving him the place of all his Generals, and the honour to eat at his table.

The peace being thus happily concluded, the troops of the mediatorial powers returned into their

In 1700.

* See *Append*. N°. 5.

their own country. Admiral *Rook*, before his departure with his fleet and that of the *Dutch*, had often the honour to salute his Majesty at his camp at *Runstadt*. A great number of *English* and *Dutch* Officers obtained likewise the same favour. His *Swedish* Majesty caused all his army to make the evolutions in their presence, which drew a great crowd from *Copenhagen* to the *Swedish* camp. The desire, which all had of seeing the King, brought this great number of people together.

The eighteenth of *August* his *Swedish* Majesty drew near to *Copenhagen*, accompanied by all his Generals, and rode round it, in order to make his observation on the out-works. The day following, all the regiments of horse as well as foot were put in motion to be transported into *Scania*. Before their departure, the inhabitants of *Seeland* and *Copenhagen* furnished them with necessary provisions and a great number of boats. The King, impatient to find himself in *Livonia*, passed the *Sound* at *Helsingburg*, well pleased to have so happily and in so little time put an end to a war so much to his glory, and which replaced his brother-in-law in the full enjoyment of all his rights and prerogatives.

Whilst the negotiations of peace were carrying on, the *Czar* prepared to attack *Ingria*, a frontier province of *Sweden*. His design was to act in concert with King *Augustus*, in consequence of the secret alliance which he had concluded with that Prince. The *Czar's* conduct with regard to *Sweden* had long given reason to believe, that he meditated something to the disadvantage of that Court, in spite of all those assurances to the contrary, which *Matweof*, his Ambassador at the *Hague*, continually gave to the

the *Swedish* Minister; whilst that Prince made 1700. the same protestations to the Resident of his *Swedish* Majesty at *Moscow*.

The better to deceive the Court of *Sweden*, and dissipate, if possible, all her suspicions, the *Czar* sent an Ambassador to *Charles* XII. named *Knees Andrew-Jacobowiz.Chilkow*, who arrived in *Seeland* the 29th, and transmitted to the King a letter from the *Czar*, by which he assured his *Swedish* Majesty of an inviolable friendship. This Envoy, who had travelled in *Italy*, harangued the King in *Italian*, and assured him, that the *Czar* his master would take the first opportunity of sending a solemn Embassy, to give him fresh proofs of his friendship.

The King gave this Ambassador a very gracious reception; and as he said, that he had orders from the *Czar* to attend the Court every where, he accompanied the King to *Christianstadt*, where this Prince was come to press the transportation into *Livonia*. But affairs soon began to change their complexion. As soon as the *Czar*'s troops were ready, he caused them to defile towards the frontiers of *Ingria*. By degrees, as these troops approached thither, the *Czar*'s Ministers in foreign Courts began to change their language: They alledged, above all, I know not what affront, supposed or true, done partly to the person of the *Czar* himself, and partly to his Ambassadors at *Riga*; ‖ on which subject a writing was publish'd and dispers'd every where[m].

‖ See Append. N° 6.

The

---

[m] The four following articles of this declaration of war, which was published at *Moscow* the 30th of *August*, seem calculated rather to divert than impose on *Europe*.

‘ 1. That his reception at ‘ *Riga*, when he passed that ‘ way in 1697, with his ‘ grand embassy, which was ‘ going into *Germany* and ‘ *Holland*, was not sufficient- ‘ ly

1700. The King of *England* [a] and the *States General* gave themselves much trouble to calm the temper of the *Czar*: They promised him, that the *Swedish* Court would be very ready to give him all kind of satisfaction, as soon as she should precisely know in what she had offended. All these representations were fruitless: The *Czar* laid siege to *Narva* with an army of 80,000 men; and, without making any other declaration of war, he put all to fire and sword.

This irruption awakened the hopes of King *Augustus*, who was much alarmed at the peace of *Travendahl*, and the clause therein inserted, by which the King of *Denmark* was engaged not to assist either directly or indirectly the enemies of the King of *Sweden*.

As *Augustus* could not besiege *Riga*, he contented himself with sending parties into the neighbourhood of that town, to carry off all the cattle and forage that they could find. The news of the *Czar*'s irruption determined him to quit the

'ly magnificent: That the provisions which he wanted were sold him too dear by that town: That they had retained his attendants as prisoners, without permitting them to go out of their houses: And when he was to pass the *Duna* with his numerous train, they did not furnish him with convenient yachts or boats, and had exacted too much money of him for those they did provide him. 2. That the coaches and baggage of one of his *Czarish* Majesty's ministers, returning from *Turkey*, had been lately plunder'd by the *Livonian* peasants. 3. That the Post-master at *Moscow* having complained in *Sweden* against the Post-master of *Riga*, on account of some differences risen between them, demanded to have him turned out of his employment; which had not been comply'd with. 4. The fourth consisted of certain unsettled pretensions, which some *Russian* merchants had on some *Swedish* merchants, &c. Memoir. *du regne de Pierre le Grand*, tom. 2.

[a] His letter is inserted at large in the above-cited *Memoirs*, tom. 2. pag. 412.

the neighbourhood of *Riga*, and to content himself with the conquests which he had already made on the other side of the river, and endeavour to maintain them, till having drawn together greater force he was in a condition to act with more vigour. To open a communication between this river and *Livonia*, he caused some troops to appear at seven in the morning before *Kokenbusen*, a little fort on this side of the *Duna*, where there was a garrison consisting of a Major and 200 men. *Augustus* repair'd hither the day following with the army, and gave orders to Veldt-Marshal *Steinau* to summon the Commandant to surrender; which this Commandant refusing to do, he resolved to open the siege in form.

The trenches were opened the same night, and after some days continuance of the siege, the Commandant seeing the enemy at the very brink of the mote, and ready to attack the rampart, found himself obliged to capitulate. The garrison marched out with all their baggage, and repaired to *Riga*. The Commandant was instantly put under arrest, for not having done his utmost in the defence of the fort.

The King of *Sweden*, who was repaired from *Christianstadt* to *Carlshaven*, where was the rendezvous of the greater part of the troops designed for *Livonia*, had yet heard nothing of these first hostilities of the *Czar*. Here this Prince's Ambassador had his audience of leave from the King, who received him in a very gracious manner.

The transports were ready to sail, when his *Swedish* Majesty received the news of the siege of *Narva*, and of the first hostilities exercised by the *Muscovites*, who put all to fire and sword.

He

He was extremely surprized at hearing it; for, notwithstanding all the reports which had been spread abroad of the march of the *Russian* troops, he could not persuade himself, that the *Czar* had taken a resolution to declare war against him; nor was he entirely convinced, till after he had an account of this last step of his *Czarish* Majesty.

Charles was touched to the quick at the extremity to which the town of *Narva* was reduced. The *Russians* having presently summoned the Governor to surrender, threatened to push the siege with all possible vigour. On the refusal of Baron *Horn*, who commanded in the place, the trenches were opened before the castle of *Ivanogrod* and before the town.

In this condition stood the siege of *Narva* when his *Swedish* Majesty embark'd at *Carlshaven*, accompanied by the Duke of *Holstein*, who was arrived from his own estates three days before. The Counts *Piper* and *Polus*, and a great number of officers and persons of distinction, embarked also with his Majesty. The Duke accompanied the King some leagues at sea, and thence repaired to *Stockholm*, to see the Dutchess his spouse, who had been delivered of a Prince in *April* this year. As troubles were likewise to be apprehended from the quarter of *Pomerania*, the Duke repaired thither to command the troops, and at the same time to put the town of *Stettin* in a condition of defence.

The King arrived happily at *Pernau* with part of the transports; his arrival revived the courage of the *Livonians*, and inspired them with the greatest hopes. The University of *Pernau* signalized itself on this occasion by many pieces both in prose and verse, which they took care to make publick. The King stopt there near a week,

week, during which stay the other vessels arriv'd with the troops; he made them disembark, and suffer'd them to repose there some days to refresh themselves after the fatigues of the sea. The first news that the King heard at his arrival was, that the *Czar* had made many attacks upon the town of *Narva* without any success. He afterwards understood, that the country was entirely laid waste ten leagues round; and that this Prince designed to burn the *Swedish* magazine at *Wesenberg*, and thence intended to march towards *Reval*.

It was to ward off this blow, that the King went to *Ryen*, where *Welling* had posted himself after his leaving *Riga*. His Majesty, having reviewed the body of troops under that General, ordered him to march towards the enemy, to cover *Wesenberg*, and to provide quarters of refreshment for the army, which was incessantly to follow. At the same time the Colonels *Schlippenbach* and *Skytt* were detached towards the town of *Dorpt*, to observe the motions of the *Russians* and *Saxons*; the first being encamped opposite to the lake *Peipus*, and the *Saxons* on the side of *Kockenhusen*. *Schlippenbach* surprized at *Ismen*, near *Rapin* on the *Peipus*, twelve *Russian* vessels, which had come thither from the neighbourhood of *Narva*.

The King, in his return from *Ryen* to *Pernau*, stopt there again some days, whence he afterwards marched to *Reval*, where he was received under a discharge of the cannon from the ramparts. The day of his arrival, the provincial colours of *Plescou*, which Colonel *Schlippenbach* had taken at the battle of *Ismen*, were presented to him. This ensign ° is extremely large, on which

---

° It is 5 ells square, made of crimson-damask, embroider'd with gold and silver. Besides the *Russ*-spread-Eagle, there

which are figures very largely painted. When the *Ruffians* of this province formerly went to war, they used to carry it with them, and to accompany it with much respect and devotion; their superstition making them believe, that if ever they lost it, they should be very unfortunate.

The King, at his departure from *Pernau*, had detached some regiments to join at *Wesenberg* General *Welling*, who was already arrived without having met any body of the enemy's troops in his march; but a Lieutenant detached from his van-guard, was encountered near *Purts* by a party of 200 men, whom, tho' he had with him no more than 20 men, he nevertheless defeated and put to flight.

General *Welling* having learnt at his arrival at *Wesenberg* that 3000 *Circaffians* were lodged some leagues off in the villages, sent a Major, named *Patkul*, with 300 horse to surprize them; and Major *Tifenhaufen* had orders to support him with an equal number. They arrived the same evening, and having come up with the enemy, who had not put themselves in a posture of defence, attack'd them, and set fire to their villages. The greater part of them perished in the flames; most of the others were killed, some few only had the good fortune to save themselves under favour of the night and the smoke, which concealed them from the *Swedish* pursuit. The fugitives repaired afterwards to General *Scheremethoff*, who kept himself at *Pybajoki* with a considerable body of horse.

there was painted on it an emblem of the Trinity, and the figure of a Patriarch above the Crown which is over the eagle. *Memoir. du regne de Pierre*, &c.

At this news the *Muscovite* General, putting himself at the head of twenty-one squadrons, went to deliver the rest of these troops. He found the *Swedes* yet busy in killing those whom the fire had spared. He attacked them on all sides, and possessed himself of the pass of *Purts*, to cut off their retreat.

The *Swedes* seeing themselves hem'd in, undertook to break through the enemy sword in hand; which succeeded; they overthrew a great number, and thoroughly disengaged themselves. General *Seberemethoff's* son was dangerously wounded in this action. On the side of the *Swedes*, Major *Patkul* and a Captain named *Adercass* were made prisoners by the starting of their horses, and were delivered some time afterwards at the battle of *Narva*.

Charles, who wished nothing more than to come to blows with the enemy, stay'd not long at *Reval*. The Count *de Guiscard*, the *French* Ambassador, was arrived from *Stockholm* to make the campaign; he endeavoured to persuade the King to wait for the rest of his army, that he might be more on an equal foot with the enemy: But nothing could cool the courage and ardour of this Prince; and the formidable forces of the *Czar*, together with the strong fortifications of his camp, instead of holding him back, only animated him the more.

His resolution was taken, and nothing was capable of dissuading him. Confiding therefore entirely in the justice of his cause, he departed from *Reval* with the few troops that he had, and went to join Mr. *Welling* at *Wesenberg*. The horse-guards, or body-regiment, which was arrived at *Reval*, departed immediately after the King. This Prince, notwithstanding his few forces,

forces, detach'd *Welling* with a body of 1050 men on the side of *Dorpt*, in order to support Colonel *Skytt* and cover the frontiers.

All the baggage, with every thing which could retard their march, was left at *Wesengberg*, which is fifteen good leagues from *Narva*, and the soldiers were forbid to take any thing with them, which was not absolutely necessary for their subsistence. The army then marched thro' *Purts* to *Pyhajoki*; crossing a country deserted, wasted, and where the enemy had throughout left marks of their cruelty; the 17th of *Novemb.* after a laborious march, and at a time when provisions began to grow scarce, they arrived at last at *Pyhajoki*, a very difficult pass, and which a small number might dispute against a whole army. General *Scheremethoff* was here posted with 600 horse, fully resolved to make the *Swedes* pay very dear for their gaining it.

Major-General *Meidel*, who commanded the van-guard of 400 horse, met at about a league distant a troop of *Russian* foragers; he had with him the Quarter-masters of the army, who were to mark out a camp.

As the *Russians* had a strong escort, Mr. *Meidel* desired the King's leave to attack them; on which this Prince advancing with his army, hastened thither with a great number of officers, and charged the foragers in an instant, some of whom he took prisoners, and the rest he put to flight, pursuing them at their heels with his few people to that dangerous pass where *Scheremethoff* was posted, in the midst of a great fire, as well of the small arms as the ordnance.

The King being impatient to carry this important post, brought up some of his foot, at the same time taking the advantage of the darkness

of

of the night to plant some field-pieces. The Russians were attacked with so much vigour, that *Scheremethoff*, instead of making head against us, fled with all his horse full speed, and was himself the messenger to the *Czar* of the enemy's approach.

Mr. *Palmquist*, Lieutenant-Colonel, was order'd with a battalion of guards to take possession of that important defile, of which we had made ourselves masters, and which was so much the more dangerous to attack and easy to defend, for that between two steep hills there is in the middle a torrent, with a steep and marshy bank, in which place, the valley, being extremely narrow, may be defended by a few men against a whole army; add to this, that the plain higher up on the *Swedes* side was entirely open, and exposed to the fire of the cannon on the opposite bank, where a great number of bushes cover'd the enemy.

After we had carried this post, the King judg'd it proper to be diligent, and take an advantage of the fright of the enemy, without giving them time to recover themselves; the rather, as our provisions began to fail us, and we could not hope to find any more in a deserted and ruin'd country. The army then continued its march thro' *Silleenegi*, and arriv'd the 20th of *Nov.* at *Lagena*, a league and a half from *Nerva*. We had but 5000 foot and 3000 horse, the greater part of which were sick, and in no condition of fighting. Indeed, considering the condition of these troops, no one would have believed that the King would so soon have attacked the enemy; the soldiers and horses being so extremely fatigued: but as it was to be fear'd that the enemy would soon put themselves in a posture of defence, the King thought proper to prevent them,

them, and attack them without waiting for other succours.

As soon as *Charles* had taken these measures, he quitted *Lagena*, and came in sight of the enemy at eleven in the morning. The *Czar* had advantageously fortified his camp, which extended from the mill of *Portei* on the river which runs through *Narva* quite to *Joola* on the other side of the town, on the same river, which makes a league in length. The intrenchment was provided with a bulwark, armed with a *Chevaux de Frise*, with deep ditches, flank'd on the outside with some works, and on the inside with several batteries placed in the most advantageous manner, and with a strong line of countervallation.

Notwithstanding the continual fire of the enemy, the King drew up his army in order of battle, conveying himself to different places to examine the most favourable ground for the attack. The foot were then employed in getting together the necessary fascines. After his Majesty had reconnoitred the weak part of the enemy's intrenchments, he resolved on two general attacks.

General *Welling* commanded the right wing, which was to enter on the side of *Rathsboff*. The attack was conducted by Major-General *Poss*, in the following manner: Lieutenant *Rhenschild*, at the head of fifty Granadiers of the Guards, began the attack. He was followed by the battalion of Granadiers of the regiment of Guards, commanded by Count *Sperling*, supported by three battalions of Guards; that in the middle under Mr. *Palmquist*, that on the right commanded by Major *Nummers*, and that on the left by Captain *Ehrensten*. Next marched the

Captains

Captains of the Guards, *Charles Pofs* on the right, and Captain *Sparr* on the left.

These were supported by Colonel *Knorring* at the head of a battalion of *Helfingers* on the right, and on the left by Captain *Cazimir Wrangel* at the head of a battalion of *Wefmanland*. Colonel *Tifenhaufen* followed with a battalion of *Finland* on the right, Major *Wulff* in the middle with a battalion of *Helfingers*, and Captain *Kurck* with a battalion of *Wefmanland* on the left. All the horse on the right wing, commanded by Lieutenant-General *Wachtmeifter*, were order'd to support the foot, and afterwards to enter the enemy's lines fword in hand.

The left wing, which was ordered to attack on the side of *Wepfckyle*, was commanded by Lieutenant-General *Rhenfchild*. We formed two attacks; the firft of which, confifting of two columns, was led to the right by Major-General *Meidel*. The firft column on the right was under the command of Lieutenant-Colonel *Roos*, who commanded a battalion of *Wermland*. He was followed by Captain *Fock* with another battalion of the fame regiment, by Major *Von Feilitz* with a battalion of *Wefmanland*, and by Captain *Safs*, who clofed this column with a battalion of *Finland*. The second column to the left had Lieutenant-Colonel *Gryndel* at their head with three battalions of *Finland*; the firft commanded by Colonel *Melin*, the fecond by Lieutenant-Colonel *Lode*, the third by Major *Berg*.

These two columns on the right were ordered to attack the intrenchment of the enemy on that fide where they had raised a battery, which commanded the country and the lines of the intrenchment, in order to make themfelves mafters thereof. The fecond attack to the left was commanded

manded by Count *Stenbock*, a Colonel, supported by a battalion of *Finland* commanded by Lieutenant-Colonel *Hastfehr*. They were provided with a great number of fascines, to mount the intrenchments.

The King was himself on this wing with his Drabans, where he had flattered himself to be able to encounter the *Czar*; but this Prince departed that morning for ᵖ *Moscow*, having left the command of his army to the Duke *de Croy*. *Charles* had with him Lieutenant-General *Rhenschild*, Count *Arwid Horn*, Major-General and Captain-Lieutenant of Drabans, and all the horse of the left wing, whereof Major-General *Ribbing* commanded the *Corps de Reserve*.

Mr. *Sioblad*, Grand Master of the Artillery, had placed his battery on the left wing, which consisted of twenty-one field-pieces; and Major *Appelmann* had another on the right of sixteen pieces.

As soon as the King had made these dispositions, the signal of attack was given, which was the discharge of two fusees, and these words, *With the Assistance of God*, which resounded through the whole army. The foot were instantly in motion, and march'd directly to the intrenchment. It was now two o'clock in the afternoon; and the weather, which had continued hitherto serene, was all of a sudden over-cast with a thick cloud, which discharged itself in a storm of hail and snow full in the face of the enemy, and caused them not to perceive the

---

ᵖ According to Mr. *Voltaire*, the *Czar* was not gone for *Moscow*, but towards *Plescow*, to hasten the march of 40000 men which were advancing from that quarter; with which other accounts seem likewise to agree.

approach

The LIFE *and* HISTORY *of*

d by Count *Stenbock*, a Colonel, supported
ttalion of *Finland* commanded by Lieute-
olonel *Haſtfehr*. They were provided
great number of faſcines, to mount the
hments.

King was himſelf on this wing with his
s, where he had flattered himſelf to be
encounter the *Czar*; but this Prince
d that morning for *Moſcow*, having left
nmand of his army to the Duke *de Croy*.
had with him Lieutenant-General *Rheny*
Count *Arwid Horn*, Major-General and
-Lieutenant of Drabans, and all the horſe
eft wing, whereof Major-General *Ribbing*
nded the *Corps de Reſerve*.
Sioblad, Grand Maſter of the Artillery,
ced his battery on the left wing, which
d of twenty-one field-pieces; and Major
unn had another on the right of ſixteen

oon as the King had made theſe diſpo-
the ſignal of attack was given, which
diſcharge of two fuſees, and theſe words,
be Aſſiſtance of God, which reſounded
the whole army. The foot were in
motion, and march'd directly to the
ent. It was now two o' clock in the
; and the weather, which had continu-
to ſerene, was all of a ſudden over-caſt
ick cloud, which diſcharged itſelf in a
hail and ſnow full in the face of the
and cauſed them not to perceive the

ding to Mr. *Vol-* of 40000 men which were ad-
Czar was not gone vancing from that quarter,
, but towards with which other accounts
haſten the march ſeem likewiſe to agree.

approach

Vol. I. Page 54.

Radtshoff

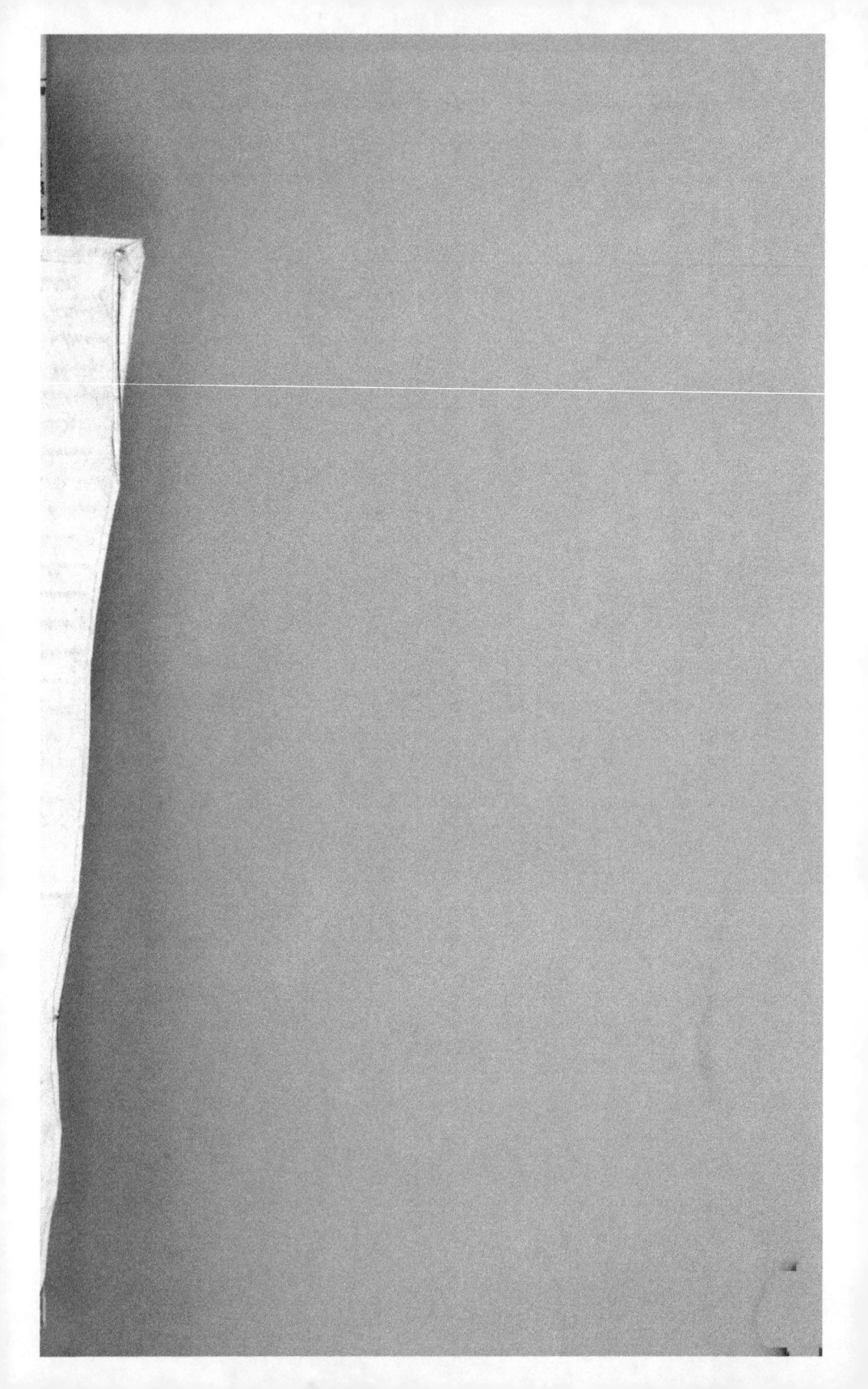

approach of the *Swedes* till they were under their cannon, and almoſt on the brink of their ditch.

The attack of the intrenchment was made with ſo much bravery, and followed every where with ſo happy a ſucceſs, that the foot made a lodgment in leſs than a quarter of an hour, and prepared a way for the horſe to enter. The *Muſcovites* were now put to flight, and diſperſed themſelves, notwithſtanding all the Duke *de Croy* could do to rally them. Our left wing chaſed the right of the enemy along the intrenchment toward the river, whither they ran to gain the bridge which they had built.

One part of theſe frightened troops attempted to get out of their intrenchments, to ſave themſelves the better; which the King perceiving, he attacked them at the head of his Drabans and Dragoons of the left wing, and forced them back in haſte. In the mean time our infantry advanced briſkly, and made a dreadful ſlaughter of all they met. Several of thoſe who were purſued to the river had the happineſs to ſave themſelves; but the bridge being at length broken down under them, a great many periſhed in the water.

The others being hemmed in between the *Swedes* and the river, reſolved to defend themſelves like men in deſpair. They had yet at their head a great part of their Generals; but the Duke *de Croy*, General *Allart*, and many others, had already ſurrender'd themſelves to the King. They found ſome houſes and barracks, behind which they took ſhelter, and barricaded themſelves with their waggons and every thing they could meet with. There they defended themſelves with more bravery than was expected; and notwithſtanding the terrible and

continual

continual fire of the *Swedes*, we could not force them.

The battle became the more fierce and bloody, by reason of the darkness which now came on. The King, who was now with some horse on the outside of the intrenchment, ran to a place where he heard a noise, followed only by his Chamberlain, whose name was *Axel Hordh*. As he passed by a morass he sunk in, whence some Valets, who were near, having drawn him out, he left his sword and one boot behind, which were afterwards found. This accident did not hinder him, with one boot on only, from putting himself at the head of his foot, whom he yet found engaged with the enemy, the fire continuing on both sides with great violence.

In the mean while the right wing of the *Swedes* had as good success as the left. They had already put the enemy to flight, and the greater part of the foot came afterwards to join the left wing at their attack.

The night coming on put a stop to the battle, and the King made use of that time to prepare for a new attack. He drew out his army between the town and the intrenchments, in such a manner that it could not be surprised. He gave orders at the same time to Mr. *Sioblad*, Grand Master of the Artillery, Major-General *Meidel*, and Count *Stenbock*, to go with some troops and attack a hill where the enemy had their principal battery, which commanded all the intrenchments, by being masters of which, the *Swedes* might henceforth hinder the communication between the two wings of the enemy.

The *Muscovites* seeing that at last they should be forced to surrender, their right wing being shut

shut up on the river of *Narva*, sent the same evening to the King to submit to his mercy. *Charles* having consented to their request, the Knez *Jacob Feodorowits Dolgoruki*, Commissary-General of War, the General *Affemon Michalowits Golowin*, and the Prince of *Melita*, Grand Master of the Artillery, came to surrender to his Majesty, and lay their arms at his feet. They declared they submitted themselves with all their men prisoners, and instantly delivered up that post which they had so long defended, which was presently ordered to be kept by two battalions of Guards.

The King, contented with the submission of these troops, permitted them to retire with their arms, which they did the next day at four in the morning, over the bridge that they had repaired. The Conqueror however reserved all their colours and standards, and retained all their officers of distinction as prisoners of war.

As soon as General *Weide*, who commanded the broken remains of the enemy's left wing, had learnt the fate of the right, which he was cut off from joining, he sent at break of day his *Aide-de-Camp* with a Drum and a letter directed to the General who commanded in chief, to submit himself at discretion. The King, having opened the letter, answer'd, that he granted the troops leave of returning into their own country, but without their arms.

Charles received all these *Muscovite* regiments, who threw their colours and standards at his feet. They afterwards filed off, as well officers as soldiers with their heads bare, and a stick in their hands, along the intrenchment and the camp towards the river, and passed over the same bridge which we just now mentioned: There was so great a number of them, that the march continued till the next morning.

Such was the success of this great day, which will be always famous in history, in which a young Hero entirely defeated an intrenched army of 80,000 men.

The *Swedes* found a great quantity of riches in the enemy's camp; but nothing was comparable to the fine train of artillery which fell into the hands of the Conqueror: It consisted of 145 pieces of brass cannon, all new cast and of different bores; 28 new mortars, of different sizes; with a quantity of warlike stores, six pair of kettle-drums, 151 colours, 20 standards, without reckoning those taken in the action, and those which were afterwards found in the field of battle; a prodigious quantity of fire-arms, the *Czar*'s military ᑫ chest, all their tents, and vast provisions of victuals and forage.

The *Muscovites* lost at least ʳ 18000 men, including those who were drowned in the *Narva*; of the *Swedes* there were not above 2000, either killed or wounded.

Among the prisoners of war were the Duke *de Croy*, their Commander in chief; *Dolgoruki*, Commissary-General of war; *Golowin* and *Adam Weid*, Generals of foot; the Knez *Iwan Jurgenits Trubetskoi*, Governor of *Novogrod* and General; *Artschelowits*, Prince of *Melita* in *Georgia*, and Grand Master of the artillery; *Allart*, Lieutenant-General and chief Engineer; Baron *Lang*, Major-General, and Envoy of *Poland*; *Iwan Iwanowits Buturlin*, Major-General; *Blumberg*, Colonel of the *Czar*'s guards; *Von Kragen*, Colonel of artillery; the Colonels *Fort*, *Von Deelen*, *Jacob*

ᑫ It contained 262,000 crowns.

ʳ 22,000 according to the author of the *Memoirs*.

Jacob Gordon, *Schnecberg*, *Gulitz*, *Pindegrand*, *Weithoff*, *Jordan*, and *Iwanitski*; not to mention a great number of Lieutenant-Colonels, Majors, and Captains.

We must not here forget what the Duke *de Croy* said to Mr. *Guiscard* speaking of this battle: He assured him, that when he saw the *Swedish* army, after it had come out of the wood of *Lagena*, drawn up in order of battle and approaching him, that he thought it was only their vanguard, not being able to believe that the King of *Sweden* would have dared to attack an army so well intrenched, and so infinitely superior to his own. This Duke, to whom the *Czar* had left the supreme command of his troops, died a year afterwards at *Reval* in his way to *Moscow*.

The King signalized himself in a very extraordinary manner on this famous day, exposing himself in all places where the fire was the briskest: He received however no wound, but in the evening a ball was found in his black cravat, which had lodged there without doing him the least mischief.

As soon as every thing was quiet, the King encampt his troops along the intrenchment, and sent the sick and wounded into *Narva*, into which town he made his victorious entry, followed by a great number of officers, and by his Drabans, amidst the repeated acclamations of the inhabitants, who were transported with joy at seeing themselves delivered by their own master,

after

---

* Mr. *Voltaire* tells us, that the King received a slight flesh-wound in his left arm, and that he had two horses killed under him, the second of which had his head taken off by a cannon-shot; and on his vaulting with activity on the third, he cry'd out, *These fellows make me perform my exercises*; and continued to give his orders with the same presence of mind.

after having suffered the inconveniencies of a siege which had lasted near ten weeks. Colonel *Horn*, who had defended this place, was very well received by his Majesty, who made him a Major-General.

The King's first care, after his victorious entry into *Narva*, was to return solemn thanks to God for the victory which he had won. The 26th was appointed for this ceremony. *Te Deum* was sung, with the discharge of the cannon of the town, of the castle of *Ivanogrod*, of the camp and the intrenchments; and all the troops, which were under arms, gave a double salvo from their small arms.

As 'twas much to be fear'd that the army would want provisions, the King thought that inconvenience was to be timely prevented. On an account therefore which he receiv'd, that the enemy had abandoned a magazine of corn at *Jama*, a castle situated some leagues from *Narva*, he went thither himself in person, and order'd the whole to be conveyed to *Narva*, together with two brass mortars which the *Muscovites* had left behind them in the castle. However, as these provisions were not yet sufficient, the King was under some uneasiness on this account.

In reality, the country was entirely destroy'd, and his Majesty would not resolve on sending parties into the neighbouring provinces of the enemy, fearing lest the inhabitants should withdraw themselves from the frontiers with all their cattle and provisions; they therefore took other measures. The King thought proper to give his protection to those provinces which depended on the *Muscovites* bordering on *Ingria*, allowing them the same liberty of commerce which they had before. This method produced for some time

King CHARLES XII. *of* SWEDEN.

time the defired effect; the neceffary provifions were brought to the camp, for which the money was not only paid, but advanced before-hand.

In the mean while the *Czar*, fomewhat recovered from his confternation, occafioned by the lofs of the battle of *Narva*, drew together the difperfed remains of his army, which he afterwards quarter'd at *Plefcow*, at *Pitfchur*, at *Iburfki*, and on the frontiers of *Livonia*, where he detached them feveral ways to burn and pillage the country.

While Colonel *Schlippenbach* coafted the river of *Aa*, near *Dorpt*, to obferve the motions of the enemy, 2000 *Mufcovites* were pofted at *Neuhaufen*, an old caftle near *Rapin*, where they intrenched themfelves, in order to lay the neighbourhood under contribution.

Lieutenant-Colonel *Romanowitz* was detached on that fide with 400 men, both foot and horfe, to diflodge them. As he had no cannon, he endeavoured to draw them into the open field, and there give them battle. With this view he difmounted his dragoons, and advancing with his foot up to the pallifades, he made a difcharge on the enemy, by which fome of them fell. He afterwards feigned a retreat, and that with fuch precipitation, that the *Mufcovites* looking on it as a flight, came out of their intrenchments to charge the *Swedes*; on which they faced about, and received the enemy fo vigoroufly, that they immediately overthrew them. The *Mufcovites*, being put to flight, attempted to regain the caftle, but were purfued fo brifkly, that great numbers of them were killed. Some of thofe, who were able to fave themfelves, took the road to *Pitfchur*, and the reft fhut themfelves up in *Neuhaufen*.

The

The *Swedes* by this means gave liberty to a great number of peasants, whom the *Muscovites* were carrying into slavery. As the enemy might receive succours from *Pitschur*, *Romanowitz* retired during the night into the next village, whence he sent out little parties to make discoveries: These reported, that the enemy had abandoned *Neuhausen*, leaving more than 200 dead behind them; and that the *Muscovites* had done the same thing at *Rapin*.

In the mean while provisions grew every day more scarce at *Narva*, which the troops felt the more by reason of their fatigue in their late hard campaign. The King, seeing it impossible to take up his winter-quarters in that town, resolved to enter into *Livonia*, where he might be able to make head against all his enemies. Before his departure, he sent Major-General *Meidel* with the *Finland* troops towards *Vasknarva*, where the enemy seemed to have a design of approaching, with orders to hinder them from committing any destruction.

The King quitted *Narva* the 13th of *December*, with his army, to put them into winter-quarters near *Dorpt*, on the frontiers of *Livonia*. The regiment of horse-guards was gone before, and had already posted themselves at *Koikel*, on the lake *Peipus*, to cover the frontiers.

As Baron *Spens*, Colonel of that regiment and a Major-General, was then absent, the Lieutenant-Colonel marched a detachment to *Neuhausen*, where he left Captain *Muller* with 100 horse to defend that post. *Muller* was presently attacked by some thousand *Muscovites*, who gave him a furious assault, which he sustained three hours together with great valour, obliging the enemy

enemy at length to retire with the loss of 300 men.

The 19th of *December* the King arrived at *Lais*, an old castle six leagues from *Dorpt*, which he chose for his head quarters: His troops were quartered in the neighbourhood and on the frontiers; Baron *Spens* at *Sagniz*, Colonel *Schlippenbach* in the neighbourhood of *Marienburg*, and Colonel *Albedyhl* at *Ronnenburg*. The King cast his eyes on *Volmar* as a proper place for his magazine.

Charles, who was always indefatigable, failed not to visit all his troops with the utmost exactness, and to provide for their safety, by covering and securing them against the frequent excursions of the *Muscovites* and *Saxons*.

As to *Ingria* and *Finland*, Major-General *Cronhiort* was ordered to repair thither with a body of 6000 men, and post himself on the frontiers. Towards the end of *December*, Count *Guiscard*, Ambassador from *France*, arrived at *Lais*, and had immediately a very gracious audience of his Majesty, whom he congratulated in the name of the King his Master, upon the victory which he had gained at *Narva*.

The troops now suffer'd much in their winter-quarters, by a distemper which was almost general, occasioned by the laborious marches and continual enterprizes in the late season, and through those miserable huts in which they were obliged to lodge their soldiers for want of houses. The King, who was extremely touched with their sufferings, went about continually amongst them to inform himself of their condition: He prevailed so much by his presence and the infinite care which he took, that the distemper abated by little and little, and did not do so much mischief

chief as it seemed to threaten. This Prince's Court was not exempt from it; and amongst many persons who were attacked by it, Count *Wreed*, the King's Chamberlain, died on the 10th of *January*, universally lamented on account of his merit and fine qualities.

Towards the end of the preceding year, Count *Stenbock*, Major-General, was ordered to make reprisals on the *Russians*, who had set fire to many places on the lake *Peipus*. With this view he passed the frontiers with 1000 men, horse and foot, near *Andowa*, to surprize that little town; but the rigour of the season, a thick mist, together with the strong garrison of *Strelitzs*, which were there, added to his want of cannon, made him change his resolution. After having gained many advantages over those parties of the enemy which he could come up with, and after having set fire to several places, he repassed the frontiers in the beginning of *January*.

On the other hand Colonel *Schlippenbach*, who had been ordered to coast along the river of *Aa*, and to observe the motions of the *Saxons* at *Kokenhusen*, being informed that they had appeared about *Marienburg*, took a resolution to make himself master of that place, and to drive them farther off. It was to be feared, that they would have fortified themselves here, on account of the situation of the place, which was very advantageous to them, and very proper to incommode all the adjacent parts.

Schlippenbach acquainted the King with his design of possessing himself of this post; and he advanced immediately, that he might be in readiness to execute his Majesty's orders. Two days afterwards a large body of *Cossacks* having appeared before the place, Major *Zoge* was detached

tached with 150 men to pursue them. He killed 30 of them, and made some prisoners. The King, who very much approved Mr. *Schlippenbach*'s design, sent him a reinforcement of 200 foot-soldiers, drawn out of the garrison of *Dorpt*, with some pieces of cannon. The Colonel made so good use of them, that in a few days, having raised the rampart, he put this place, which was of itself environ'd with a morass, into so good a condition of defence, that he not only hindered the excursions of the enemy, but made some very successful ones himself, having established his quarters here for the rest of the winter.

In the mean time the King, who was not pleased at the frequent irruptions of the *Russians*, went to *reconnoitre* the lake *Peipus*; and as the body-guards were yet in their quarters of refreshment, Baron *Spens*, now Lieutenant-General, was ordered to march towards *Sagnitz*, to enter into winter-quarters. There remained now at *Neuhausen* but one Lieutenant with 30 horse, who three days afterwards were attacked by 400 *Muscovites*, whom they bravely repulsed.

As to Colonel *Schlippenbach*, having received advice that the *Saxons* had laid up a magazine at *Sesswegen*, and had forced the inhabitants of the country to bring in their corn, to be afterwards conveyed to *Kokenhusen*, he detached Lieutenant-Colonel *Brandt* thither, who with 400 horse made himself master of the magazine, and conducted to *Marienburg* near a thousand ton of corn.

The King seeing the *Saxons* desert every day in great numbers, thought proper, after distributing money amongst them, to send them all to *Reval*. This Prince, who was always in action,

1701. action, to amuse the rest of his time, discover'd some taste for hunting ; to entertain which, Count *Stenbock*, on his return from his last expedition, made a great hunting-match for his Majesty on St. *Charles*'s day, which was followed by a fine entertainment and other diversions.

Publick rejoicings were every where celebrated through *Sweden* and the conquered provinces, on account of the victory of *Narva*, but above all at *Stockholm*, where they made the most magnificent entertainments and illuminations. *Te Deum* was sung, accompanied with a discharge of the cannon, and the whole city was illuminated in the evening, to which Baron *Tessin*, afterwards made Marshal of the Court, and one of the greatest architects of his age, contributed by a thousand beautiful devices ; the most remarkable of all was a triumphal pyramid of his invention, the design whereof was perfectly elegant, and which was erected at the expence of the city : It was placed on a hill named *Brunkeberg*, almost in the middle of the city, which commanded the whole neighbourhood, and was set off with several thousands of lamps. On the four sides were a great number of devices of Mr. *Kheder*, an able antiquary ; and above all these formidable words, *Ecce, veni, vidi, vici*, which had been before so well verified.

There was a *French* Opera at Court, which was followed by a fine fire-work, and by several balls and entertainments. The Ambassadors and foreign Ministers emulated each other in shewing honours to this day, which was so glorious for *Sweden*.

Whilst they were busy in celebrating this victory, the King, who was always attentive to every opportunity, resolv'd to surprize and burn

Pitschur,

Pitfchur, a place situated on the frontiers of *Livonia,* and which afforded the enemy a retreat after every excursion; for which purpose Lieutenant-General *Spens* was dispatched with the regiment of horse-guards, and was joined in his march on the frontiers by Colonel *Schlippenbach* and his Dragoons, with some foot from the garrison of *Marienbourg,* and a great number of peasants proper to ravage the enemy's country. *Spens* being arrived before this town at break of day, on the 13th of *February,* attacked the *Russians* who were posted here, so briskly, that our men kill'd more than 500 before they came up to the barrier. We pursued them into the town, where a great number of *Russians,* who had barricaded themselves within the houses, whence they discharged on us with great violence and despair, were burnt by the *Livonian* peasants, who set fire to the four corners of the town, and also to a quantity of hides and dress'd leather, and a large magazine of hemp; the loss arising from this conflagration amounted in all to near a million.

Some of those who fled saved themselves in a convent surrounded by a strong wall mounted with cannon, and situated on an hill which commands the town; of which the enemy taking advantage, made a hot fire on the *Swedes,* who were scattered in the several parts of the town, and thereby obliged the General, who had no ordnance, to retire, after having caused the peasants to bring off all the booty which they could save from the flames. We had 30 men killed in this rencounter, amongst whom was a Major, whose name was *Wallenstedt,* and about 60 wounded. Mr. *Spens* returned directly to *Sagnitz,* and *Schlippenbach* to *Marienbourg,* whence,

1701, on the 20th of *February*, he sent out a party of 200 men, horse and foot, who penetrated between *Pitschur* and the *Polish Livonia* as far as *Iburski*, having with them a Captain named *Axel Green*, an Engineer, to *reconnoitre* the ground and the situations of places.

These troops defeated several *Russian* parties in their way, and brought off a quantity of provisions and a number of prisoners. The town of *Iburski*, which lyes in a triangle with *Plescow* and *Pitschur*, is situated on an high mountain, and defended by some works. The Czar, after the rout at *Narva*, had placed good garrisons in these three towns; viz. 6000 of his best troops at *Plescow*, four regiments of Circassians at *Iburski*, and 4000 men at *Pitschur*, to cover the frontiers, and make frequent excursions into *Livonia*.

That Prince, after his hasty return to *Moscow*, proceeded from thence to *Birsen* in *Lithuania* the 21st of *February*, to have there an interview with the King of *Poland*. Here these two Princes, after three weeks conference [f], renewed their alliance, and

---

[f] Mr. *Voltaire* says, they were only 15 days together, in which they carried their pleasures to a great excess; for the *Czar*, says he, who was desirous of reforming his people, could not correct in himself his dangerous propension to debauchery. A treaty was here made between them, by which it was agreed to take from the King of *Sweden* all his possessions on this side the *Baltick*, either in *Poland* or *Germany*; to which purpose it was stipulated, that his *Czarish* Majesty should bring into the field, in the month of *June*, 20,000 men: That as the *Russians* could not so soon be brought to the *German* discipline, the King of *Poland* should procure his *Czarish* Majesty 50,000 men from different Princes, to enter into his pay; namely, 22 thousand of the house of *Saxony*, 16 thousand *Danes*, and 12 thousand *Poles*: That the

and the *Czar* promised to supply 20,000 men, and large sums of money, to push on the war with vigour against the common enemy. After this interview the *Czar* repaired to *Dunamund*, passed through *Mittau*, and returned by *Birsen* to *Moscow*; and the King of *Poland* took the road of *Warsovia*.

Colonel *Schlippenbach*, encouraged by the successful excursions of his men, sent out a new party, who, after having made great destruction, brought back a large quantity of provisions and many prisoners. General *Spens* on his side de-

the *Czar* should pay to King *Augustus* 3,000,000 rixdollars in two years for the support of his *Saxon* troops; in consideration of which his *Polish* Majesty should keep up 28 thousand foot and 3 thousand horse, to which his *Czarish* Majesty should join 50 thousand *Russians*, and 10 thousand of those foreign troops which we have mentioned: That all these troops should act together in *Livonia* against the King of *Sweden*, whilst the *Czar* himself in person, at the head of another body, should invade *Finland*, and penetrate into the heart of the *Swedish* dominions: That the Knez *Menzikoff* with 50,000 *Russians*, to which should be joined the troops of *Sapieha*, and all those of *Poland* which were in the service of King *Augustus*, should be posted on the frontiers of *Lithuania* to give a diversion. King *Au-gustus* engaged moreover to discipline 50 *Russian* battalions, who were to be always employed in his service, to be dress'd in the *German* fashion, instructed in the *German* exercise, and put on the foot of old troops, which were from time to time to be recruited by the *Czar*, who was likewise to send men on the *Rhine*, to be incorporated in those regiments which *Augustus* there supported as his quota, in quality of Elector of *Saxony*. The *Czar* likewise received from King *Augustus* a plan of the rules of military discipline, promising for the future, that all his army should be raised, payed, dressed, exercised, and disciplined after the *German* manner. *Mem. du regne de Pierre,* &c. *tom.* 2. *fol.* 466. This treaty, says *Voltaire*, if it had been executed, might have been fatal to the King of *Sweden*.

tached

tached a Captain with an hundred horse, followed by a great number of peasants, who passing over the *Peipus*, which was frozen, advanced within four leagues of *Plescow*. This expedition was not fruitless; for having met a body of *Strelitzes*, they entirely defeated them, and returned laden with booty and prisoners, after having burnt all the places they found in their road.

About this time a phænomenon appeared at noon-day at *Lais*; this was two suns, each surrounded with different arches, and seeming to form a double X. The ignorant and superstitious immediately cried up this appearance as a miracle; and there were some, who even attempted to make use of it as an opportunity of making their court to the King, who only laughed at and treated them as dreamers, having too good sense and too good an understanding to form any superstitious judgment on the occasion.

Adolphus John Stegeborg, Prince Palatine, and the King's nearest relation, who after his descent in *Seeland* had returned to *Stockholm*, died at *Lais*, whither he had repair'd after the battle of *Narva*, to make a campaign against the *Saxons*. He was attacked with a purple fever, which, after a few days illness, carried him off the 25th of *March*.

He was of the family of the Princes of *Deuxponts*, and uncle according to the custom * of *Britany* to the King, his father having been the younger brother of *Charles Gustavus*, King of *Sweden*. He had one brother and many sisters: In *Sweden* they were commonly called Princes of *Stegeborg*, from an appennage situated in *Ostrogothia*, given

to

---

* This is what we call *Wekb* uncle: for these people and the *Welch* are deriv'd from the same ancestors.

to them by *Charles Gustavus*, together with some other revenues which they drew from *Bremen* and other places.

This Prince *Adolphus John* wanted neither bravery nor understanding; but he was inconstant and fantastical; for which reasons he could never advance himself. His body was carried from *Lais* to *Riga*, and thence to *Stockholm*, where he was buried in the tomb of the Kings of *Sweden*, as a Prince of the blood.

The King was at *Lais*, when he received a petition from the *Swedish* Ladies, to desire a year's prolongation of the permission to wear foreign stuffs, which this Prince had lately forbidden through all his dominions, in order to promote the silken manufactory some years since established at *Stockholm*. This petition was in verse, and well written; and tho' the King was not naturally fond of women, he had however so much complaisance for them, that notwithstanding the usefulness of the ordinance, he granted their request in the most gracious manner, which favour produced a second piece of poetry full of thanks and acknowledgments.

In the mean while Colonel *Schlippenbach*, having understood that the *Russians* were drawn together on the side of *Pitschur*, detached a party of 60 troopers and 20 dragoons to observe their motions. These met near *Newhausen* a party of some hundred *Cossacks*, detached from the garrison of *Iburski*, to make excursions into *Livonia*. The *Cossacks* were entirely defeated, pursued three leagues, and 40 of them with a *Circassian* officer taken prisoners.

General *Spens*, on his side, sent out Major *Creutz* with several hundred men of his regiment. The Major advanced close to *Plescow*, defeated

F 3 several

several *Russian* parties on the road, and brought back a considerable number of prisoners.

About this time Colonel *Schlippenbach* detached from *Marienbourg* Lieutenant Colonel *Brandt*, with 130 horse and a great many officers, who served as voluntiers; these scouring round *Pitschur* and *Iburski*, without any interruption from the garrisons, set fire to several thousands of houses, which they reduced to ashes, and spread an universal terror and alarm. These excursions were afterwards continued with sometimes greater and sometimes less parties, in order to curb the enemy, and keep him in continual fear.

During all the month of *April*, the King took the pains to visit the quarters and review the troops, which had been weakened by distempers, of which however they began now to recover. He sent at the same time courier upon courier, to hasten the embarkation of 12,000 men from *Sweden*, in order to act with more vigour against the *Saxons*, who worked without ceasing on the fortifications of *Kokenhusen*, and had for that purpose conveyed thither a reinforcement of 300 horse and 600 foot, with some cannon, and had likewise heaped up a great quantity of corn at *Erla*, some leagues off, which they designed for the defence of *Kokenhusen*. Colonel *Albedyhl*, who was then quartered at *Ronnenburg*, being advised of this, detached Captain *Trautfetter* with 120 horse, to which was joined a small detachment from the garrison of *Marienbourg*, with orders to bring away all the corn which they should find at *Erla*. The Captain heard at his approach, that the enemy were ready to depart with all their provisions, and that the escorte, in great certainty of success, had marched before, without fearing the least

accident

accident to their convoy. *Trautfetter* attacked them immediately, took 37 waggons loaded with provisions, and brought them back safely to *Ronnenburg*, without the enemy's taking the pains to pursue him. This plunder was conveyed to the magazine which was preparing at *Volmar*, whither Colonel *Albedyhl* went a few days afterwards with all his detachment to cover and defend it, leaving at *Ronnenburg* only Captain *Lorentz*, a famous partisan, with a small detachment for the defence of that post.

As soon as the transports, which were preparing in *Sweden*, were in a condition to put to sea, several regiments of horse, foot, and dragoons, embarked at *Stockholm* and other ports of the kingdom, and arrived by the middle of *May* safe at *Reval*. The King was highly delighted with their arrival, seeing himself now able to open the campaign with a considerable force. He sent them immediate orders, after a few days rest, to come and join him, intending a very early march toward the enemy.

The transports returned to *Sweden* with the Generals and other *Russian* officers taken at *Narva*, who were all conducted to *Stockholm*, except the Duke *de Croy*, who by very earnest instances obtained leave to stay at *Reval*, where he died the year following.

On the 22d of *May* the artillery first began to quit their winter quarters; all the regiments were immediately thereon put in motion. Towards the end of the month the King encamped with the army half a league from *Dorpt*. As it might be easily foreseen that this country, as soon as we had quitted it, would be certainly infested by the *Russians*, several detachments of horse and foot, with a strong militia, which had been

been raised in the winter, were ordered to guard the frontiers, and to act against the *Russians*. The command of these troops was given to Colonel *Schlippenbach*.

Admiral *Nummers* received orders to equip a small squadron on the lake *Peipus*, to cruise there, and hinder the descents of the enemy. Major-General *Cronhiort*, at the head of 6000 men, covered *Ingria*; and *Narva* had a strong garrison against any attack which the *Russians* should make on that place.

The *Saxons* having received an account of the King of *Sweden*'s preparations, neglected nothing on their side to put themselves in a posture of defence. Colonel *Boos*, Governor of *Kokenhusen*, after having raised the ramparts, and added several new works with batteries, built a bridge over the *Duna*, to open a free communication; and the *Saxons* formed a camp of several regiments under the cannon of the fort.

A report was industriously spread, that this camp consisted of 10,000 regular troops; but it was certainly not so strong, the regiments being weak, and for the most part consisting of *Lithuanians* and *Cossacks* dress'd in the *German* fashion. They were ordered by continual excursions to carry off all the provision and forage; which they did a great way up in the country, finding the peasants of those parts sufficiently inclined to furnish them with whatever they demanded.

What had been foreseen of the *Russians* came to pass; for no sooner had the King quitted his winter-quarters, than they appeared in great numbers on the frontiers near *Kirumpa* and *Koikel*. Colonel *Patkul*, who commanded there, had the advantage of them in several little skirmishes. The

The *Saxons* on the other side, enraged at the frequent excursions of Captain *Lorentz*, an able and succesful partisan, resolved to attack him in his post of *Ronnenburg*. He had with him in that miserable town no more than 60 dragoons and 50 foot, with 40 voluntiers, who followed him every where. He was attacked with all possible vigour, but defended himself so well, that the *Saxons*, after three furious subsequent assaults, retired, leaving a Captain, a Corporal, and 12 men prisoners, and carrying with them 12 waggons full of their dead and wounded.

The King, after the arrival of his new regiments, having all the forces which he had designed against the *Saxons* ready to march, decamped from *Dorpt* on his birth-day, at the head of a fine well-cloathed army, inflamed with eagerness to come to blows with the enemy. He marched the first day but three leagues to *Terrafer*, and on the next arrived at *Ringen*, an old castle [t] (2 ½ leagues) where he halted one day.

On the 20th he continued his march to *Ramalybla*, or *Platers-Krug*, (3 ½ leagues.) On the 21st he advanced to *Walk*, a small town, (3 ¾ leagues.) The same day the *Saxons*, after having passed thro' *Venden* with 400 horse, attacked at *Neumublen*, near *Riga*, two Captains of horse, whose names were *Fittinghof* and *Kleebek*, who commanded a detachment of 80 troopers; these they entirely defeated, having killed 50, and made the rest prisoners, together with their two Captains, of whom *Fittinghof* was mortally wounded. The

---

[t] We have followed the *French* copy, in inserting the distances between the towns through which the *Swedes* marched in this short manner in a parenthesis, by which the reader will suffer the less interruption.

1701. The 22d the King received advice, that the *Saxons* had appeared near *Volmar*; on which General *Spens* had orders to detach four companies of the horse-guards to attack them: He followed himself with the rest of the regiment, and passed the river *Aa*; but the *Saxons* were gone before his arrival. On the 23d the army decamped from *Walk*, and went (3 ¼ leagues) to *Strenitz*. The 24th they arrived at *Volmar*, (3 leagues) where they halted two days.

The 27th they marched to *Lindenhof*, a Gentleman's seat, (2 ½ leagues), and arrived the next day at *Arrachs*, or *Old Venden* (2 ½ leagues.) They passed thro' the town of *Venden*, where a *Saxon* party of some hundred horse had carried off a quantity of victuals. The 29th the army arrived at *Nietau*, (3 ¼ leagues), where they rested one day. On the second of *July* they continued their march to *Lindberg* (3 ¼ leagues,) and the day following came into the neighbourhood of *Rodenpois* and *Siffegallen* (4 leagues) where they staid some days.

To give the enemy some diversion, the King detached from the camp Lieutenant-Colonel *Meyerfeldt* towards *Kokenhusen*. Colonel *Helmers* was ordered at the same time to leave *Riga*, with 600 men and 12 field-pieces, and to take the same rout. General *Steinau*, thinking he had no longer room to doubt the attack of *Kokenhusen*, hastened with all diligence to settle every thing; and ordered several regiments, which lay encamped opposite to *Riga*, to follow him, he returned however presently, on advice that the King was with the army at *Riga*.

Colonel *Helmers* took in his rout 21 boats loaded with provisions, which he sent to the King at *Riga*. His Majesty passed the 7th thro'
Neumublen,

Neumuhlen with all his army, which marched that day two leagues and an half, and encamped under the cannon of the town. The 8th Lieutenant-Colonel *Meyerfeldt* returned from his expedition, having taken near *Kokenhufen* an advanced guard of 22 men, with a Lieutenant.

The *Saxons* had no sooner notice of the King's march, than they quitted their camp at *Kokenhufen*, and hastily repassed the *Duna*; which, as soon as they had done, they set diligently about making intrenchments along this rapid river, to dispute the *Swedes* passage.

As General *Steinau* could not directly know where this passage might be attempted, he was obliged to be on his guard in all parts, and to divide his forces, which continued however very numerous, without reckoning the strong garrisons of *Dunamund*, *Cobrun*, and *Kokenhufen*. The old Veldt-Marshal Count *Dahlberg*, who saw the works of the *Saxons* advancing daily, placed some prames over the *Duna*, mounted with a great number of cannons, which they fired incessantly on their redoubts and breastworks, as well on the isle of *Dahlholm*, as on the other side of the river. Whatever mischief the *Saxons* received from hence, it did not hinder them from continuing their works, which it was their interest to finish with the utmost expedition.

The *Swedish* army was soon in a condition to pass the river. This was owing to the indefatigable care of Count *Dahlberg*, an old experienced General, with whom the King had many conferences on this subject at *Riga*, whither he often came from *Hodenpois*. They worked very hard at *Riga* on their floating bridge, on which the horse were to pass over, but 'twas not finished till after the battle; and as for the foot, they had

had got together all the vessels and ferry-boats which they could find. The King went often himself to *reconnoitre* the banks, and then gave his orders to Baron *Stuart*, to make the necessary dispositions for an attack.

The 8th, at nine in the evening, all the infantry filed off with profound silence towards the river to the place of embarkation, called *Fassenholm*; and, under favour of the night, they embarked as many as they had vessels to carry over, without giving the least suspicion to the enemy. As to the horse, for want of boats, no more than the Drabans, 100 of the horse, and as many of the dragoon guards could be got over.

The foot which embarked consisted of four battalions of guards, two battalions of the regiment of *Upland*, commanded by Baron *Lowen*, two of *Dahl-Carlia* under Count *Stenbock*, a battalion of *Helsinghers* under Colonel *Knorring*, two battalions of the regiment of *Wesmanland* under Baron *Axel Sparr*, and one of *Westerbothn* under Mr. *Ferson*; the rest of the foot remained behind for want of transports.

The Generals appointed for this attack were General *Welling*, with the Lieutenant-Generals *Spens* and *Horn* for the horse; and for the foot, Baron *Liewen*, Lieutenant General, and the Major-Generals *Stenbock*, *Poss*, and *Stuart*.

This disposition was afterwards totally changed at the attack, which was carried on in a manner entirely different from the first plan which the King had formed; all these Generals being placed indifferently at the head of their regiments in the same order as they came to land. It was at first proposed, that the horse should pass over with the artillery, and attack the redoubts directly, before they advanced towards the enemy; but this was found impracticable. On

On the 9th, at four in the morning, all the troops, notwithstanding the bad weather, which had continued several days, began their march within a short quarter of a league of the town, to pass over the river.

The King, attended by an *Aid-de-Camp* General, by his Equerry *Keuser-Crantz*, and his Page *Klinkenstrom*, put himself into a little boat by the side of the Granadiers of his guards, who were to begin the attack. They had got into the middle of the river[a], when the enemy, perceiving our boats, began to fire from their two redoubts.

This discharge was without effect, our two prames, which cover'd the transports, returning them full broad-sides, and the cannon of the town and citadel discharging on their works

[a] The King of *Sweden*, says Mr. *Voltaire*, had himself formed the plan of this passage. He had caus'd large boats of a new invention to be built, the sides of which, being higher than the common fashion, could be pulled up and down like drawbridges: when they were up, they cover'd the troops which they carried; and when they were down, they served instead of a bridge for their disembarkation. He made use likewise of another stratagem. Having observed, that the wind blew from the north, where he was, to the south, where his enemies were encamped, he set fire to a great quantity of wet straw, the thick smoak from which spreading itself over the river, concealed his troops and his designs from the *Saxons*. Under favour of this cloud he brought up several boats filled with smoaking straw, so that as the cloud continually thicken'd, and was driven by the wind into the enemy's eyes, it was not possible for them to discover his passage. He conducted himself the execution of this stratagem; and being arrived in the middle of the river, he said to General *Rheinschild*, *The* Duna *will not be more unlucky to us than the sea of* Copenhagen *was; believe me, General, we shall beat them.* He was a quarter of an hour in his passage, and was a little mortified, that he was only the fourth who got to land.

without

without cessation. The General [x] was now beat through the whole army of the enemy, who drew up in order of battle, in two lines, between the two redoubts, having their horse on their wings, and the foot in the centre.

They were commanded by Veldt-Marshal *Steinau*, Prince *Ferdinand* of *Courland*, and Lieutenant-General *Patkul*, the two latter commanding each one of the wings. The army consisted of four regiments of horse, all *Cuirassiers*, and fourteen battalions, with the dragoons of *Milchaw*. In their reserve were twenty-four battalions of *Russians*, but these ran away on the first repulse of the *Saxons*.

The King caused his troops instantly to disembark opposite to where the enemy were drawn up, himself leaping on the land one of the first, with his sword drawn. The foot hastened at the same time on all sides from their boats, and drew up in a single line as fast as they could get to land.

The King placed himself with Mr. *Liewen* at the head of his Granadiers, and marched forthwith with all his line directly to the enemy. The Drabans under Major-General *Horn*, and 50 of the horse-guards under Mr. *Spens*, were drawn out to cover the right wing.

At this instant the *Saxons* attacked our foot with astonishing vigour, but were repulsed by a volley from our musqueteers, which being discharged when they were almost close, obliged them to retire. On the other side, some of the enemies squadrons attacked the Drabans and the 50 horse on the right wing, who sustained their fire, and then repulsed them sword in hand, driving

---

[x] A particular beat of drum so call'd, by which the whole camp are summoned to arms.

driving them back on their second line. The enemy were not dismayed at this ill success, but returned a second time to the charge with all their foot ranged in one line; they were however obliged again to give ground, which the *Swedes* gained by little and little, especially after they had carried one of their redoubts.

As our right wing was too much exposed, the enemy, who were a third time returned to the charge, attacked it in the flank with their horse, and obliged the battalion of Granadier guards to give back with some precipitation; but rallying immediately, they sustained the efforts of the enemy with an admirable firmness, till our Drabans, attacking them in the rear, obliged them to an hasty retreat. The *Saxons* made a new attempt on the right wing with great bravery; but General *Stuart*, who was ordered to cover them with a battalion of *Ferfen* and the rest of the horse, rendered their attack fruitless. Our foot were now entirely passed, and almost as strong as the enemy.

The *Saxons* seeing themselves reduced to an impossibility of resisting any longer, gave ground by little and little, remaining however unbroke; about seven in the morning, after an obstinate and bloody fight of three hours, they retreated with precipitation two different ways. The greater part of the foot took the road to *Cobrun*, and the rest with most of the horse drew towards *Dunamund*, our horse being too weak to pursue them. The King, who had fought on foot during the whole action at the head of his infantry, pursued with his left wing those who fled towards *Cobrun*, till General *Rheinschild* came up with his regiment of Dragoon guards, but too late to overtake the enemy, who were now got at a good distance. When

The LIFE and HISTORY of

When the King came to *Cobrun*, he found the enemy had abandoned that place, the garrison being retreated to *Kokenhufen* along the *Duna*. General *Spens* was detached with some horse to cut off their retreat: In the mean time our troops entered the fort, and made themselves masters of the great magazine which the enemy had gathered together at *Marien-Muhl*. All the army being now assembled, encamped near *Cobrun*, whither Major-General *Morner* came about noon with his regiment, which had just passed the river.

The small redoubts, which the enemy had raised on the banks of the river, had surrendered at the beginning of the battle; but there remained one at *Lutzausholm* on an island of the *Duna*, and another little fort near *Kramers-hof* on the side of *Dunamund*. This latter post, possessed by 40 *Saxons* and 50 *Russians*, was carried by General *Chorner*, who obliged these troops to surrender at discretion, tho' he had with him no more than ten horsemen.

As to *Lutzausholm* beyond *Cobrun*, 400 *Russians* were entrenched there up to the teeth, whom Colonel *Helmers* and Lieutenant-Colonel *Wrangle* were ordered to attack with a body of 500 men. The Colonel embarked his command, and arriving a little after midnight, began the attack immediately; the fight was very sharp on all sides, the enemy making a desperate defence; notwithstanding which our troops enter'd by break of day, and put all they met to the sword. The King, coming up in the heat of the slaughter, saved the lives of 20 *Russians*, which were the only ones spared. Here Colonel *Helmers*, Major *Lilliestirna*, with many other brave officers, lost their lives.

The business was at end, when the King, who was yet busy in examining the works which the enemies had abandoned, saw the magazine of powder, which was at *Cobrun*, blown all at once into the air: for the enemy, on their retreat, had planted a lighted match, which taking effect, overthrew an entire bastion, and killed a centinel. The horses of our cavalry, which were encamped with the rest of the army under the cannon of the fort, taking fright at the terrible noise of the powder, broke their pickets, and fled cross the fields to the next wood. The King repaired thither instantly, and sent out parties every way, who had the good fortune to bring them all back.

Thus ended this glorious action, in which the King with an army, at first very inferior, passed a very large rapid river, defeated a formidable enemy, advantageously posted on the river's bank, and render'd himself master in twenty-four hours of five little forts and batteries, of two breast-works, the enemy's camp, thirty-six pieces of their cannon, three standards, one pair of colours, and the greatest part of their baggage.

We had in this action very few killed or wounded. Amongst the persons of note, who were killed, the chief were Mr. *Palmquist*, Lieutenant-Colonel of the guards, Captain *Blaman*, an Engineer, Major *Sparfwenfeld*, Major *Von Wolffen*, and Lieutenant *Lindhielm*; and, amongst the wounded, Major-General *Horn* and Captain *Stiernhok*. On the enemy's side, Veldt-Marshal *Steinau* was dangerously wounded in the arm, as was Lieutenant-General *Patkul*, who conveyed himself instantly to *Mittau*. Count *Ronnof*, and Colonel *Zeidler*, with many other officers were killed. Colonel *Eppinger* was wounded,

wounded, and carried prisoner to *Riga*, with more than five hundred of the enemy, chiefly *Russians*[u].

The 11th, Major-General *Morner* was order'd to go with 1500 horse and dragoons to *Mittau*, to secure the great magazine that the *Saxons* had established there. He found on the road, on one arm of the river *Bulderan*, which runs before the town of *Mittau*, some scatter'd troops of the enemy's army, who undertook to dispute the passage with him. He attacked them, and put them to flight. At his approach to the town the Burgomaster and the rest of the Magistrates came out, to demand of him the King of *Sweden*'s protection. Mr. *Morner*, after having granted their demand, enter'd into the town, and summoned the Governor of the castle, who surrender'd at discretion. As soon as he was master thereof, he made a double discharge of the cannon from the ramparts. 1050 *Saxon* Dragoons, who came from *Annenburg*, to throw themselves into *Mittau*, having heard the report of the guns, returned hastily, seeing that the *Swedes* had been before-hand with them.

The same day the King detached Colonel *Klings-Porr* towards *Dunamund*, to hinder the enemy from throwing succour and provisions into that town. He found at *Slock*, where there was a magazine, a great party of *Russians*, whom he attacked and entirely defeated, taking at the same time 48 pieces of iron cannon, and a great deal of ammunition of war and provision.

The Colonel was dangerously wounded in this action, and died a little afterwards. However,

[u] The enemy lost 2000 men, and had 1500 taken prisoners in this action. *Puff.* *Introduct. à l'Hist.* tom. 7. p. 86.

orders were given to the detachment to advance nearer *Dunamund* under the command of Colonel *Albedyhl*, to block up that place on the side of *Courland*, whilst some ships anchor'd before it, so that no person could either go in or out. There remained now to the enemy no more than *Kokenhusen*, which the King resolved to take by open force. But as Colonel *Boos* thought himself in no condition of maintaining it, and as he found his retreat not cut off, he abandoned the fort, blew up the castle, repassed the *Duna*, and then burnt the bridge.

On the 13th of *July*, the King, at the head of the army, which was divided into three columns, marched to *Rekou* (2½ leagues,) the next day they advanced (2 leagues) to *Borkowit*, and the 15th (1 league) to *Thomas-Hoff*, where his Majesty was informed that the enemy had abandoned *Kokenhusen*, where they left but 12 pieces of cannon, 4 mortars, and 2 fauconets. His Majesty sent some troops thither, and presently turned with the army towards *Courland*, detaching diverse parties to *reconnoitre* the motions of the enemy, who were retired with all haste towards *Birsen* in *Lithuania*.

The 16th the army arrived at *Linden* (two leagues,) where they halted the 17th; the next day they came to *Neuguth* (three leagues,) where the Duke of *Holstein-Gottorp* arrived, accompanied by Mr. *Dahldorff*, to make a campaign with the King his brother-in-law. This Prince had settled every thing which might be necessary for the defence of *Pomerania*, as Generalissimo of the estates of his *Swedish* Majesty in *Germany*.

The 20th the army renewed their march, and proceeded (2¼ leagues) to *Kleenbarbe*, where they halted two days, and came on the 23d to *Alten-*

1701. *rade* (2 leagues;) here the King ſtaid ſome days, during which, having heard that King *Auguſtus* had left at *Birſen* 6 large pieces of braſs cannon, and 32 braſs pontons, he detached thither Lieutenant Colonel *Roos* with 260 horſe to demand them of the Governor, who excuſed himſelf under pretence of firſt aſking the Republick's permiſſion to deliver them.

Upon this the King ordered ſome troops to advance immediately under the command of Baron *Poſs*, Major-General. The march of theſe troops produced the effect which the King expected. Mr. *Chalcouſki*, Governor of the *Poliſh Livonia*, repaired in a hurry to his Majeſty's camp with the Governor's ſon, whom he left there as an hoſtage, promiſing inſtantly to deliver the cannons, which were afterwards convey'd to *Bauſk*, and thence to *Riga*, with ſome of the pontons, the reſt being left with the army, to be made uſe of upon occaſion.

In the mean while Colonel *Albedyhl* ſent two officers to ſummon the fort of *Dunamund* to ſurrender; but Colonel *Canitz*, who commanded there, having fiercely anſwered, that he would defend it as long as he had powder, ball, and proviſions left; the Colonel contented himſelf with blocking it up by ſea and land, which he did till the month of *December* the ſame year, as we ſhall ſee a little afterwards.

The 26th of *July* the army decamped from *Altenraden*, and came to *Bauſk* ($1\frac{1}{2}$ league,) where 500 men of the van-guard had arrived the day before, to repair the fortifications of the caſtle called *Bauſkenburg*. Mr. *Morner* did the ſame at *Mittau*, where they worked very hard to put every thing in a good condition, and to encreaſe the works of the caſtle, which were

very

very much shatter'd. He had already, by the King's orders, sent circular letters to the Estates of the Province to convene them together at *Mittau,* to settle the contributions for the army's subsistence, whither the Chancellor, the Grand Master, the Burgrave, and the Chiefs of the country repaired, and immediately lamented the misery of the inhabitants, and their incapacity to furnish any thing.

Besides these reasons, they protested farther, that they had taken no part in this war, which had been begun without their consent, and even without their knowledge.

As that Province acknowledged the King of *Poland* to be their Chief and Protector, all their remonstrances were useless, and the country, as well as the towns of *Mittau, Bausk, Goldingen, Libaw, Windaw,* and others, were all taxed at certain sums of money.

In the same degree as the King penetrated into *Courland,* the flying troops of the enemy all took the road of *Lithuania* towards *Kauno,* where Veldt-Marshal *Steinau* drew them together to form a camp. The Marshal did not think however to stay there long, and he actually set out soon after, making his way in great haste and with long marches towards *Prussia,* on the side of *Marienbourg* and *Dantzick.* This precipitate retreat gave us easily to understand, that the war would not be prosecuted so briskly as it had been hitherto. We had the greater reason to flatter ourselves with the approach of a peace, as the Republick seemed very much dissatisfied with the undertaking the war, in which she declared herself to have had no share, and as there was all appearance that the *Saxons* would be soon unable to stand alone

1701. against the victorious arms of so formidable a power as *Sweden*.

Charles, displeased with the unjust proceedings of the King of *Poland*, who had invaded his estates contrary to the right of nations, was not contented with barely driving him out again, but demanded, as a farther security of his kingdom, a more solid and sensible satisfaction. His *Swedish* Majesty was not ignorant, that King *Augustus* had shewn more than once, that as long as he sat on the throne of *Poland*, no solid alliance could be hoped for with him, and that he would be always ready to renew the war on the first favourable occasion.

These reasons at last produced in the King of *Sweden* a resolution * to dethrone *Augustus*, and to persuade the Republick to elect a Prince more inclined to maintain peace with his neighbours. With this view he sent two letters from *Bauſk* to *Warsovia*, the one to the Republick, the other to the Cardinal Primate, which contained a long recital of the injuries the King of *Poland* had done him, and the damages which he had suffered. These letters represented likewise, that King *Augustus* had not only broke his oath, but that he had resolved to rob the *Poles* of their liberty, and that it was the interest of the most serene Republick to elect another King as soon as possible, who would not strike at her liberties, and would maintain the treaties of peace with her neighbours. Lastly, his Majesty as-

---

* There is a great difference amongst authors concerning the time when the King of *Sweden* first took this resolution; some referring it to that wherein he first heard of the treaty between the *Czar* and *Augustus* at *Birgen*; others say, that it was on his arrival at that place: the former of these seems the more probable.

sured

sured the Republick and the Primate of the kingdom of his assistance and protection in the execution of so just a design.

The King, having stopt at *Bausk* till the 11th of *August*, departed with his army, leaving there Col. *Nils Poss* with his regiment and some Dragoons, and proceeded (3¼ leagues) to *Klappmannshoff*, or *Schorsten*. Hither came a courier from *Bausk* with advice, that the Deputies of *Lithuania* were arrived there, and demanded an audience of his Majesty. The army halted here a day, and the King took that opportunity to make a tour to *Mittau*, being attended by the Duke of *Holstein-Gottorp* and his train. *Charles*, after having examined the works of the castle and the town, and given his orders, returned the same day to the camp to put himself at the head of his forces. The army marched the same day to *Hoff-Zum-Bergen*, (3½ leagues,) whither the Deputies of *Lithuania* repaired the same day with a train of 200 persons.

The King considered some time, whether he should give audience to these deputies, whilst the army on the 14th continued their march, and encamped at *Dobeln*, (2¼ leagues.) Here the chief of the Deputies, named *Podbereski*, had at last an audience of the King, whom he complimented on the victories he had gained, and besought him, in conformity with the peace of *Oliva*, that he would not touch the frontiers of *Lithuania*, and that he would take pity on *Courland*, which was entirely ruined by the *Saxons*, and the large contributions they had raised. But as his Majesty was apprized, that this deputation came only from one party of the Nobility of *Lithuania*, assembled at *Wilna*, which had confederated under the name of Republicans;

1701. cans; and moreover, as the Envoy could not produce full powers from the Republick, he gave them an anfwer agreeable to the fituation of affairs, and the Deputy departed without obtaining an audience of leave.

From *Dobeln* the army marched the 17th to *Birften* or *Berfenhoff* (2¼ leagues.) The Staroft *Potocki*, fon of the Great General of the Crown, arrived here from *Warfovia*, with the Cardinal Primate's anfwer to the King's letters to his Eminence and the Republick. He had immediate audience of the King, who having opened his letter, found it full of politenefs; but as to the article which concerned the depofition of King *Auguftus*, the Cardinal teftified in very refpectful terms, that the *Poles* could never confent to it. In the mean while his Eminence offered the King the good offices of the Republick to fecure his Majefty a fure and folid peace, and all the fatisfaction imaginable.

Thefe fine promifes engaged the King to ftay at *Courland*, and not to pafs the frontiers. As foon as Mr. *Potocki* had received his audience of leave, the army renewed their march the 21ft, and arrived at *Bliden* (2¼ leagues,) coafting along the frontiers of *Samogitia*. The 22d of *Auguft* they arrived at *Frauenburg* (2 leagues,) where they halted one day. The 24th they marched to *Knochenkrug* (2 leagues,) where the Colonels *Pulbufch* and *Leyonhufwud*, with their battalions, were fent to *Mittau*.

The 25th the army arrived at *Schrunden* (1½ league) an old caftle belonging to the Duke of *Courland*, where they paffed the river *Windaw* on thofe pontons which they had had from *Birfen*. Here the King ftay'd till the 29th, when he

decamped

decamped and came to *Neubaufen* (3 leagues,) where he rested two days. The 31st the army marched (2 leagues) to *Hafenpoth*; the first of *September* to *Rauen* (2 leagues,) and the 2d to *Grubin*, a small town, part of the dowry of the Dutchess of *Courland*, where there was formerly a castle, fortified by the *Swedes* during the war of *Charles Guftavus*, but now entirely demolished.

Whilst the King continued to penetrate into *Courland*, the *Czar*, who had applied himself with great industry since the defeat of *Narva* to the re-establishment of his army, had drawn together a strong party near *Plefcow*, in order to make three different inroads into *Livonia*, on that side where Colonel *Schlippenbach* commanded; viz. with 3000 men near *Rapin*, where Major *Roos* was posted with 200 foot, 300 dragoons, and 2 field-pieces; with 4000 at *Cafaritz*, whither a detachment had been sent under the command of Mr. *Berend Rebbinder*, Captain of horse; and with 6000 at *Rauk*, where Captain *Nolk*, at the head of 50 horse and 100 foot, was lodged in a church-yard.

As soon as Mr. *Schlippenbach* had received advice from *Cafaritz*, which was but one league distant from his camp, of the enemy's arrival, he hastened with some horse to the support of *Rebbinder*; but having learnt at his coming thither, that the enemy had made an irruption with greater forces near *Rauk*, at three leagues distance from *Cafaritz*, he detached thither Lieutenant-Colonel *Liewen* with 200 foot, 300 horse, and 2 field-pieces, to reinforce the Captain posted in the church-yard. He attacked the enemy at *Cafaritz* himself, and after having received 2 field-pieces more, obliged them to retire. But

1701. as it might be feared, that this detachment of the enemy would join that at *Rauk*, Lieutenant-Colonel *Stakelberg*, with some horse and two field-pieces, was ordered to join Mr. *Liewen* without delay. He met them on the road with his foot, having sent his 300 horse before to attack the enemy, and assist Captain *Nolk*. It was not at first possible to come up with him, nor to stop the enemy; but as soon as Messieurs *Liewen* and *Stakelberg* were arrived with the foot and cannon, they charged them so briskly, that, after some resistance, they forced them to retreat through great morasses, over which they had built a bridge. In this manner we opened a free communication with the Captain, who had defended himself with great bravery in the church-yard.

Our horse having pursued the enemy even to the end of the bridge on the morass, could proceed no farther; all the enemy's dragoons, which had now dismounted, attacked them in the flank, and endeavoured to put them in disorder; but the foot and cannon being come up, these Dragoons were pushed so vigorously, that they at last gave ground, and were driven fighting beyond the frontiers; near 2000 of them were killed and wounded, and a great number of officers.

Matters went not so well at *Rapin*, whence *Schlippenbach*'s camp was 6 leagues distant, as well on account of the difficulty of hastily succouring so advanced a post, as because the enemy had brought hither the greatest number of his forces; add to these, that Major *Roos* had engaged too imprudently, and was presently surrounded by the enemy, with whom however he continued fighting from the morning to three in the

the afternoon, at which time he broke through, after having left almost all his people slain on the field of battle, and joined Mr. *Schlippenbach*, who was coming to his assistance, with 30 men only. Notwithstanding this advantage which the enemy had gained, they had no stomach to wait the arrival of *Schlippenbach* at *Rapin*; but after having plundered and carried away all that they could find, they hastily repassed the frontiers.

This action reflected great honour on Mr. *Schlippenbach*, whom the King made a Major-General, and at the same time sent him a reinforcement of some regiments from *Courland*, which filed off towards *Dorpt* and *Sagnitz*, and at last obliged the enemy entirely to abandon the frontiers, and retreat to *Plescow*.

While all this passed, the King remained encamped with his army at *Grubin*, and placed a garrison in *Lilaw*, which is but half a league's distance, and where they began to build a citadel for the security of the port, and a free communication with *Sweden*. The direction of this fortress was entrusted with Major-General *Stuart*, who had formed the plan of it. The work was at first carried on with diligence, tho' the ground is very sandy; but they were at last obliged to give it over, on account of the hurricanes, which are very frequent on these coasts, and which overthrew in a few hours what they had been a whole week in raising. As to *Baukenburg*, we put the fortifications into so good a condition, that this little place served us always for the future as a safe retreat, and kept a curb on the *Poles* and *Lithuanians* in these parts.

With regard to *Mittau*, we applied ourselves only to fortifying the castle, where Mr. *Morner*

ner repaired two lodgments on the side of the river, and made a ravelin at one of the ports, with a good counterscarp all round the castle.

The Counts of the illustrious family of *Sapieha* came with pressing instances to demand the King of *Sweden*'s protection against some of their countrymen, by whom they were almost entirely oppressed. This house, which is one of the most powerful and most considerable in *Lithuania*, and which for an age had been invested with the chief honours of the country, had by its great riches excited the envy and jealousy of the rest of the Nobility, who feared to be one day overpowered by it [*]; and in reality, the two Counts of *Sapieha*, whereof one was Grand General and the other Great Treasurer of *Lithuania*, had given the Nobility some reason for their fears.

But however that was, *Augustus* took part with the enemies of this family, who encreased considerably every day; nor did he neglect any means to encourage the hatred which they bore it. He was little pleased with the conduct of the *Sapiehas*, who had done all they could to thwart his election, declaring themselves for the Prince of *Conti*. This hatred grew to such an height, that as the greatest part of the friends and allies of the *Sapiehas* had either through caprice or fear abandoned them, their enemies thought it a fit time to strip them of their estates, and deprive them of their honours.

Oginski, putting himself at the head of the party which opposed *Sapieha*, had the luck to

---

[*] *Lithuania* was then divided into two parties, the one of which was headed by the house of *Sapieha*, and the other by that of *Oginski*. These two factions, which had at first begun by private quarrels, broke out afterwards into a civil war. *Voltaire*.

defeat

defeat the body of the Grand General's army in different rencounters, and carried his vengeance so far, as inhumanly to massacre his son, contrary to his promise to do him no harm. At length the enemies of the *Sapieba*, who were joined by Prince *Wisniowiski*, got so much the advantage of them, that after having destroyed almost all their lordships and lands, they forced them to abandon the country, and throw themselves into the King of *Sweden*'s arms, King *Augustus* having refused them that protection which they had demanded of him.

His Majesty received the *Sapieba* very graciously; and Colonel *Hummerhielm* with 600 horse and dragoons was ordered instantly to pass the frontier of *Samogitia*, and march towards *Schauden*, to cover the lands of the *Sapieba*, situated in that country, against the frequent incursions of *Oginski* and those of his party. And this gave the King of *Sweden* an occasion to enter *Poland*.

At the same time *Charles* detached Lieutenant-Colonel *Meyerfelt* with some horse towards *Polangen*, to seize on the revenues designed for the support of King *Augustus*'s table. On another side, Lieutenant-Colonel *Peter Bannier* with some hundred dragoons and foot was ordered to repair to *Seelburg*, an old castle situated on the *Duna* and the frontiers of *Courland*, to cover them, and hinder the incursions of *Oginski* into these quarters, which were afterwards very frequent, as we shall soon see.

As the season was far advanced, and the weather grew too hard to keep the field any longer, the King quitted *Grubin*, where he had remained almost the whole month of *September*, and repaired to *Worgen* (3 leagues,) a castle appertain-
ing

1701. ing to a Gentleman of *Courland*. Here his Majesty resolved to canton his army, till he could put them into winter-quarters.

With this view they quartered the troops at Gentlemens houses, and in the villages about *Wurgen*, and along the frontiers of *Samogitia*. The horse consisted of the Drabans, who always attended the King, of the regiments of horse and dragoon guards, of the two regiments of horse of *Ostrogothia* and *Nyland*. The foot were four battalions of guards, two battalions of *Dahl-Carlia*, two of *Upland*, two of *Westerbothn*, two of *Kruse*, two of *Wesmanland*, two of *Nerk* and *Wermland*, and one battalion of *Hastfehr*, with a suitable train of artillery.

The King, instead of lodging in the castle of *Wurgen*, resolved to lie in his tent, which he thatched over and surrounded with boards at the bottom; and to warm him in case of necessity, he was entertained night and day with some red-hot bullets, which would have much incommoded any other sort of person than *Charles* the Twelfth.

Towards the end of *September* there was a little action at sea, which deserves to be remembered. King *Augustus* had raised sailors at *Lubec*, to cruize, with a vessel which was there equipt, on the *Swedish* merchants. As soon as this news came to *Wismar*, which is in the neighbourhood, the citizens fitted out a vessel at their own expence, on board of which they sent sixty granadiers and thirty sailors, under the command of one named *Nortman*, who, after having pursued the *Corsair* enemy some time, he at last came up with her under the island of *Femern*, attacked and took her, making twenty-eight prisoners, the rest escaped to land.

The booty, which was confiderable, without reckoning three months wages for the crew, was conducted to *Wifmar*.

Though the campaign was ended, the King, who was always indefatigable and in action, employed himfelf without relaxation in vifiting the different quarters of his army, which were fufficiently difperfed and diftant one from the other, and chiefly fituated along the frontiers, which the *Polifh* parties under *Oginfki* began to infeft. *Charles*, who commonly had very few attendants, expofed himfelf much in thefe long and frequent excurfions, wherein he was in continual danger, of which the following inftance ought not to be paffed over in filence.

His Majefty one day took the road of *Polangen*, attended only by fome officers, and after fome difcourfe with Mr. *Meyerfelt*, giving orders that he might not be made known, he fet out by himfelf on horfeback for a little town named *Repfin*. He went directly to a convent, where the Superior talked with him, and drank the King of *Sweden*'s health, without knowing to whom he addreffed it. *Charles* pledged the holy Father; and after having been well treated by the Monks, proceeded to *Polangen*, and thence to *Wurgen*.

Baron *Cranenburg*, Envoy from *Holland*, who had lately arrived at *Libaw*, had fome time afterwards an audience of his Majefty, to whom he offered the mediation of the Republick for the re-eftablifhment of peace in the North. The Marquefs of *Bonac*, who was to fucceed Count *Guifcard*, arrived alfo fome days afterwards, and made the fame propofitions. The intention of thefe Minifters was doubtlefs to bring the King into their mafters interefts, the war between

France

France and *Holland* being then on the point of being declared. As his Majesty had already in *Livonia* taken a resolution to send back the foreign Ministers to *Stockholm*, where their negotiations might be more commodiously carried on than in the army, he declared to these Ministers, that he should be pleased with their repairing to his capital. And his Majesty was ever afterwards inflexible on this article, tho' several Ministers of different Powers had made the strongest instances to obtain a permission to follow him, and be near his person. This he refused with great constancy, that he might create no odium or jealousy in them, nor give them any room to think he had the interest of one more at heart than of another. So the two Ministers took leave of the King, and repaired to *Riga*, where they remained till the spring, when they received orders to go to *Stockholm*.

Oginski and those of his party continued in the mean time to destroy the lands of the Counts *Sapieha*; and, at the instances of King *Augustus*, they appeared from time to time at our most advanced quarters, without ever making head, or it being possible for them to force us. For though *Oginski*, had brought them to attack *Ornstedt*, Major to *Hummerhielm*'s detachment, the *Poles* fled, as soon as they saw their Commander and some others killed; that, as we could never do them any great mischief, so they did but little to us, as soon as we were once used to their manner of fighting.

All these hostilities engaged the King to pass the frontiers, thoroughly resolved to have no mercy on a country which thus continued to insult him. He resolved however to pass this year

year at *Courland*, and orders were given to Mr. Stuart, Quarter-Master-General, to regulate the quarters.

His Majesty quarter'd at *Wurgen*; Mr. Sioblad, Grand Master of the Artillery, was to have the castle of *Nurrins*; General *Welling* the little town of *Neuberg*, and Lieutenant-General *Liewen* that of *Frauenburg* assigned to them; Major-General *Meidel* was to lie at *Stenden*, and Mr. *Stuart* received orders to stay at the head-quarters.

According to this plan, the regiments were distributed into garrisons in the towns and along the frontiers, which they were to cover; but this project took not place, and the troops continued to be canton'd till they began their march to *Lithuania*.

The 3d of *November*, two regiments of foot, viz. those of *Calmar* and *Skytt*, consisting of two battalions each, arrived safely from *Sweden* in the road of *Libaw*, and were put into garrison. A great number of recruits arrived at the same time from *Riga*, which considerably reinforced the army.

The 17th, the regiment of horse of *South-Scania* arrived also at *Libaw*, under the command of Major-General *Alexander Stromberg*. The disembarkation of these troops was not at all successful. Two days after they arrived, a storm arose very suddenly, and drove 7 great transport-ships on the sands, which were beat to pieces. They lost near 100 horses, but not one man, nor their baggage. The regiment was immediately sent to *Frauenburg*, into good winter-quarters, in order to refresh the men after the fatigues of the sea, and to be remounted.

On the 20th, some Deputies of *Samogitia*, having had audience of the King, intreated him not to let the army pass into their territories, nor to treat them as enemies. To this they had a very favourable and gracious answer: but as we heard a few days afterwards, that one of *Oginski*'s parties had attacked, tho' with loss, a detachment of Lieutenant-Colonel *Meyerfeld* at *Polangen*, the King, incensed at seeing himself so often harassed by such pitiful troops, resolved to chastise them once for all, and to put a stop to the continuance of their hostilities. As *Oginski* had publickly declared himself the King of *Sweden*'s enemy, his Majesty determined to go himself in quest of him, and punish his insults. He was now in the neighbouring parts, lording it in *Lithuania*, where he put all to fire and sword, and destroyed every thing belonging to the *Sapieha*.

During these transactions, the Duke of *Holstein-Gottorp* took leave of the King, and his Highness took the northern road to *Stockholm*, where he passed all the winter, and returned the next summer to the army.

The first of *December*, at night, the King put 400 of his guards on sledges, passed the frontiers of *Courland* with them, and joined Colonel *Hummerhielm*, who was posted at *Schauden* with a detachment of horse and dragoons. Taking with him this whole detachment, he set out that instant for *Calivaria*, whither Mr. *Meyerfeld* had by his orders brought his party from *Polangen*.

Charles, impatient to see the enemy, who was, they said, at *Skudi*, galloped before with the dragoons only; but could not arrive in time, the enemy having had the prudence to decamp silently the preceding night. Not judging it proper therefore to give his people any useless

fatigue,

King Charles XII. of Sweden.

fatigue, he waited there for the rest of his troops, left his foot at *Skudi*, and marched the next day with the horse towards *Tirksel* (4 leagues.) This place belonged to *Oginski*, who departed a little before the King's arrival; but the *Partorasta*, or Bailiff, was surprized by Major *Ornstedt*, and killed by his men.

The King, who was in continual hopes of overtaking the flying enemy, marched from *Tirksel* to *Triski*, a little town 4 leagues distant; but they were already retired: so that at last, giving over all hopes of coming up with them, he passed the river which runs before that town with his horse, at a ford, being able to find neither bridge nor boat. The cavalry were quartered upon the citizens, and were permitted to unsaddle their horses and repose themselves. As to the King, he went to lodge at a castle without the town, leaving only a small picquet-guard of a few men at the town's end. About 11 in the evening, *Oginski*, who had been advertised by the Curate of the town of the security in which our troops lay, returned with all his force to the number of 6000 men, who, finding no resistance, went with a great cry to the market-place, where they set fire to several houses. The *Swedes*, who expected not this visit, and were most of them in their beds, dressed themselves with all haste, saddled their horses, and drew together as well as possible. Mr. *Sak*, Captain of the horse-guards, Count *Laurence Flemming*, and some others, were the first ready, and feared not to attack the enemy, notwithstanding his infinite superiority in numbers.

This handful of *Swedes* fought with extraordinary bravery, and kept the enemy so well in play, that they gave time to the horse and dragoons to get together, and draw themselves into order; who then attacked them on all sides with such constancy and vigour, that they were presently overthrown and put to flight. Our people, who were for the most part in their shirts, pursued them at their heels a great way out of the town. The King, who had call'd for his horse at the first alarm, hastened to them, and having found the enemy already put to flight, he drew together the rest of his horse, which were scattered through the town, rallied them in haste, and marched forth himself to support the others in case of necessity. He came up with Mr. *Thomas Funk*, Captain of the dragoon-guards, who was yet engaged with a party of the enemy's troops, that had at first made head, but ran away at the King's arrival. They were closely pursued; but notwithstanding all the haste of our troops, could not be overtaken. Mr. *Claes Bond*, Captain of the horse-guards, pursued them so smartly, that he took *Oginski*'s led horse with a pair of kettle-drums, and made the Groom, who led it, prisoner.

Such was the success of *Oginski*'s undertaking, who, if he had had more courage and conduct, might here have struck a decisive stroke, and put an end to the war.

The King, seeing it was in vain to persist in the pursuit of those fugitives, returned to the town, and caused the fire to be extinguished, which was kindled in the beginning of the action to disorder our troops. At the same time his Majesty reinforced the guard, and retired to his repose. He remained the rest of the day in the town, and gave orders to have the wounded conducted into *Courland*, who were about 18 men, amongst

amongst whom Mr. *Sak* was dangerously wounded in many places.

The Curate of the town, who was suspected to hold intelligence with the enemy, was presently put under arrest, and Mr. *Canifer* was commanded with 30 men to watch the enemy's motions. He return'd the same day, and brought back some of the wounded, who had been left behind, without being able to learn what was become of *Oginski*, who was nevertheless not far off; and an old woman informed the King in the evening, that he was at *Lubinski*; on which a resolution was taken to march thither, and the King advanced (4 leagues) the next day.

Oginski was retired a little before their arrival, having left several wounded men behind him. The King continued his rout, without stopping, to *Uzwetta* ($1\frac{1}{2}$ league,) where he found no body. Here the foot, which had been left at *Skudi*, joined his Majesty on the sledges; and he continued his march the same night towards the town of *Kelm*, where there was a castle belonging to one *Grusinski* of *Oginski*'s party. The King caused this castle to be plunder'd, and then demolished. He stopt at *Kelm* that day and the next, and the 10th he marched to *Sittowiani* (3 leagues,) and the next day to *Grynkiski* (4 leagues.) He yet flatter'd himself with being able to come up with the enemy; but as they had no other view than to escape from our troops, they found means to save themselves.

The fort of *Dunamund* was now surrender'd to the *Swedes*. We have already said, that Colonel *Albedhyl*, after the battle of *Duna*, had block'd it up straitly by sea and land with the help of some frigats, which kept out all succours both of

1701. men and provisions. Mr. *Albedhyl* had several times summoned Colonel *Canitz* to surrender; but this Governor was * too brave to suffer the besiegers to carry the place, unless at the dearest rate. *Albedhyl* found himself obliged to a bombardment, which was begun towards the end of *August*; for which purpose all the mortars and heavy cannon, which they thought they should want, were brought from *Riga*. The enemy defended themselves with great bravery; but notwithstanding all the fine artillery which was in the place, they did us but little mischief, only one Captain being killed all the time. Our batteries having soon reduced their mill and magazine to ashes, with some of their cazerns and houses, and the garrison beginning to grow weak by their distempers and want of provision, the Governor found himself obliged to capitulate and surrender; for which purpose he sent an officer to Mr. *Albedhyl*, and it was agreed that they should march out with their arms and baggage, which they accordingly did the 12th of *December*, with all the honours of war.

The fort was delivered to the *Swedes* in a condition infinitely better than it was when taken. We found here thirty-two 24 pounders, twenty-one of 12, ten of 6, all of brass; and 18 mortars, 49720 cannon-balls, 9345 granades and

---

* The King of *Sweden* was so pleased with the conduct of this Colonel, that, as he marched out of the fort, he told him, *You are my enemy, and yet I love you as well as my best friends; for you have behaved yourself like a brave soldier in the defence of this fort against my troops; and to shew you that I can esteem and reward valour even in my enemies, I make you a present of these* 5000 *ducats*. Of 1700 men which were in the fort at the beginning of the siege, there remain'd no more than 60 at the surrender.

bombs,

bombs, 2385 cartridges, 3000 quintals of powder, 800 muskets, 4000 ton of corn, without reckoning other ammunition, and an arsenal well stored.

The King was not at first content with this capitulation, because he had expected the garrison to surrender at discretion: but he approved of it afterwards, when he consider'd the number of men this fort would have cost, had they determined to carry it by storm. Here they placed a good garrison, and changed the name of *Augustusburg*, which Mr. *Flemming* had given it, into *Neumund*, its true name, and by which it had been always formerly known.

In the mean time the King, who continued in *Samogitia*, in pursuit of *Oginski*, marched the 13th to *Kyedum*, where he stay'd a few days to gain intelligence of the enemy. Here he was present at divine service, which was perform'd in the *Lutheran* church in this town; from thence he marched into a little village full of poor Gentlemen, to whom they commonly gave in *Poland* the name of *Slattitz*. Here the King learnt that *Oginski* was at *Kauno*. To prevent his knowledge of our march, his Majesty set a guard on all the places through which any one might pass to give him advice. Towards midnight he marched towards *Kauno*, and arriv'd thither about break of day. Unhappily, the river *Niemen*, which ran before the town, was thaw'd, and as it could not be passed without much difficulty, the enemy had on that occasion sufficient time to retreat. For they could find in all places thereabouts only one little prame, on which the troops could defile, each man holding his horse in his hand, which swam by the prame side. By this

1701. this the reader may judge, what time we were obliged to spend in passing this water.

The King was one of the first who went over, and though the enemy might have easily obstructed us, a pannick had so seized them, that, except some few, who were fuddled, and made prisoners, all the rest ran away full speed towards *Wilna*. The King sufficiently convinced, that it was in vain to pursue an enemy farther, who would have gone to the end of the world rather than have fought, resolved to leave all the detachments at *Kauno*, where they were quarter'd upon the citizens. His Majesty himself, to prevent his being known, performed the office of Quarter-master during the whole march, sending out at the same time several parties on all sides to raise contributions on the adjacent parts; and after having put all things in order, and presented a sum of money to the *Lutheran* Church of *Kauno*, he left the command of these troops to Colonel *Hummerhielm* till farther orders.

Charles, notwithstanding all the remonstrances which could be made him of the danger which few persons must run in crossing a country of more than 40 leagues extent, where the enemy made frequent excursions, took the road of *Courland* with a few attendants; in which road tho' *Oginski* did not dare to appear, his parties however continually scoured the country, as we shall see presently by the relation which Baron *Nils Poss* sent the King from *Bauskenburg* the 18th of *January*, 1702.

The King met with no accident during his journey, and arrived safely at his quarters at *Wurgen*. He was escorted part of the way by Major-General *Arwed Horn*, who came to meet him with a detachment of Drabans. His safe

return

King CHARLES XII. *of* SWEDEN.

return gave an unspeakable joy to the whole army, who had been under dreadful apprehensions during his absence, having had no news of him during the expedition, which lasted near a month.

Whilst all this past in *Courland* and *Lithuania*, the *Russians*, who were assembled in great numbers on the frontiers of *Livonia*, had made a new irruption, which the rigour of the season had rendered easy and advantageous, of which Mr. *Schlippenbach* sent the King the following faithful and exact relation, written in *High Dutch*.

S I R,

'Lieutenant-Colonel *Borckhusen*, who was canton'd between *Aja* and *Eratsfer*, with
' orders to post himself in case of necessity in
' the latter place, without waiting fresh orders,
' or at least to assist both the one and the other,
' and to make an immediate report to the head-
' quarters, having received advice the 28th of
' *December* from Colonel *Pahlen*, who was post-
' ed at *Aja*, of the enemy's approach with con-
' siderable forces, marched instantly with the
' regiment of horse of *Carelia*; upon which
' orders were given through all the quarters to
' get the ammunition ready, and to hold them-
' selves prepared to march at the first signal.

' Lieutenant-Colonel *Borckhusen* returned im-
' mediately, and reported, that it was only a
' false alarm, caused by the peasants, who had
' taken some *Russian* maroders for their whole
' army, and who had given this notice to Colo-
' nel *Pahlen*.

' The next evening at four there was a like
' alarm of the enemy's arrival, at Lieutenant-
' Colonel *Platen*'s quarters, who was posted at
' *Varban*

'*Varban* with a battalion of militia. He took
' immediately some horse of the regiment of the
' Nobility of *Esthonia*, to go and *reconnoitre*;
' and after he had leisure to judge of their forces,
' which were considerabe, he brought me an
' account at nine in the evening. He told me,
' that the enemy had near 2000 sledges loaded
' with *Chevaux de Frise*, and 30 pieces of can-
' non and mortars; so that we had all the rea-
' son to believe they had some design of im-
' portance.

'I presently gave orders to Baron *Reinholdt
' von Liewen*, who was a Lieutenant-Colonel,
' to go, during the night, and *reconnoitre* and
' divert the enemy with 300 horse of the regi-
' ment of *Esthonia*, till I could bring up the bat-
' talions of *Skytt, Liewen, Gardie,* and *Stakelberg*,
' which I had ordered to march up to me the
' same night. Mr. *Liewen* falling in with the
' advanced guard of the enemy, on the 30th, at
' break of day, which consisted of 10 or 12000
' men, attacked them with all possible bravery,
' but was at last obliged to yield to numbers,
' almost all his men being slain on the field of
' battle, with two Captains named *Wrangle* and
' himself made prisoner.

'The enemy, finding now no more resistance,
' fell instantly on our most advanced quarters, and
' first on that of Mr. *Fritsch*, Captain of horse.
' This Captain did his utmost to stop the enemy,
' but lost his life in the action. The greatest
' part of his men having the happiness to come
' and join me. Having then drawn together
' the battalions of *Skytt, Liewen,* and *Stakelberg*,
' with six small field-pieces, four of brass, and
' two of iron, which I took with me, I went to
' join the two regiments of horse of *Esthonia*
'and

'and *Abolehn*, and then marched directly to the
' enemy. I came up with the van-guard, which
' had defeated Mr. *Liewen*, a league beyond
' *Eratfer*, near the village of *Camar*; and hav-
' ing encouraged all my officers and soldiers to
' do their duty, who all unanimously testified
' their zeal for your Majesty's service, I put my
' self at the head of the horse, with the Colonels
' *Wachtmeister* and *Ehnskiold*, and the army
' marched couragiously to the enemy, whom
' they charged so fiercely, that they forced them
' to give ground.

' As I apprehended the enemy, who was infi-
' nitely our superior in numbers, might fall on
' our rear, and cut us off from the foot, which
' we had left a little behind with the cannon, I
' resolved to go and join them with the horse,
' which was performed in good order. Colonel
' *Ehnskiold*, who was too much exposed, was
' taken prisoner on this occasion.

' The enemy having presently followed us,
' were so well saluted on their arrival by the
' foot and the cannon, that they were broke,
' and retreated in great disorder towards the
' body of their army, which I did not see, but
' knew to be in full march to attack me. After
' they had staid some time to observe us at a
' distance, I judged proper, to make the parties
' a little more equal, to retreat to *Eratfer*, where
' I expected to meet the regiment of foot of
' *Campenhausen*, with the dragoons of *Stenbock*
' and the horse of *Carelia*.

' The two last regiments having joined me on
' the road, I ordered them to cover the rear-
' guard, which the enemy harassed continually,
' and where the combat became at last very
' bloody. Baron *Gabriel Horn*, a Major, stood
' a long

'a long time firm with his squadron almost sur-
'rounded with the enemy. He was mortally
'wounded in this action, which obliged him to
'be carried out of the field of battle, after he
'was relieved by Major *Liewen*, with his squa-
'dron.

'As the enemy continued to press us, scarce
'giving us time to draw up, Lieutenant-Colonel
'*Liewen*, who was in the van-guard with the
'cannon, turned them readily against the ene-
'my. Lieutenant-Colonel *Stakelberg*, with his
'battalion, posted himself on a cross-way to stop
'the enemy, till the battalions of *Liewen* and
'*Skytt* had time to pass and form a line toge-
'ther. The horse were ranged on the two
'wings in the best manner we could.

'The action became now very sharp, and the
'fire continued on both sides without ceasing
'with terrible violence, especially after the ene-
'my had received their artillery and mortars,
'which incommoded us extremely. As I per-
'ceived their forces to encrease every minute,
'and that by attacking our two wings they en-
'deavoured to hem us in on both sides; besides
'that of the twenty-five cartridges, with which
'each of our cannon was furnish'd, there remain-
'ed but four; I set myself on retreating, with
'design, if necessary, to cut through the enemy
'sword in hand.

'To this purpose I ordered the foot to form
'the van-guard with the cannon, and the horse
'to cover them, and to stop the enemy by fre-
'quent discharges. This scheme had not the
'success I had flattered myself with. The horse
'no sooner perceived the foot to retreat, than
'they ran away without its being possible to ral-
'ly them. The regiments of *Carelia* and *Abo-*
'*lebs*

' *lehn* began to run first, then that of *Esthonia*,
' and lastly one squadron of *Stenbock*'s dragoons.
' One battalion of this regiment, with Count
' *Lowenhaupt* at their head, continued with the
' others to second the battalion of *Stakelberg*.

' All these horse running back on the foot
' put them in disorder, notwithstanding all my
' efforts with the greater number of officers to
' rally those that were flying, there was now no
' possibility of stopping them, by reason of the
' vast number of the enemy that pursued us;
' who seeing the foot without support, and aban-
' doned, broke them on all sides, and cut them
' almost all to pieces. It is true, they at first
' attempted to defend themselves with great
' bravery, but were at length forced to yield to
' the prodigious multitudes of the enemy, and
' were totally defeated.

' Of all the foot-officers who were present at
' the action, there remained with me no more
' than Lieutenant-Colonel *Liewen* with four of
' his officers, Lieutenant-Colonel *Stakelberg* with
' a non-commission officer, two soldiers, and
' Major *Meyer Krantz*, who, after the battalions
' were overthrown by our own horse, had the
' happiness to find horses, and save themselves
' through the enemy, under favour of the
' smoke and the darkness of the night. The
' Captain-Lieutenant of *Liewen*'s battalion saved
' the colours; all those belonging to *Stakelberg*'s
' were ordered by him to be torn to pieces be-
' fore the retreat; this was faithfully executed
' by all the Ensigns, as we learnt from a soldier
' of *Skytt*'s battalion, who likewise assured us,
' that several officers and soldiers had happily
' preserved themselves in the woods.

' I continued

'I continued always with the horse-officers, exhorting those that fled to rally; and Adjutant-General *Freymann* killed some who refused to obey, which example, together with some others of a like kind, obliged them at last to stand their ground near *Eratfer*, and to rally. Here I found Count *Gardie's* battalion, commanded by Major *Stabl*, who had with him the rest of the cannon. I now resolved on a retreat, with Mr. *Stabl* and Colonel *Wachtmeister*, who had commanded the horse, which I performed in good order.

'The enemy pursued us very briskly towards *Kebrart*; and as I saw they had set fire to the church of *Canepoëbe* and the village of *Korart*, I thought my self obliged to burn the little magazine at *Kebrart*, fearing lest the enemy should seize it. As night now drew on, I sent Lieutenant-Colonel *Stakelberg* towards *Sagnitz* with the cannon and the remains of his people, who were posted at *Korart*, as likewise Count *Gardie's* battalion and *Stenbock's* dragoons. As for myself, I staid some time at *Koikul* with the rest of the horse, and towards break of day took the same road hither.

'I was much surprized at hearing nothing from Colonel *Campenhusen*, to whom I had sent orders to bring his regiment to *Eratfer*, and join the other troops; but as these came not to him till very late, by reason of the messenger's losing his way, he could not be there in time. However, when he approached the head-quarters, and by the noise of the cannon and small arms, found we were at blows with the enemy, he hastened to my assistance; but he unhappily missed the road, and had only time to defeat a straggling *Russian*

" fian party, who had taken up their quarters in
" some houses about *Eratfer*. *Horn*, his Lieu-
" tenant-Colonel, attacked this party, and made
" most of them prisoners. Mr. *Campenhusen*
" drawing afterwards to *Dorpt*, after he had
" heard of our being routed, made a thousand
" windings to join me, which he hath just per-
" formed.

' The enemy have kept themselves very quiet
" since the battle, till yesterday. As soon as the
" parties which I have detached to *reconnoitre*
" them shall be returned, I will order my affairs
" according to their report, and shall not fail to
" give your Majesty the speediest information.

Sagnitz, Jan. 1.
1707. SCHLIPPENBACH.

The enemy did not at all improve the advantage which they had gained. General *Scheremetof*, who had at first intended to lay siege to *Dorpt*, thought proper hastily to repass the frontiers; whether they feared a second battle, which Mr. *Schlippenbach* seemed to prepare for, by drawing his troops together from all parts, or whether the last battle had cost them too many men through the desperate defence of our foot, which rendered their loss much more considerable than ours.

The King, at his return from *Wurgen*, found that Mr. *Stuart* had made all the necessary dispositions for the winter-quarters, no person doubting but that the army were to enter into them; but his Majesty all of a sudden changed his mind, and order'd several regiments of horse, foot, and dragoons, under the command of Lieutenant-General *Spens*, to file off in several columns

through

1701. through *Samogitia*, to be nearer the detachment which was at *Kauno*.

The King at the same time wrote a letter to the Cardinal Primate, declaring the reasons which had induced him to pursue the enemy, and attack him wherever he might be met with.

This firm resolution, declared in so authentick a manner, was very disagreeable to King *Augustus*, who, having all things to fear from so formidable and justly-provoked an enemy, had already very earnestly applied himself to solicit the mediation of the States General, as well as of several other powers of *Europe*: But as he found every where an infinite number of obstacles, and saw the King of *Sweden* inflexible against him, he thought proper to employ one of the fair sex's endeavours to work on her cousin.

The Countess of *Koningsmark*, a *Swede* by birth, and a Lady of great beauty, assisted by all the charms of a rich and cultivated genius, was chose for this business; on which account she repaired to *Libaw*, confiding in her charms, and believing she should have as great an ascendant over the mind of the young *Swedish* Monarch, as she had gained over the King of *Poland*.

The Countess laid hold of certain pretensions of her brother-in-law Count *Charles Lowenhaupt*, who was then in the *Saxon* service, to disguise the true intentions of her journey. She offered the most advantageous conditions of peace on the part of King *Augustus*, at the same time demanding a particular audience of his *Swedish* Majesty: But whether these propositions were not agreeable to the interest of the Republick, whose friendship the King was resolved inviolably to maintain, or whether this Prince suspected his enemy to have some private views in

this

this affair, he refused to see this beautiful Ambassadress, notwithstanding all the complaisance which on other occasions he shewed to the fair sex; and tho' this Lady used all imaginable stratagems to come at an audience, even to the sending him some fine copies of Verses on his Winter-Campaign, she could not obtain it. The Countess was therefore obliged to return without attaining what she had proposed [b].

The King now departed from *Wurgen* on the 15th of *January* with the rest of the army, which he brought to an encampment about *Goldingen*, and took up his own lodgings in the castle.

There had been during these transactions several skirmishes between the parties of *Oginski* and the little garrisons the King had left at *Seelburg* and *Bausk*. The Governor, Lieutenant-Colonel *Peter Banner*, who was at *Seelburg*, had detached in the month of *December* in the preceding year a Captain of Dragoons, who fell on a party of the enemy, discomfited them, and took some prisoners. Colonel *Nils Poss* sent the following relation, in the *Swedish* language, from *Bauskenburg* to the King, to inform his Majesty of what passed in this action.

---

[b] She endeavour'd to meet him on the road in some of those excursions which he frequently made on horseback, which one day she accomplished in a very narrow place; and as soon as she perceived his approach, she alighted from her coach: The King saluted her, without saying a single word, and presently turn'd back; so that the Countess gained nothing more by her journey than the satisfaction of believing that she was the only person who was fear'd by the King of *Sweden*. *Voltaire*.

The author of the *Memoirs* informs us, that the *Czar* conceived an esteem on this occasion for his enemy, which he preserved ever after the King of *Sweden*'s death.

SIR,

The Life and History of

SIR,

'Concerning the expedition of Major *Trautfetter*, I have the honour to tell your Majesty, that the Major departed from hence the 22d of *December*, 1701, upon those orders which he had received, with 150 Dragoons of Colonel *Gustavus Albedhyl*'s regiment, for *Gulbin* in *Lithuania*, to serve as a guard on the territories of the Great General *Sapieha*, against the frequent incursions of *Oginski*, who put all to fire and sword.

'Being arrived the 23d at *Gulbin*, he heard that a large party of the enemy was scatter'd in the neighbouring villages, where they entertained themselves with plunder. He instantly attacked them, killed a great number, and took the rest prisoners, namely, four officers, and 20 soldiers, which have been sent from hence to *Riga*. He took from them at the same time one standard, two kettle-drums, and five *Tartarian* standards.

'This loss, which the enemy received, obliged him to retire for some time from the lands of the *Sapieha*. As to Major *Trautfetter*, he posted himself at *Gulbin* to observe the motions of the enemy.

'The 11th of *January* I was informed, that a Colonel of *Oginski*'s party, whose name was *Berg*, was arrived from *Janitzieck* with twelve troops of horse; that he had passed near *Schonberg* on the frontiers in his way to *Birsen*, one league from *Gulbin*, and that he had destroyed all that belonged to the *Sapieha* in his road.

'Upon this news I ordered Major *Trautfetter*, on the 12th, to bring up his detachment from *Gulbin*, which I intended to employ in

'* levying

'*levying contributions on those Nobles of *Cour-*
' *land* which had not paid them. He came to me
' the 13th, and after he had acquitted himself of
' that commission, I gave him on the 15th in the
' evening some orders sealed up, which he was
' to carry with his detachment, and not to open
' until a certain distance. These orders were, to
' resume his post at *Gulbin*, and drive off the ene-
' my; and, in case he could not find them there,
' to look out for them and attack them. The
' Major, coming to *Gulbin* the 16th at break of
' day, learnt that the enemy, after having been
' defeated some days before near *Dunenburg* by
' Captain *Ramfelt*'s party, had been so terribly
' frightened, that they retired 3 leagues from
' *Gulbin* into a town called *Coppieha*. Major
' *Trautfetter* learnt farther, that these troops,
' having been advertised of his departure from
' *Gulbin* for *Courland*, were separated, leaving
' five companies at *Coppieha*, where they thought
' themselves in security; and the rest were lodg-
' ed in the adjacent village, after having had
' the precaution to barricade all the passages.

' The Major, in consequence of his orders,
' departed from *Gulbin* the same evening with
' 100 dragoons, the rest being sick, or out on
' parties, and arrived the 17th at break of day
' at *Coppieha*, where, after having forced the
' guard, he made some of his party dismount,
' and attack those who were shut up in the
' houses, and discharge their muskets and gra-
' nades on them, by which they were driven
' from house to house to the end of the town,
' more than 100 of them being slain on the spot.

* The *French* has it, "to *lands*," which, I apprehend,
execute some Nobles of *Cour-* is a mistake.

' As

The LIFE and HISTORY of

'As this action lasted near an hour and a
' half, the enemy, who were posted near at hand,
' ran up from all parts at the noise of the firing;
' upon which the Major was obliged to retreat,
' as well on the account of their great num-
' bers, as the fatigue of his horses. This retreat
' was however performed in good order; and as
' the enemy feared an ambuscade, or that the
' Major might receive some succours, they durst
' not attempt to pursue him. They retired into a
' neighbouring wood, and afterwards went to
' join *Oginski*, who was posted at two leagues
' distance with all his forces, which, as they pre-
' tended, amounted to 6000 men. He is since
' gone, as I am informed, to *Vichur*, where he
' has some cannon, and has fortified himself.

'All the booty, which was at first made, was
' gotten by the peasants, except the colours of
' Colonel *Berg*. We brought away one Lieute-
' nant and five soldiers prisoners. On our side
' we lost Lieutenant *Bachman*, two non-commis-
' sioned officers, and seven dragoons, who were
' killed. We likewise missed the two drums,
' with three dragoons; and as the enemy must
' be certainly informed of the weakness of the
' Major's party, I resolved to recall him from
' *Gulbin*, lest he should be attacked by all their
' forces, and he hath joined me accordingly. I
' now wait your Majesty's farther orders.

Baukenberg,   NILS POSS.
Jan. 18. 1702.

All these excursions of *Oginski*, with those of the *Lithuanian Poles*, joined to the slowness of the Republick in declaring herself and giving his Majesty satisfaction, determined him at last to enter *Poland* with the rest of the army. He de- parted from *Goldingen* at the end of *January* to
Rosienne,

Rosienne, 12 leagues from *Kauno*, whither Mr. *Spens* had gone before, as we have already said.

The artillery and heavy baggage had been sent back to *Riga*; and we left in the towns of *Courland* a sufficient number of horse and dragoons to keep that province in order, of which Baron *Stuart*, Major-General, was made Governor. He chose *Mittau* for the place of his residence, and neglected nothing which might contribute to the defence of the country during his Majesty's absence.

The army passed the frontiers in three columns, the first and second of which took separate routs to *Lubenick*, where they joined again; whilst the third column continued to follow in another rout. The general conjunction of these troops happened some leagues from the frontiers.

First Rout.

From *Schwenden* to *Caubelick*,	1½ league.	*Judelein*,	2 leagues,
Kalvaria,	4,	*Solanten*,	2,
Telloe,	3,	*Olscadi*,	2,
		Schorani,	3,
	Lubenick,		4,
	Yzwela,		2.

Second Rout.

From *Ratzo* to *Plattel*,	1½ league;	*Kurleisten*,	7 leagues;
Ploncain,	2,	*Taurogola*,	4,
Rettau,	3,	*Gaurin*,	2,
Teidan,	3,	*Jurburg*,	5,
Sufing,	2,	*Ponimon*,	2,
Ciulin,	4,	*Raudani*,	1,
Rosienne,	4,	*Willeja*,	8,
Girtokela,	1,	*Kaun*,	4,
Euvogala,	3,	*Wiellon*,	1,
		Seradnelle,	1.

1702.   The King was extremely fatigued during this march, always riding from one regiment and one column to another, notwithstanding the rigour of a very severe winter, without giving himself any relaxation, or taking any repose. He would never repair to his head-quarters, named *Bielowice*, the seat of a Gentleman of that name, a long half-league from *Rosienne*, before he had distributed the whole army into good quarters in the neighbourhood, where they remained till the end of the month of *March*.

One of the first things which his Majesty did, was, to drive away a great number of lewd women, who had slipt in amongst the troops, and introduced libertinism and disorder; but he took such measures that very few women durst remain amongst them.

King *Augustus* in the mean time flatter'd himself with I know not what ill-grounded hopes, with which the Countess of *Koningsmark* had fed him of success in her negotiation. She had ever since her departure from *Wurgen* coasted along the frontiers of *Samogitia*, and was now come to *Tillsen* in *Prussia*, which is situated on the frontiers, and at a little distance from *Rosienne* and from his Majesty's head-quarters.

King *Augustus* sent hither Mr. *Witzthum d'Eckstedt*, his Chamberlain, to confer with her, and to remain till farther orders. Madam *Koningsmark* very dextrously prevailed with him to go to the King of *Sweden*, and make a second trial; which he did. Count *Piper*, his Majesty's first Minister of State, to whom he notified his arrival, at the same time demanding an audience, was very much surprized to find him arrived before he had asked leave to come; however, he agreed to see him; but when Mr. *Witzthum* would

have

have delivered him a letter from King *Augustus*, the Count excused himself from receiving it without his *Swedish* Majesty's permission.

The King was incensed at this proceeding, which was a liberty that ought not to have been taken in time of war; he therefore order'd Baron *Buchwaldt*, his Aid-de-Camp General, to put Mr. *Witzthum* in arrest, and at the same time set an Ensign of the guards with twelve men over him.

Mr. *Witzthum* was treated with all imaginable civility, and waited on by the King's servants. Amongst his papers, which were instantly seized, was found, with his instructions, a letter written by King *Augustus*'s own hand to the King of *Sweden*, in which he engaged in the most complaisant and even submissive terms, to attend his *Swedish* Majesty in person, and to clear up by a conference all the difficulties which obstructed the conclusion of a sure, solid, and lasting peace.

Mr. *Witzthum* remained in arrest all the time of the King's stay at *Bielowice*; he was afterwards conducted under an escort to *Riga*, where he had liberty on his parole to walk where he pleased; till at last, the King being arrived at *Warsovia*, permitted him to return into *Saxony*.

About this time Count *Sapieha*, Great General of *Lithuania*, sent a Captain of horse to *Bielowice*, to ask the King's leave to pay his respects to him, which he immediately obtained; and having set out for the head-quarters, attended by a numerous train of Nobility and domesticks, he was much surprized to meet his Majesty on the borders of *Prussia* with only four or five attendants. He appeared very well satisfied with the favourable reception which was graciously given by his august protector.

I 4 As

1702.

As the affairs of King *Augustus* grew worse every day, he now thought himself in so dangerous a situation, that he determin'd to convene a Diet at *Warsovia*. He then imparted the King of *Sweden*'s resolution to the assembly, with the perplexity he was in on that account. A great number of mal-contents took this occasion to exclaim against the present government, which they now ventured to do in the most publick manner. However, a resolution passed to send a solemn embassy to the King of *Sweden*, and offer him the intercessions of the Republick.

Baron *Sacken*, the Chamberlain, was sent to communicate to his Majesty the Republick's resolution to send an embassy to him. The Baron had been formerly sent by the Cardinal Primate to *Stockholm*, to notify the death of the late King of *Poland*. He arrived the 12th at *Bielowice*, and had an immediate audience. He demanded of his Majesty the time and place in which he would be pleased to give the Ambassador, who was on the road, the honour of attending him. He was told, that the King's intention was to spare him half his journey; and he departed thence without being able to obtain a more positive answer.

It might have been imagined, that since the King of *Sweden* was with his army in the heart of the enemy's country, they would not have dared to undertake any thing to molest our quarters: However, *Oginski* and Prince *Wisniowiski* committed continual hostilities, scouring about daily with their little parties; in which attempts they were generally worsted, tho' they never attacked our small detachments unless with three or four times their number.

These

These daily skirmishes chiefly incommoded the detachment at *Kauno*, whither the King sent Lieutenant-General *Liewen*, who was posted at *Kudani* with his regiment of foot, to reinforce them. Colonel *Hummerhielm*, who had hitherto commanded there, had had the good fortune some days before to defeat a party of twelve companies, belonging to *Wisniowiski*, near the castle of *Jesna*, which is the property of a gentleman named *Paix*, and to take ten pieces of brass cannon; but as he could not carry away more than four, for want of boats, he resolved to return soon after in order to fetch off the six others.

Having put himself with this view at the head of 130 troopers, he departed from *Kauno*, and at the same time embarked in two large boats 110 men of the regiment of foot-guards, commanded by Captain *Gustavus Siegroth*, to bring back the six cannons by water on the river *Memel*, near which the castle is situated.

Prince *Wisniowiski* being advertised of this design, drew near *Jesna* with 6000 men, amongst which were four regiments of *German* foot and horse. *Hummerhielm*, who had heard nothing of this, or perhaps would not believe it, having passed the river near *Jesna*, and continued two days march by the water side, that he might not be at too great a distance from the foot, quitted the river the third day, and marched before towards a little town named *Dorsinski*, six leagues from *Kauno*, where he waited the arrival of the infantry.

When *Wisniowiski* saw that he was separated from his foot, he thought proper to attack him, and with that design brought forward his vanguard, which was repulsed with great bravery by by Mr. *Hummerhielm*. The enemy returned again to the charge with all their force; and Mr. *Hummerhielm*, being advanced to *reconnoitre* them, was unhappily intercepted and made prisoner. Mr. *John Siegroth*, Major to *Morner*'s regiment, had now with the rest of his officers no other game to play, than to break through sword in hand. The *Swedes* had the advantage in the beginning of this action, having overthrown all those who opposed their passage; but getting by misfortune into a morass, they could neither advance nor retreat, and were there, after defending themselves with incredible valour, all cut to pieces, there being neither officer nor soldier who had not received several wounds.

Twenty only were taken prisoners, and those all covered with wounds; two troopers of this number had the courage to throw themselves into the *Memel*, and swam over to the other side; one of whom was killed by the peasants, so that only one escaped to bring the news of this defeat to Mr. *Gyllenkrok*, Major of the guards, who was detached with a party into the neighbourhood to raise contributions.

After this action, the enemy being advertised of the approach of the foot with the cannon, went to meet and attack them. They were commanded by *Gustavus Siegroth*, brother to the Major of whom we have just spoken, and who, being ignorant of Colonel *Hummerhielm*'s fate, had landed a non-commission officer with some soldiers to bring him news. These met with the van-guard of *Wisniewiski*'s army, and, after having stood some musket-shots, returned to their body, to give them advice of the enemy's approach. *Siegroth*, who could not believe it, landed

landed himself, with about 20 men; but after a discharge on the scouts of the enemy, whom he now perceived to be advancing, he retreated in good order to his boats, intending to defend himself till the arrival of *Hummerhielm*, from whom he expected assistance: But in that instant while he was preparing to pass to the other bank of the river, his boats unluckily ran on the sands, nor was it possible for him to get them off again. In this conjuncture *Siegroth* presently saw, that he had no way left but to defend himself to the last extremity, especially as the enemy had now planted six cannons against him, from which they fired incessantly on our boats, and pierced them in such manner, that our soldiers were up to the middle in water; however, they lost not their courage, which when *Wisniowiski* saw, and found with what resolute troops he had to do, who had by a volley just repulsed his men as they were endeavouring to plant a cannon on the brink of the river, he ordered a trumpet to be sounded, which was answered from *Siegroth* by a drum.

A Colonel of the enemy, whose name was *Grothusen*, approached *Siegroth* at this interval, and acquainted him with the total defeat of *Hummerhielm*, who was taken prisoner, and then summoned him to surrender also with his men; but *Siegroth*, very far from accepting his summons, plainly declared his intentions of defending himself to the last extremity, or till he had received those succours, which he could not fail of from *Kauno*.

Grothusen then represented to this brave officer the great danger to which he exposed himself and his people, Prince *Wisniowiski* being present with his whole army; but he could not
move

move *Siegroth*, who continued his firing, while he had powder or ball left. In the mean while the enemy, who faw with aftonifhment the extraordinary defence made by this handful of people, and perhaps feared the arrival of fuccours from *Kauno*, as *Siegroth* had artfully infinuated, offered him the liberty of returning to *Kauno* with his men, which he was at laft obliged to accept, feeing no room to flatter himfelf with hopes of better conditions.

The capitulation ftipulated, that the foldiers fhould lay down their arms, but that the officers, even the fubalterns, fhould keep theirs; and that they fhould be allowed an efcort, and waggons to carry off their wounded and their dead.

In this manner this brave officer extricated himfelf with honour out of fo dangerous a fituaation; fix men only of his detachment were killed and nine wounded, and he returned with the reft to *Kauno*.

Lieutenant-General *Liewen*, who commanded at *Kauno*, no fooner heard of this defeat, than he inftantly recalled all the detached parties from the other fide of the river, that he might be in a condition to make head againft *Wifniowifki*, in cafe that Prince fhould think proper to attack him. At the fame time he encreafed all his guards, and fent advice to the King. But the enemy, inftead of improving their advantage, had haftened directly to *Wilna*.

As foon as the King heard what had paft, he ordered all the army to decamp, and march towards *Kauno*; and Major-General *Morner* and Count *Stenbock*, who were pofted with their regiments on the fide of *Wilna*, had private orders to march and furprize Prince *Wifniowifki* at that place. To

To haften this expedition, the horfe took the foot up behind them; and marching through forefts and thick woods, that they might not be perceived by the enemy, they arrived at break of day before the town, forced the barrier, and inftantly began the attack.

The enemy, who had no mind to fight, took the fureft method to fave themfelves, which was to run away full fpeed. This however they could not execute fo expeditioufly, but that feveral were made prifoners, and fo many killed, that the ftreets of the town were all cover'd with dead bodies.

Wifniowifki was in great danger himfelf of being taken by a trooper, who purfued him fo clofely, and preffed him fo fharply, that, if the trooper had not been unluckily killed, that General would have fallen into our hands. He loft all his cannon, his horfes and his equipage.

General *Morner* remained at *Kauno*, in conformity to the orders he had received; and, as he was to ftay here fome time, he laid the town and the adjacent parts under heavy contributions, having firft received a reinforcement of fome troops.

The King was ftill at *Bielowice*, tho' all the army was already decamped; and as the Great General *Sapieba* and his brother were in the neighbourhood on the frontiers of *Pruffia*, his Majefty paid them a vifit, and held a conference with them. He ftay'd with them all night, and returned the next day.

The Duke of *Holftein-Gottorp* arrived fome days after at *Bielowice*. He came by fea to *Riga* from *Stockholm*, and performed his voyage in eight days. His defign was to make a campaign with

with the King, who received him with all the tokens of a perfect friendship.

At length the King with his Drabans began his march towards *Kauno*. He left in *Somogitia* Colonel *Charles Cruus* with his regiment of horse to levy the remaining part of the contributions; and as the Colonel remained some time at *Rosienne*, there were frequent skirmishes between his parties and the *Poles*.

His Majesty on his arrival at *Kauno*, 112 leagues from *Bielowice* by the rout which I have set down above, took care to bring the sick safely up into *Courland*, and then continued his march directly into *Lithuania*; and that the army might not want provisions, he divided them into two columns, one of which was commanded by Lieutenant-General *Spens*, and the other by his Majesty, who had with him the Duke of *Holstein*, and some other Generals. This latter column coasted along the river *Memel* through *Rumifski* (3 leagues,) whence it marched to *Doesinski* (3 leag.) the place where Colonel *Hummerbielm* had been defeated.

The King surveyed the field where the action had been, of which Captain *Siegroth* related to him all the circumstances. The next day he gave orders to bury the dead; and having caused the officers and soldiers to be put into coffins, they were buried with the usual ceremonies, the King himself assisting at the funeral, and the troops honour'd the memory of those brave men by several vollies. They set fire to the town, which, except the church, was burnt to the ground.

The column afterwards continued its march towards *Punia* (3 leagues,) which place had likewise some days before been partly reduced to ashes

King CHARLES XII. of SWEDEN.

ashes by Mr. *Roxman*, Captain of horse, who commanded a party of *Swedes*. One of the Ecclesiasticks of this place had given the enemy timely notice of Mr. *Roxman*'s arrival, who was attacked by them, but he repulsed them with loss. From *Punia* the column drew towards *Olita*, where his Majesty staid some days.

In the mean time Prince *Wisniowiski*, enraged at the surprize of *Wilna*, thought of nothing else but how to revenge himself. He believed that *Easter*-day (old style) would be a most favourable time for the execution of his design. As he maintained an intelligence with some of the citizens, he repaired thither with little noise, forced the guard, who suspected nothing, and entered with his troops, who set up an universal outcry and most dreadful howling. This was done at noon, when all our people were at dinner.

They did at first some mischief; Lieutenant-Colonel *Treffenberg* and some others were killed: But they did not long maintain this advantage; for our troops running instantly to arms, attack'd them so briskly on all sides, that tho' they were our superiors in number, they were drove back, broke, and at last entirely dispersed.

Wisniowiski was again in danger of being taken; but having saved himself through a convent, he escaped Mr. *Morner*, who eagerly pursued him: he left however a great number dead and wounded behind him, with some trophies in our possession; and he had the shame and vexation to fly with loss before an enemy who was much weaker than himself, and whom he had at first surprized. We took in their retreat without the town a Captain of horse and some troopers wounded. This action having taught

Wisniowiski,

Wiſniowiſki, that the *Swedes* were an improper people to be play'd with, he for some time lost all desire of giving us fresh disturbance.

The King marched from *Olita* to *Merecz* (4 leagues,) where his Majesty remained some days, till the army had passed the *Memel*, on such floats as they could get together, and then he marched to *Liepuni* (3 leagues,) where the army rested till the 17th, and then decamped and came to *Sopotſkini* (4 leagues,) leaving the town of *Grodno* (1 league) on the left.

The *Poliſh* Ambassadors, who were already arrived there, and who saw the King pass by the town, sent to his Majesty to know in what place he would permit them to attend him. The King, who easily penetrated into the design of this embassy, the end of which was only to amuse him till King *Auguſtus* had time to bring his troops into *Poland*, and to form there an army with the permission he had obtain'd of the greatest part of the Senate, firmly resolved not to hearken to any propositions which the Ambassadors should make to retard the course of his victorious arms; the rather, as the chief of them was a declared partizan and creature of King *Auguſtus*.

In the mean time his Majesty was pleased to hear what they had to say, and acquainted them by Mr. *Cederhielm*, Secretary of the Chancery, that he would expect them at *Dlougowitz*, five leagues from *Grodno*, one of the largest villages in *Europe*, which extends five *Poliſh* leagues in length, and is several hundred paces wide.

The army being come hither on the 22d of *April*, the Ambassadors immediately followed it; but it was presently discover'd, by the difficulties which they started concerning the ceremonial, that

that they thought of nothing farther than to gain time; on which the King very plainly declared to them, that, if they persisted in their chicanery on those small points, he would pass on without giving them any longer hearing. This declaration at last obliged them to accommodate themselves to his Majesty's pleasure.

These Ambassadors were five in number, of which the two chief, Mr. *Lipski* Waiwode of *Calis*, and Mr. *Crispin* Waiwode of *Witepsk*, were Deputies from the Senate; and the three others, namely, Count *Tarlo*, Mr. *Oginski*, and Mr. *Crispin*, from the Nobility.

The King had prepared a tent at some distance from the village to receive them. The Drabans were drawn up on horseback before the tent, with 600 of the foot-guards, colours flying and drums beating. Lieutenant-General *Liewen* received them at two o'clock in the afternoon to conduct them to the audience, whither they repaired with a train of 200 horsemen. They were received before the tent by Mr. *Hard*, who performed the office of Marshal, and by the Officers of the Court, who conducted them to the antichamber. Baron *Knut Poss*, Major-General and Colonel of the guards, met them at the entrance of the King's apartment, and conducted them to his Majesty, who was seated on a chair of state, with the Duke of *Holstein*, Count *Piper*, and several other General-Officers and Colonels on both sides of him [c].

The Waiwode of *Calis* first spoke in the *Latin* tongue; and, as soon as he began to speak, the King arose, and remained standing during the

---

[c] He had a constant disdain for this sort of pomp; but he thought it necessary on this occasion. *Voltaire*.

whole audience, in which Count *Tarlo* afterwards spoke also in *Latin*.

These two Ambassadors desired his Majesty to be pleased to make a peace; not to advance farther into *Poland*; to abandon *Courland*; to restore the cannon and artillery taken at *Dunamund* and other places, which King *Augustus* had made a present of to the Republick, to make an amends for the damages caused by the war, and the heavy contributions raised in *Courland*, *Samogitia*, and *Lithuania*; lastly, to name Commissaries to treat with them on all these articles, and those other propositions which they had to make on the behalf of the Republick.

Count *Piper* having answered them in *Latin*, that the King would appoint Commissaries, the Ambassadors withdrew, and his Majesty presently named Count *Piper*, Mr. *Wachshager*, formerly Resident in *Poland*, and Secretary *Hermelin*, to treat with them; but as their demands were very exorbitant, and on the other hand the King, who was the most jealous Prince in the world of his glory, would not suffer them to prescribe laws to him, most part of the appointed time for the conferences passed in supporting the arguments which were suggested on both sides, without bringing any thing to a conclusion.

Violent disputes happen'd among the Ambassadors themselves, which almost came to blows. The Waiwode of *Calis* was the person who chiefly embroiled the affairs, being a creature of King *Augustus*, who had made him a present of a Starosty, the better to support his interest, and which cost him dear, as we shall see hereafter. This Ambassador, who was a violent man, and shewed no respect to any one, and always spoke
in

in a magisterial voice with great fierceness, at last incensed his Majesty so much, that he resolved to be no longer amused, and to march directly to *Warsovia* to find out the enemy.

The regiment of horse of *Scania*, commanded by Major-General *Stromberg*, being arrived during these transactions with some field-pieces taken at *Kauno*, the King caused the army to decamp from *Dlougowitz*, and march to *Sykinkuri* (4 leagues,) and on the next day to *Knysin* ($3\frac{1}{2}$ leagues.) And to rid himself at once of the Ambassadors, who always followed him, the King resolved to quit his column, and with a small train, to join that under the command of Mr. *Spens*, which was some leagues distant from the other.

His Majesty having learnt that the *Saxons* appeared at *Brzescia*, a town advantageously situated on the river *Bug* and the confines of *Great Poland* and *Lithuania*, he presently marched thither with Major *Creutz* at the head of 300 of his horse-guards, where he soon arrived, and made himself master of that pass, which the *Saxons* had just abandoned.

This column continued its march towards *Tykozin*, a little town belonging to the son-in-law of *Sapieha*, a well-built place, and in which there are a great many *Jews*. Here is a little castle, situated in the middle of a morass, which the *Swedes* had formerly fortified, and kept a long time, but the Republick had now a little garrison therein.

The Ambassadors persisted in following the King's column, and never ceased pressing Count *Piper*, continually flattering themselves that some resolution would be at last taken in their favour. But all their instances were useless, their demands

1701. appearing so exorbitant, that it was thought proper to give them no satisfaction. At last, finding the King resolved to see them no more, they quitted the army, and repaired to King *Augustus* at *Warsovia*, giving that Prince an account of the ill success of their negotiation, and assuring him that he had nothing to hope from the King of *Sweden*, whom they had found inflexible.

Upon this *Augustus* set out instantly for *Cracovia*, whither the army which he had brought from *Saxony* had orders to march, to oppose the enterprize of the King of *Sweden*. He was attended by several Senators, and particularly by those who had consented to his bringing his *Saxon* troops into *Poland*. In the number of his attendants in this journey were the Princes *Lubomirski*; one of which was lately made Great General of the Crown, in the place of *Potoki*, who had succeeded the brave *Gablonofski*, and had been Great-General no longer than a fortnight, which gave room for a suspicion, that the death of these two brave noblemen was not natural: as to the Cardinal-Primate, and the other Senators, they retired home, to wait the issue of an adventure which held all *Europe* in a suspence [d].

During

[d] It is proper to remark here, that in the *Senatus-Consultum* held at *Warsovia*, and in which they deliberated on the methods which King *Augustus* had to take, several Senators advised this Prince to remain here, and receive the King of *Sweden* as his friend and relation, submitting himself entirely to his discretion; suggesting, that a King, who aspired at nothing but what was great and magnanimous, would be too generous not to be softened by an action which express'd so much confidence in his virtue.

The other Senators on the contrary, especially the favorites, dissuaded King *Augustus* from these measures, as unworthy of his Majesty; and upon this latter advice he resolved to depart, and put

During the king's absence, Count *Piper* continued to conduct the column through *Pembrawa* (three leagues) to *Oſtrowia* (five leagues) where he publiſhed his *Swediſh* Majeſty's Manifeſto, and his Proclamation, addreſſed to all the Eſtates of *Poland*.

'The unjuſt proceedings of King *Auguſtus* were herein ſet forth at large; and the Wrongs done his *Swediſh* Majeſty by that Prince; in what manner he had violated the oath made the Republic, and how little dependance was to be had on ſo troubleſome a neighbour, that the Republic could take no better meaſures than to ſet a Prince on their throne, whoſe peaceable inclination and conſtant friendſhip with *Sweden*, would put her into a flouriſhing condition, and render her formidable to all thoſe neighbours who would undertake to give her any trouble. As to the reſt, his Majeſty promiſed to cauſe the troops to obſerve an exact diſcipline, provided that they furniſhed them with proviſion and neceſſary ſubſiſtence, during the whole time that he ſhould be obliged to purſue the enemy in *Poland*, and as ſoon as he ſhould have entirely quitted the country, he aſſured the Republic to put them to no farther charge.'

From *Oſtrowia* the column marched to *Perembi*, (three leagues) where the King joined them; and they marched the next day (three

put himſelf at the head of his troops, to decide the affair by force of arms.

It is certain, that if King *Auguſtus* had given in to the former counſels, the peace had been ſecured; nothing being ſo capable to bend the high and noble heart of *Charles* the Twelfth, as a recourſe to his clemency. This his Majeſty did me the honour to tell me in the preſence of Count *Piper* and Mr. *Hermelin*.

leagues)

1702. leagues) to *Wiskowa* on the *Bug*, to pass which they set about a bridge, which was finished the third day. *Axel Gyllenkrock*, Major of the Guards, then received orders to go before with a detachment, and post himself at *Prague*, which is the suburbs of *Warsovia* on this side of the *Vistula*.

The King followed with the army, and encamped at *Radzimin*, half-way between *Warsovia* and *Wiskowa*; here they halted one day, and marched on the following towards *Prague*, taking their way through a plain, where his Majesty's grandfather, of glorious memory, CHARLES GUSTAVUS King of *Sweden*, gave battle, with FREDERICK-WILLIAM, sirnamed the GREAT, Elector of *Brandenburg*, to the *Polish* army, which he entirely defeated, after a battle which lasted three days, notwithstanding the superiority of the enemy.

Charles XII. who had a happy memory, and well understood history, took great pleasure in recounting to the Generals, who were about him, such particulars as could have only been known by a great General, shewing them the places of attack, and informing them in what manner the squadrons and regiments were drawn up.

The King lodged at *Prague*, and the army was distributed along the *Vistula*, and in the neighbouring villages. Towards the evening his Majesty commanded Baron *Charles Poss*, Lieutenant-Colonel of the guards, with 400 men, to pass the *Vistula* in boats. *Poss* presently took possession of the castle in the town without the least opposition from the little garrison of the Republick's troops. He was made Governor of that place, where he maintained good order,

notwith-

notwithstanding the ordinary insolence of the populace and the inferior gentry thereabouts, who are much given to insurrections. The same day they set about a bridge, in order to pass over the army; but instead of choosing the easiest place, where there is always a floating bridge during the Diets, his Majesty made them begin it on the side of the suburbs of *Cracovia*, opposite to Prince *Radziwil*'s palace, in the most dangerous part of the river, where it often runs over its banks, especially in rainy seasons, which had now continued several weeks, notwithstanding which it was remarked that the water was not risen at that time.

The King at the same time was careful to give his troops some rest after the laborious and severe marches they had made. To furnish them with subsistence, he proposed to the town to contribute 20000 crowns, besides other things of which they were in want. The town at first found this demand so much the more grievous, as the greater part of the merchants were retired with all their effects. They offered 12,000, without reckoning beer and other daily provisions which they were obliged to furnish.

The Convents only were exempted from this tax by the express orders of his Majesty, as well as the house of *Marienville*, which belonged to the Queen Dowager of *Poland*, and which was inhabited by a great number of servants. These measures, joined to the King's manifesto printed and made publick, by which he declared he was come as a friend to the Republick; and lastly, the good orders carefully observed among the soldiers, brought back all the inhabitants which had fled at the King's approach; who could not sufficiently

1702. sufficiently praise and admire the perfect discipline which reigned in our army.

Colonel *Cruus*, who had been employed in levying contributions in *Samogitia*, was now returned into *Courland* with his regiment; but as recruits were daily expected from *Sweden* for the whole army, and as we wanted a magazine for their subsistence, he detached a Captain from his regiment, called *Rutenschild*, towards *Janiska* on the frontiers to gather together provisions. He had scarce taken his post before he was surprized by a *Lithuanian* party, and taken with all his people.

Upon this news Baron *Stuart* detached Colonel *Cruus* with Count *Adam Lowenhaupt* and Baron *Pudbusch*, each with his battalion, to give chace to the enemy.

Mr. *Cruus* was very successful in his expedition; he surprized a *Lithuanian* partizan, named *Zaraneck*, between *Janiski* and *Schaud*, and took from him a standard, three pair of kettle-drums, and all his baggage, having pursued him three leagues without losing a single man of his own in this action.

One of the enemy's parties attacked, a few days after, a Captain of horse, named *Roxman*, who had orders to go from *Libaw* to *Janiski*. This enterprize did not succeed; he was so well received by our troops near *Raumkaski*, that having been pursued into a morass, he had 40 men killed, more than 100 wounded, and 24 made prisoners. Those who escaped having rejoined *Zaraneck*, he undertook to attack *Roxman* a second time, who was posted at *Janiski*, with all the forces which he could draw together; but he succeeded no better than before, being obliged

after

after a bloody fight, which lasted from 11 in the morning to 6 in the evening, to retreat with the loss of some hundreds of his men killed and wounded; the Captain had on his side no more than 7 killed, and 28 wounded.

Upon the *Peipus* there was a very bloody battle between our little squadron and a great number of *Russian* vessels, which were transporting troops into *Livonia*, of which the following relation was written to the King in *High Dutch* by *Loscher*, who commanded that squadron in chief.

'SIRE,

' ON an information which I received the 27th of *May* from our peasants of *Porcasaar*, that the enemy prepared to attack our block-house, in order to render themselves masters of the mouth of the river, I resolved to weigh anchor with those vessels under my command, namely, the galley *Charles*, the galley *Vivat*, with a yacht and six great shallops, and to sail the day following towards *Plescow*.

' This I executed on the 28th, by sailing out of the mouth of the river; and being arrived near *Ismen*, I learnt that the enemy had transported some troops into *Livonia* on 200 *lodiens* or barques, amongst which there were 5 or 6 mounted with three cannons each. I presently attacked them, and put them to flight.

' In the mean while, as I was in pursuit of them, I was much surprized, at doubling a promontory, to find myself surrounded on every side by 200 little vessels, which had on board the transports, with whom I fought for three hours, from 6 in the morning till 9. I sunk three of the greatest, out of which not a
' single

"single man was saved; this put the others on
"tacking about, and regaining their own coast.
"The Yatcht distinguished herself very much,
"having received above fifty cannon shot in her
"flag and her sails, which were shot through
"and through. The *Russian* vessels had each
"from forty to sixty men, amounting in the
"whole to about 10,000. I had but one man
"killed, with six others very much wounded.
"Upon my pursuit, I found the rest of the ar-
"my, horse and foot, encamped by the side of
"a wood, near the sea-shore. I then began to
"salute them with my cannon, which obliged
"them to strike their tents, and remove farther
"up into the country, at the same time firing on
"me from a battery which they had raised and
"mounted with five cannons, but without any
"success. At my return toward our coast, I met
"a *Russian* vessel, which I sunk. We have not,
"however, taken any prisoners, the enemy be-
"ing too strong. I have sent to Colonel *Skytt*
"for a reinforcement of fifty men, with some
"powder.

LOSCHER.

From on board the *Charles*,
May 29, 1702.

This action did in truth hinder the enemy from making an invasion on *Livonia*; they had however many rencounters on the *Peipus*, till they had an opportunity of being reinforced, and getting the advantage of us, as we shall see a little lower.

The column of Lieutenant-general *Spens* arrived at last in the suburbs of *Prag*, where he applied himself without ceasing, to put the bridge in a condition of passing over the army. The Count

Count *Sapicha* Great-Treasurer of *Lithuania* was arrived here, to put himself in a place of safety, and to make a campaign with his Majesty; he had with him his son the Commissary-general of *Lithuania*, and a small train of *Polish* Gentlemen.

As the King earnestly wished to see the Cardinal-Primate, Mr. *Watchlager*, the Resident, was sent to desire him to hasten to *Warsovia*. He at first raised some difficulties on that proposition, pretending that he would avoid giving any suspicion in so delicate a conjuncture; but at last he thought better on it, and arrived at *Warsovia* the 30th of *May*, and had the next day a publick audience of the King, who afterwards took him into his closet, where that Prelate employed all his eloquence, in endeavouring to bring about an accommodation with King *Augustus*, representing to him, 'That the deposition of that Prince was not so easy a matter as it was imagined; and that he could never contribute to it; however, he offered to use his utmost care and good offices, to bring affairs to an amicable determination, and in that way to procure his Majesty all the satisfaction he could desire*.'

The

---

* The other historians have set the Cardinal in a very different light from that in which our author hath represented him. We are not therefore to doubt his integrity, who very likely might not have been admitted into all the secrets which passed between the King of *Sweden* and his Eminence; nor is it indeed certain that his *Swedish* Majesty himself was openly dealt with by that cunning Prelate, who was afterwards rather a tool to execute that King's designs, than able, by means of the *Swedish* force, to execute his own. His name was *Radjouski*, and he was Archbishop of *Gnesnia*; governed, says Mr. *Voltaire*, by an ambitious woman, whom the *Swedes* called *Madam the Cardanaless*, who continually pushed him

on

The King was the more surprized at this unexpected change in the Cardinal, as that Prelate on to intrigue and faction. King *John Sobieski*, the predecessor of *Augustus*, had at first made him Bishop of *Warmia*, and Vice-Chancellor of the kingdom, and he afterwards obtained the Cardinal's hat by the favour of this King, which dignity soon opened to him the road to the Primacy. After the death of King *John*, he used all his credit to set Prince *James Sobieski* on the throne, but the torrent of that hatred which they bore to his father overwhelmed the son. The Cardinal then joined the *French* Ambassador, in favour of the Prince of *Conti*, who had been in effect elected, had not the *Saxon* money and troops got the better of all their negotiations. He then went along with the party who crowned the Elector of *Saxony*; and waited patiently for an opportunity to sow division between the nation and their new King. The victories of *Charles* XII. who was the protector of Prince *James*, the civil war of *Lithuania*, and the general discontent with King *Augustus*, made the Primate believe that the time was now come, in which he might send *Augustus* back into *Saxony*, and pave Prince *James*'s way to the throne, who, though formerly the innocent object of the *Polish* hatred, began to grow their darling, from the time that they cast their hatred on *Augustus*; but he himself could never conceive any hopes of this great revolution, of which the Cardinal was insensibly laying the foundation. He at first seemed willing to reconcile the King and the Republic; he sent circulary letters, dictated, in appearance, by the spirit of unity and charity, which, though they are the common and known snares, do never fail to catch mankind. This interview with the King of *Sweden* was of the Cardinal's own seeking: and to prevent any umbrage being taken at it, he went to King *Augustus*, and told him, that *Charles* was disposed to an accommodation; upon which hope *Augustus* permitted him to go to the King of *Sweden*, in company with Count *Lesckynski*, Great-treasurer of the Crown. And in the conferences which they had with this Monarch, the project of dethroning King *Augustus* was brought on the carpet; to which purpose all the Cardinal's future actions very apparently tended, tho' he still played the hypocrite in his words. *Voltaire, Pufsendorf, &c.*

had

had himself made the strongest instances to his Majesty, when he was in *Courland*, to induce him to come to *Warsovia*. This discourse therefore of the Cardinal gave him great reason to suspect that he had been well paid for it by King *Augustus*.

His Majesty nevertheless gave no token of his displeasure; but continued to caress him very particularly, and ordered Count *Piper*, as his first Minister, to pay him a visit. The Cardinal received the Count with great civility, and discoursed with him near two hours, in the presence of the Little-General of the Crown.

The result of the conference was, that the *Poles* were ready to submit to whatever else the King of *Sweden* should exact of them, but would never attempt to dethrone their King. In all the conferences which were had with the Cardinal, he always spoke in this language, whether for the reason which we have above alledged, or whether he feared the approach of the *Saxon* army; or lastly, whether it was that he would not render himself suspected by the Nobility, whose favour he very much courted.

This conduct of the Cardinal did not hinder the King from marching directly to the enemy, to put an end to all the difficulties which obstructed his designs by a battle. However, he entered first into another private conversation with him in *Lubomirski*'s closet; but the Primate stood firm, and gave not the least symptom of ever intending to change his resolution. He alledged as his reasons, ' That he was considered by the
' Republic, out of the Diet, as only a private
' Gentleman; that during the King's life, no
' other person could convene a Diet; that if
' they should elect another King, there would
' never

' never be any peace in the Republic, the Elector
' of *Saxony* being a very powerful Prince, and so
' near a neighbour; and lastly, that he would
' never be reproached with having dethroned his
' King.'

The Primate concluded his discourse by making several propositions to his Majesty, which, as they were only for the interest of *Poland*, and very far from amounting to such an entire satisfaction as the King desired, were all rejected. The Cardinal seeing the King very steady in his first resolution, and not thinking himself safe at *Warsovia* after his Majesty's departure, had his audience of leave, and retired with Count *Leszinski*, to an estate of his in the Palatinate of *Lublin* [f].

---

[f] We have not here room to set down all the entertainments and diversions which were at *Warsovia*, while the King remained there with his army, of which there is an exact account in the journal; it shall suffice therefore to observe, that on the part of the *Poles* the Cardinal, the Counts *Sapieha*, *Tarlo*, and *Leszinski*, gave very splendid entertainments to the Duke of *Holstein* and all the persons of distinction both of the court and army; the Grand Marshal *Biolinski*, the Palatine *Towiauska*, who was said to be much in his Eminence's favour, and Mr. *Poniatouski*, who had followed the army from *Punia*, distinguished themselves likewise at this season. On our part Count *Piper*, who kept open house, sometimes treated the Cardinal; Mess. *Welling* and *Horn* gave also several entertainments; as did the Colonels *Bergholz*, and Baron *Goertz*, both in the Duke of *Holstein*'s service. The *French* Envoy treated the Duke of *Holstein*, and all the persons of quality of both sexes, as well *Swedes* as *Poles*, who were at *Warsovia*, at the garden of *Casimir*. The King was at none of these parties of pleasure; but, what is something remarkable, his Majesty, who had never seen King *Augustus*, repaired the 18th of *May*, being four days after his arrival at *Plotsko*, to see that King's picture, which was drawn by a celebrated painter, whose name was *La Croix*, and was viewed by his Majesty with great attention.

The King, before his departure from *Warfovia*, sent an exprefs to *Pomerania*, with orders to the General Baron *Nils Gyllenstierna* to enter *Poland* immediately with his Army of 12,000 Men, which he had drawn together near *Stettin*, and to come and join him. Baron *Morner* and Count *Stenbock*, Major-Generals, who had remained at *Wilna*, received orders at the same time to leave some troops with Count *Sapieha*, the Great-General, and with the reft to join his Majefty on the road to *Cracovia*.

As the bridge on the *Viftula* was finifhed, the King ordered Mr. *Gyllenkrok*, Major of the Guards, to march before, with 500 horfe and 300 foot, to gather up provifions, and raife contributions for the army; and then, after giving an audience of leave to the Ambaffadors from the Republic, who had remained at *Warfovia*, and a particular audience to the Marquifs *de Heron*, the *French* Envoy, his Majefty departed the 16th of *June*, and encamped with his army at *Tarczin*, (five leagues) in the road of *Cracovia*, paffing through *Novemiafto*, which is the fhorter rout, but very deftitute of provifions, the Palatinates of *Sendomir* and *Cracovia*, through which he was to pafs, having declared for King *Auguftus*, and the inhabitants having carried away all their effects and provifion.

The army continued its march through *Lecziezki* (3 leagues,) whence it came to *Novemiafto* (3 leagues,) where it refted fome days. Thence proceeding to *Drzewioe* (3 leagues,) thence to *Gowarkow* (3 leagues,) and then marched to *Radozicza* (4 leagues,) where they encamped and refrefhed themfelves for fome days, before they marched to *Gablonova*. Major *Gyllenkrok*, who was now returned from his expedition, being at *Malogocz* with his detachment. The

The difficulty of meeting with provision, caused a resolution in the King to turn to the left, towards *Kielce*, where the country was in a better condition, and there were not so many defiles and forests to pass through, besides that he could that way more conveniently join *Morner*'s brigade.

The army decamped the first of *July* from *Radozicza*, and marched to *Kielce*, a town belonging to the Bishop of *Cracovia*. Here they rested the next day, which was the feast of the Visitation. We now received advice that *Morner* and *Stenbock* had already past the *Vistula* at *Casimir*, and were but 8 leagues from us. This determined the King to stay some days at *Kielce*, during which we learned that King *Augustus* had marched from *Cracovia* towards *Pinschow*, with 5000 *Saxons*, and that the army of the Crown, under the command of Prince *Lubomirski*, was to join him near *Sendomir*.

Colonel *Meyerfelt* was detached with 600 horse, to *reconnoitre* the enemy. He returned the fifth, without having met with more than an hundred *Valoche* guards, whom Captain *Fund* pursued to no purpose ; but as to the peasants and inhabitants of the country, they had all abandoned it, retreating towards the *Saxon* army. The King in the mean time, attended by the Duke of *Holstein*, and a small number of officers, went to look after General *Morner*, who used all possible diligence to join the army. His Majesty returned the 6th in the evening, and gave orders for the army's decamping the next day, and marching (three leagues) to *Opietza*, which is three quarters of a league from *Clischow*, and that one league and a half from *Pinschow*.

Augustus was already come to *Chlischow* with his army, where he waited for that of the Crown,
which

which was making great haste towards him, Lubomirski had desired *Augustus* to stay for him, that he might have a share in the victory, which he promised himself over our army, which he knew was not above 12,000 strong; nor was our number of effective men greater, for we had a great many sick, besides our vast loss of horses, occasioned by our long marches.

The day after our arrival at *Opietza*, there was an alarm in the camp. A *Saxon* party had attacked our advanced posts, commanded by Major *Ornstedt*, at eight in the morning. The Major repulsed them with such bravery, that several of them were killed, several taken prisoners, and their commander wounded. This shock put them out of any humour of returning that day. We lost in this action Captain *Fagerskioldt*, who was killed, with some troopers. The King, who hastened up at the first discharge, and caused the picquet to advance to engage them in the action, found it all over at his arrival.

Mr. *Morner* came to the camp the same evening with his troops, which were very much fatigued, and a great many of them sick. The arrival of these troops gave his Majesty much pleasure, who now took a resolution to give battle to King *Augustus*'s army, notwithstanding the superiority of the numbers of the latter, and the very advantageous situation in which they were posted; and accordingly, orders were given to march the next day towards the enemy.

We shall here give a perfect relation of that glorious day, as it was written by Mr. *Ehrenschants*, a Lieutenant-colonel, who was always near the King during the whole action; which

L   relation

relation was afterwards presented to his Majesty in the *Swedish* language.

In order to a perfect comprehension of what passed in this battle, it will be necessary to recapitulate some circumstances which passed a few days before it.

The King being arrived the 1st of *July* with his army at *Kielce*, an episcopal town of *Cracovia*, being informed of King *Augustus*'s march from *Cracovia*, detached Colonel *Meyerfeldt*, with 600 horse, to *reconnoitre* the enemy. This detachment marched out of the camp on the 2d of *July* in the night, and advanced (three leagues) to a village called *Opietza*, near which 200 Cossacks lay in ambuscade, in a wood which covers the village; they fell in with a small advanced body of 30 horse, commanded by Mr. *Funk*, Captain of the King's dragoons, who repulsed them so bravely, that he dissipated and put them to flight, killing and wounding many of them, without being able to make a single prisoner.

On this news of the enemy's approach, the King ordered the army to march on the 7th from *Kielce*, and to encamp at *Opietza* three quarters of a league from *Clischow*, where King *Augustus* lay with his army; and without waiting for Mr. *Morner*, Major-general of horse, who had passed the *Vistula* at *Casimir*, and was but a day's march from us, his Majesty resolved the next morning at the break of day to attack the King of *Poland* in his Camp; however, he at last yielded to the instances of his Generals, who advised him to defer the attack till the day after, in hopes that Mr. *Morner* would not fail to come up, which he did accordingly, and joined the army the evening before the battle.

The

The eighth of *July* in the morning, while the King was busy in observing the foragers, he perceived a party of the camp-guard, under the command of Mr. *Ornstedt*, Major of dragoons, engaged with some of the enemy's troops; he ran directly to them, with as many as he could get together; and gave orders, at the same time, to the picquet to march: the business was over before he came up, and the enemy, which consisted of about 200 *Saxons*, and about 100 *Cossacks*, put to flight; we pursued them, killed twenty, and took about eight or nine prisoners. On our side, Baron *Fagerskioldt* a Captain in the King's regiment of horse, was killed, and Captain *Tyrol*, of the same regiment, with some troopers, were wounded.

The night which preceded the day of battle seemed extremely long to the King, who was impatient to see the event of an action, which could scarce fail of being decisive. The 9th, about six in the morning, his Majesty drew up his army, which was composed of 12,000 fighting men, in order of battle at the head of his camp. This day had been already rendered famous by the glorious passage of the *Duna*, which happened on the 9th of *July* in the preceding year.

The army was drawn up in two lines, the horse on the wings, and the foot in the center; the King placed himself at the head of the first line on the right, having with him Baron *Rheinschild*, a Lieutenant-general, Baron *Morner*, and Baron *Horn*, both Major-generals of horse: this wing was composed of thirteen squadrons, *viz.* one of royal dragoons, under Colonel *Hamilton*, one of the King's Drabans, commanded by Count *Wrangle*, a Colonel, and Lieutenant of the Drabans,

bans, who had with him Lieutenant-colonel *Otto Wrangle*, of the same corps; seven squadrons of the regiment of horse-guards, under the command of Baron *Creutz*, a Major; and four squadrons of the *Oſtrogoths*, which were led by Mr. *Burenſkold*, Lieutenant-colonel of that regiment.

His most serene Highneſs the Duke of *Holſtein-Gottorp* led the firſt line of the left wing, having under him Baron *Welling*, General of horſe, and Major-general *Stromberg*: this confiſted of twelve ſquadrons, the firſt being of the King's dragoons, under Lieutenant-colonel *Rotblieb*; two ſquadrons of the horſe-guards, commanded by Lieutenant-colonel *Skyttenhielm* and Captain *Lybecker*; three ſquadrons of *Smoland*, commanded by Lieutenant *Stahlhammar*; and ſix ſquadrons of *Scania*, under the command of Lieutenant-colonel *Ridderkants*.

Baron *Liewen*, Lieutenant-general, and Count *Magnus Stenbock*, Major-general, both of foot, were in the main body, at the head of the foot of the firſt line; which confiſted of twelve battalions, four of the guards, of which Count *Sperling*, Major, commanded the granadiers; Lieutenant-colonel Baron *Poſs*, the ſecond battalion; Quarter-maſter-general *Gyllenkrok*, the third; and Baron *Arfvidſon*, a Captain, the fourth; two battalions of *Upland*, under Lieutenant-colonel *Holſt*, and Major *de Poſt*; two battalions of *Wormland*, commanded by Colonel *Roos*, and Lieutenant-colonel *Cronmann*; two battalions of *Waſmanland*, under Baron *Axel Sparr*, and Lieutenant-colonel *Feilitz*; laſtly, two battalions of *Dahl-Carlers*, led by Lieutenant-colonel *Siegroth*, and Baron *Swinhufvud*, a Captain.

In

In the second line, Lieutenant-colonel *Spens* led eight squadrons on the right; the first of royal dragoons under Captain *Funk*, three squadrons of the horse-guards under Captain *Wetzel*, and four of *Ostrogoths*, commanded by Major *Sturkenfelt*. On the left, Major-general *Nieroth* was at the head of eight squadrons, one of royal dragoons, under Baron *Creutz*, a Captain; five squadrons of *Smoland*, commanded by Baron *Morner*, a Major, and two squadrons of *Scania*, led by Major *Ridderkiold*.

The foot of the second line consisted of six battalions, commanded by Major-general *Poss*, whereof the two first of *Westerbothn*, on the right, were led by Colonel *Ferfen* and Major *Biornhufvud*; the two other of *Calmar* and *Smoland* on the left were commanded by Colonel *Rank* and Lieutenant-colonel *Silwerfparr*; and the two battalions of *Tremanning* in the middle, were led by the Lieutenant-colonels *Ekebladt* and *Hammerhielm*. The reserved body consisted only of 100 dragoons of *Albedyhl*'s regiment, under the command of Major *Trautfetter*, who was afterwards commanded with a battalion of *Tremanning* to cover the baggage.

The King chose Baron *Taub*, Aid-de-camp-general, to carry his orders through the right wing; Mr. *Ducker*, Aid-de-camp-general, for the left; and Mr. *Buchwald*, Aid-de-camp-general, for the centre. His Majesty kept only Major-general *Albedyhl*, Colonel *Lagercrona*, Aid-de-camp-general, Colonel *Meyerfelt*, Lieutenant-colonel *Ehrenfchants*, and Mr. *Scheven*, Fort-Major, near his person, to receive his orders in case of necessity.

The King having ordered this disposition, in which we were afterwards obliged to make some

1701. small alterations in the time of action, according to the occurrences, giving, with a loud voice, his usual word, *With God's assistance*, waited with impatience for the enemy's army, which we had heard in the morning were in full march to attack us; but as they did not appear, and we heard no farther news of them, his Majesty resolved, according to his first project, to go and attack them in their own camp.

To which purpose he made all the army pass through the wood about nine in the morning, and gained the plain, which is on the other side; the right wing marching in two columns, and the left in order of battle, because the wood is more open and more passable on that side; when we were arrived here we discovered two bodies of the enemy's troops near the wood on the left; but they retreated, without mistrusting any more than that a large body of *Swedes* were advancing.

King *Augustus* was said to have been here in person; and that having only seen our left wing, (the columns of the right being hidden from him by some hills) he gave himself no trouble about us; an error which afterwards cost him dear. The army continued their march in four columns, through the extent of the plain, at the end of which, there being a wood, the King made them all wheel half round to the right; passing along by the side of the wood, which was on their left, and leaving the village of *Groscow* on their right. Now we discovered the enemy's camp, it being precisely noon. The King, to prevent the enemy's knowledge of the arrival of his whole army, ordered all the horse to lower their standards, and the foot to furl their colours, and carry them down, as well as the pikes, which made the enemy judge it was

only

only a large body, detached to *reconnoitre* them; in which false opinion they remained very quiet in their camp, thinking they had nothing to fear.

The King then ordered the right wing to pass round the corner of the wood to the left, while the left wing, under the Duke of *Holstein*, marched directly forward with the foot; so that all the army drew up at once, in the order we have above represented, within cannon-shot of the enemy, and on the back of the wood they had just passed.

The enemy now took the alarm, seeing all our army advancing in order of battle, they presently beat the general, and gave the signal by the discharge of two cannon, the third not going off.

The King, attended by the Duke of *Holstein* and the Generals, went instantly to *reconnoitre* the ground in person, and found the attack very difficult, not to say impracticable, on account of the morasses with which the enemy's camp was almost surrounded. The head of the camp was fixed on a rising ground, which commands all the country round it, and whence the cannon which was there mounted, played on all the avenues, and hindered our approach. Before this place, there were two morasses, at a mile distance from each other, that on the right beginning at a village named *Coquot*; and the other between *Coquot* and the village of *Virbitza*; reaching the whole length of their camp, and ending in a pond or brook on their left, surrounded with bogs, near the village of *Rembowa*, which protected their wing; and beyond this pond a third morass was extended in the form of a half moon, behind their camp almost as far as their right; and was flanked by a thick and shady wood:

wood: in short, a post so advantageously situated for defence, and so difficult to be attacked, would have disconcerted any but *Charles* XII.

His Majesty seeing the absolute impossibility of attacking the enemy, as they stood in battalia, at the head of their camp, making a very smart fire on us from their artillery, performed the part of a great General, and ordered the army to wheel a little to the left, to gain the rising ground, and disengage themselves from the morasses, which absolutely hindered them from acting.

This motion obliged the enemy to change their disposition; and quitting their advantageous situation, to draw towards the right, passing through some marshy ground, and the village of *Coquot*, where the defiles produced the effect which the King of *Sweden* had promised himself.

The enemy now ranged the crown army, consisting of 12,000 men, on the right, with the *Cossacks* in their flank, and lined them with the other *Pancemes* and *Poles*, armed cap-a-pee, in ranks at certain distances, according to their manner, before the village of *Kye*; wherein they committed a great error, the ground there being properer for the *Saxons* to act in, whose situation was by this means embarrassed. Their right wing of horse was ranged before the village of *Coquot* in several lines, and from thence to their left was a line of *Saxon* foot, with a morass both before and behind them.

Whilst the two armies made these motions, we perceived the enemy's left wing of horse beginning to defile along the village of *Rembowa*, to fall on the right flank of the *Swedish* army: his Majesty being acquainted with this, answered sternly, *Let them do it*; not doubting but that they

they would be repulsed with vigour. About two in the afternoon, the King, having thus gained the rising ground, as well as all that which lay between the wood and the morass, thought proper to line the squadrons with some regiments of foot, *viz.* those of *Dahl-Carlers*, *Wesmanland*, and *Wormland*, commanded by Lieutenant-general *Liewen* and Count *Stenbock*; at the same time ordering the regiment of *Calmar* to have an eye on the flank.

The Duke of *Holstein* was now ordered to begin the attack; but while this brave Prince was preparing to march, he unfortunately received a shot from a falconet in his body, which obliged him to have himself conveyed to a poor cottage hard by, where he died a few hours afterwards. This wing, however, began the attack with all imaginable vigour, and with such success, that the *Poles*, after having stood the two first shocks, found themselves unable to support a third; and as the *Swedes* always gained ground on them, without giving them time to consider, they began to turn about, and at last ran away full speed, through the village of *Kye*; nor was it possible to bring them any more back to the charge.

General *Welling*, who, after the Duke of *Holstein*'s death, commanded on the left till the King came thither himself, seeing the *Saxon* Horse drawn up in several lines, and led by Mr. *Flemming*, proposed to attack them front and rear, himself making head against them with four squadrons of *Scania*, and ordering one squadron of that regiment, at the same time, to attack the enemy in the flank; by which means they were so vigorously pressed from all quarters, that after a very bloody and obstinate

dispute

dispute on both sides, the *Saxons* began to give way, and retreated full speed to the village of *Coquot*; in their way to which place they were exposed to the fire of our regiments of foot, namely, the Guards, *Upland*, and *Westerbothn*, who by their discharges on them completed their rout.

Our foot in the mean time having safely past the morass, prepared to attack the enemy's foot, who had several pieces of ordnance and a *Chevaux de Frise* before them, which defended their whole line from one end to the other. Notwithstanding which advantageous situation, Major-General *Poss*, who commanded our foot, attacked those of the enemy so roughly, and with such valour, that he broke and routed them several times, took their cannon, put them to flight, and pursued them over a morass which was in the enemy's rear, beyond that rising ground which led to their camp, where being all broke and disordered, they dispersed themselves several ways.

A battalion of *Saxon* guards met in their retreat with the battalion of *Tremanning*, newly raised, and commanded by Mr. *Ekebladt*, which made a great slaughter of them. Those under young *Steinau*, brother of the Velt-Marshal, attempting to retreat in order, fell in with a battalion of the regiment of *Upland*, which attacked them with such vigour, that, after killing a great many of them, they drove them on a battalion of *Calmar*, and three squadrons of *Burenskioldt*, who entirely defeated them, and forced them to throw down their arms, without suffering one to escape.

While all this past in the centre and on our left, where the King was, the left of the enemy, commanded

commanded by Velt-Marshal *Steinau*, after having leisurely defiled through the village of *Rembowa*, as we have said above, fell with great fury on our right, which they attacked in front, in flank, and in the rear. The fight was very bloody, and the victory very stoutly disputed. In the mean time the Generals *Rheinschild*, *Spens*, *Morner*, and *Horn*, who commanded there, and had at the first shock very bravely sustained all the efforts of the enemy, who were very much superior to us in horse, perceiving that their second line endeavoured to gain the wood which was in the rear of the *Swedes*, and that their first line had got between them and the village of *Brotzin*, to cut them off from that village; these Generals, I say, seconded by the incomparable bravery of our squadrons, which were in very close order, took an immediate resolution to draw up with a double front; and Mr. *Spens*, at the head of some squadrons of the horse-guards, and of the *Ostrogoths*, facing those who approached on the side of the wood, overthrew them after a bloody battle, and obliged them to join their first line, having however first done all that could be expected from brave men.

The *Saxons*, surprized at a defence so much beyond their expectation, and at the incredible efforts of bravery in our Drabans and other troops, which, without firing, defeated sword in hand all that they encountred, and, attacking their squadrons, overthrew them one after another, resolved at last on an hasty retreat; which they executed with great precipitation, left it should be cut off by the *Swedish* foot, who were yet engaged with that of the enemy, and from whom they were separated only by a morass. But as our horse pressed them too close at their heels to permit

an

an orderly retreat, so, being put into confusion, they ran over each other, and, after the greater part of the squadrons had passed the defile, the rest threw themselves all together into the village of *Virbitza*.

Our troops having surrounded them on all sides, they had nothing left them but to cut their way through sword in hand, which they attempted; but after having cut through our horse, they had the misfortune to meet our victorious foot, to whose fire they were so terribly exposed, that most of those who were not killed or wounded, were mired in the morass; and, to complete their distress, the few who escaped endeavouring to take the road by which the left wing had fled above the village of *Virbitza*, met three squadrons of *Scania*, commanded by General *Welling*, who were returning by the King's orders from the pursuit of the enemy to join the right wing; these pushed them into the village of *Coquot*, and put them to the sword, except some few, who were drowned in the canal in that village.

In the mean time the *Saxon* horse of the left wing, which had escaped the heat of the action, took possession of a rising ground, very commodious to draw up in; where perceiving the approach of our squadrons, they gave them time to defile over the morass and range themselves, and then attacked them with all imaginable bravery. Both sides fought with great fury; and had it not been for the extraordinary exploits of our squadrons, especially the Drabans, the enemy had penetrated through to our foot; but finding every where an equal resistance, that brave body of horse was broke, and, after having perform'd as much as could be expected from them, was
at

King Charles XII. of Sweden.

at last entirely routed, and pursued into the morass behind their camp, between the villages of *Clissow* and *Rembowa*, where many of them were drowned, and the rest owed their escape to the extreme drought of the season. The *Saxon* foot had already saved themselves the same way under favour of the last fight, and through the prodigious efforts of their horse.

King *Augustus*, now seeing all lost, hastened at the head of the right wing and the crown-army to *Pinschow*, whence he took the road of *Cracovia* with the scatter'd remains of his army, the *Poles* having secured themselves at *Sendomir*.

The ardour of the King's troops still remained, after a battle of four hours; but his Majesty, who since the death of the Duke of *Holstein* had fought at the head of the left wing, perceiving that they were much fatigued, recalled all those who were in the pursuit, and at 6 in the evening entered the enemy's camp to the sound of kettle-drums and trumpets.

We found in the camp 48 pieces of cannon, 12 of twelve-pounders, and 26 of three-pounders, with all their artillery and ammunition. We had 300 men killed, and 800 wounded in this action. The foot-guards, who performed wonders that day, suffered the most; Major-General *Poss*, who commanded them, being very dangerously wounded.

The enemy lost near 2000 [h] men killed and wounded, besides 1700 made prisoners. In the morass behind the camp, through which the enemy

---

[h] According to *Puffendorf*, there were 4000 *Saxons* kill'd, and 2000 taken prisoners, without reckoning the *Poles*; which is indeed a number more agreeable to a victory that is agreed on all hands to have been complete, and also to the account which our author himself gives of the action.

1702. enemy fled, we found all their baggage, which was there mired, particularly King *Augustus's* magnificent equipage, with his mules, plate, and military chest; likewise all the waggons belonging to the *Russian* Envoy, who had saved himself at the beginning of the battle, and had left 12000 crowns in specie behind him.

All this was the next day given up to be plundered, which, together with the fine tents, and the rest of what was found in great abundance in the camp was very convenient for our troops, who having left all their heavy baggage in *Courland*, were very thinly provided with equipages.

We took likewise some Ladies in the same morass, with a great number of women and children, who were all civilly treated, and soon after sent back. The evening of the battle the King caused *Te Deum* to be sung in the camp, to give God thanks for that signal victory which he had just obtained.

The only thing which cast a damp on this publick joy was the death of the great Duke of *Holstein-Gottorp*, with which the King was sensibly afflicted, and which all the army extremely lamented, on account of his bravery, generosity, and greatness of soul. His body was embalmed, and some time after carried to *Holstein*, as we shall see below.

The day after this glorious battle, in which we gained so complete a victory over an enemy so advantageously posted, and so much stronger than ourselves, the King caused all the dead to be buried, and ordered great care to be taken of the wounded, and that they should be conveyed as soon as possible into houses for their better accommodation. He then detached Major

Creutz

Creutz with some hundred horse and dragoons to make himself master of *Pinschow* castle, 1½ league from the camp, through which the *Saxons* had pass'd and repass'd to *Cracovia*. The Major presently took possession of the town and the castle, whose advantageous situation on the river *Nida* render'd it very difficult to be attack'd.

The King, who came hither the next day with a small train, seemed surprized, that the enemy had not expected us in this place, instead of marching forwarder, and posting themselves, as they had done, between two morasses; by which means *Augustus* might have defended himself with more advantage, and the victory would at least have been longer disputed. It is very certain, that King had very bad counsellors on this occasion; and 'tis as true, that the loss of this battle was a fatal blow to *Saxony*.

The King gave immediate orders to conduct all the wounded, both *Swedes* and *Saxons*, to *Pinschow*, where the air is much wholesomer, and the water better. The officers, who lodged in the castle, were treated at his own table. His Majesty resolved to leave them here under a good guard, and not to burden himself with them when he should pursue the enemy, as he proposed. The *Saxon* artillery arrived first the next day under a good escort, the sick and wounded the day afterwards; then followed all the army, and encamped on the banks of the *Nida*, in a fine plain below the town. Count *Zinzendorff*, who succeeded Count *Weltz* in quality of Envoy from the Emperor, arrived now at his Majesty's camp. As the King had no leisure to give him audience, he departed instantly for *Cracovia*, to wait for a more favourable opportunity.

1702. portunity. He had already been at *Kielce* for that purpose, but could not speak with his Majesty there. We now sent back all the Ladies, who had been made prisoners, with an escort to the frontiers of *Silesia*; amongst whom was the wife of a Colonel, and the wives of several other officers.

As to the *Saxon* prisoners, who beside the wounded amounted to 1100 men, the council of war was divided in their opinions concerning what methods were to be taken; but at length his Majesty found out a mean, which was, neither to send them back, nor to keep them all prisoners, but retaining only the natives of *Saxony*, permitted the others, which amounted to 900 men, to enter themselves, with some of their officers, into his service. He formed a small body of them, which he sent to *Pomerania*, to be distributed among the fortresses, causing two months pay to be advanced to them. But these troops were scarce arrived on the borders of *Silesia*, when they mutinied, abused their officers, and disbanded, many of them returning back to King *Augustus*.

After his Majesty had settled every thing for the wounded, sick and prisoners, he left Lieutenant-Colonel *Feilitz* at *Pinschow* to cover them with a small body of foot and dragoons, which were also to levy contributions, and keep the *Polish* parties and *Cossacks* thereabouts in order. The army then decamped, and advanced (three leagues) to *Skalmiers*.

We ought not here to forget to give an account of some actions which happened about this time, as well in *Courland* as *Livonia*. *Bandomir*, a *Polish* partizan, having on the 15th of *June* surprized the quarters of our dragoons near *Seelburg*

burg during the absence of Lieutenant-Colonel *Banneer*, who was at *Mittau*, carried off all their equipage, and killed them 29 dragoons and a drummer. Captain *Swab* was also made prisoner in this rencounter, with a Lieutenant and some dragoons. We shall soon see in what manner our troops found an opportunity of being revenged.

The battle of *Einbeck* in *Livonia* is of somewhat more importance, and deserves to be here reported. The following is a relation of it. After Mr. *Loscher*'s action, whereof we have before spoken, the *Czar*, being desirous to take an advantage of the King of *Sweden*'s absence, had drawn together a very considerable army on the frontiers near *Plescow* and *Pitschur*, to make an irruption into *Livonia*, and put all to fire and sword. The better to spread his army, he had divided it into different bodies, some stronger than others. That which marched on the side of *Waskenarva* was very roughly handled by Lieutenant-Colonel *Stahlbom*, who at the head of 400 men only took from the *Russians*, who were infinitely his superiors, a post called *Ahlfang*, and drove them quite out of that country.

Fourteen vessels having appeared on the *Peipus* in the latitude of *Porkazari*, *Loscher*, who commanded our squadron, gave orders to Captain *Hokenflycht* to go with the armed galley named *Vivat* to *reconnoitre* them. As soon as he had doubled the promontory, he saw himself immediately surrounded on all sides by the enemy's squadron. Our vessels, which saw this, could not come to his assistance, on account of the calm which happen'd at that instant; so that the Captain of the galley, after having defended himself two hours together with astonishing bravery,

1702. very, and having spent all his ammunition, he waited till the enemy which approached him on all sides had boarded him; he then blew up his vessel and a great number of *Muscovites* at the same time. All the crew perish'd, except a single Priest, who had saved himself at first in a small shallop, and brought the news of the defeat. This passed on the 11th of *July*.

The 16th of the same month Major-General *Schlippenbach* had advice, that the main of the *Muscovite* army, consisting of 50,000 men, had passed the frontiers, and was already arrived at *Eratfer*. The 17th the advanced guards were alarmed by the enemy's parties. Mr. *Schlippenbach*, who had in all but 6000 men, detached Baron *Ungern* of *Sternberg*, Great Hunter of *Livonia*, who perfectly knew the topography of the country, with 300 horse to *reconnoitre* them. Having met a party of 2000 horse, he attacked them, and after having routed them, he drove them back to the body of their army. He then retreated, and was pursued home to the picket of *Schlippenbach*'s army, which was drawn up in order of battle; and coming to his assistance, obliged the enemy to stop, and retreat with great precipitation.

Mr. *Schlippenbach* now went himself without loss of time to *reconnoitre* their forces and designs; and seeing the enemy cause their troops to defile cross the morass at *Taggaval* to surround them on all sides, he instantly retreated towards the river *Embach* to dispute the enemy's passage, in case they should follow him. This retreat was performed in good order over two bridges, which he had made; but as the heat of the season had brought the river very low, and the enemy had passed over the ford and on pontons

in

King Charles XII. of Sweden.

in several places, the General found himself obliged to stand his ground, and draw up in order of battle.

The fight began at six in the morning; and notwithstanding the enemy's superior number, our troops, after a fight of two hours, repulsed them, broke them, and put them to flight, and pursued them as far as the river *Embach*, taking from them six field-pieces, and a great part of their baggage: Here the action was very hot; the enemy, who could not save themselves by flight, defended themselves in despair, and, having received succours, they at last made our horse give ground, who throwing themselves on the foot, put them in disorder, whilst themselves ran away full speed; nor could Mr. *Schlippenbach* or the officers make them rally, or bring them back to the charge.

The abandon'd foot were now entirely defeated, except a small number which saved themselves in the woods. The General seeing all lost, retreated towards *Pernau*, with as many of his broken troops as he could get together. He was obliged after this defeat to abandon all this country to the *Russians*, who plunder'd it, set fire to the little town of *Walk*, where they inhumanly murder'd the inhabitants, and carried all those who fell into their hands, as well young as old, into slavery: However, they did not as yet undertake the siege of *Dorpt*; and instead of improving the advantage they had gained, they repassed the frontiers according to custom.

Augustus, who had retreated to *Cracovia* after the battle of *Cliffowa*, thought of nothing but of drawing up the remainder of his army, and to put himself in a condition to oppose the new enterprizes of the King of *Sweden*. This King, having received a reinforcement of eight regiments,

1702. ments, which General *Robel* had brought him from *Saxony*, caus'd an intrenchment to be made, which should cover his camp, in case that the King of *Sweden* should attack him, as he had great reason to apprehend. He sent back Baron *Sack* to his *Swedish* Majesty; the Baron was a Captain of the King of *Sweden*'s own regiment of horse, and had been made prisoner at the battle of *Cliffowa*, through the impetuosity of his horse, which had carried him into the middle of his enemy's squadrons.

This Baron returned to the King's camp with several propositions of peace on the behalf of King *Augustus*; but they were all rejected. In the mean time his *Swedish* Majesty, that he might not be behind hand with the King of *Poland* in generosity and politeness, returned him thirteen *Saxon* officers the same evening, having first magnificently treated them at his court. And as he heard on all sides that the King of *Poland* had a design to repair to *Leopold*, to avoid a second battle, Count *Stenbock* was detached the same night the shortest way towards the *Vistula*, to prepare a bridge, and cut off the enemy's march, in order by that means to bring them to a new battle.

To this purpose the army decamped the next day early in the morning, and passing through *Conary* (3 leagues) found at their arrival a bridge already thrown over the *Vistula*. The King presently caused the foot with the artillery and baggage to pass over the river, which being not very deep in this place, tho' pretty wide, the horse, to gain time, passed at a ford; so that the whole army was got over by the evening, and encamped near *Solomna*, where they rested one day, and the next proceeded (3 leagues) to *Bochnia*,

nia, a little town, where there are salt-pits, five leagues from *Cracovia*.

Augustus, having timely notice by the *Cossacks* and his parties of the King's march, departed suddenly, and prevailed so much by their long marches, that his army decamped from *Bochnia* the same morning that ours was on their march thither. His rear-guard appearing on a high mountain to observe us, his Majesty mistook them for the van-guard, and made the army hastily pass a little river which empties itself into the *Vistula*, and there ranging them in battalia, advanced briskly towards the mountain, not doubting but that he was on the point of giving them battle. But the rear-guard of the enemy, contented with having observed our motions, and covered the march of the main body of their army, which had already gained a league of us, hasted to join them full speed. The King therefore, on his arrival at *Bochnia*, seeing that it was impossible to overtake them, encamped his own army near a castle before the town, in which there remained a few *Saxons* with one baggage waggon and some tents.

The next day the King, as he was riding out on horseback with Count *Stenbock*, and twenty officers, hearing that the *Valoches* had come to a village near his camp, and had killed some soldiers who were looking after provisions, his Majesty hastened thither; and whilst he was riding backwards and forwards to discover whether any of the enemy were there, he was all of a sudden attacked by a large party, who had lain in ambuscade among the houses, who came out upon him with a great outcry.

The King, who was insensible of danger, presently engaged them, repulsed them, and pursued

sued them near a quarter of a league out of the village; but as their number continually increased, it was necessary for him to think of a retreat before it was cut off, especially as the *Valoches* were in possession of a bridge over which we were to return. The King then resolved to go directly up to them, and to present his pistol without firing till he was sure of his mark. This boldness discomfited them, and gave his Majesty with Count *Stenbock* and several officers an opportunity to pass.

Colonel *Dahldorf* and Mr. *Nils Rosenstierna*, Captain of the guards, were wounded and made prisoners, their horses being too much fatigued to save them. A Page named *Klinkowstrom* was shot through the arm by an arrow, and several of those officers who escaped were wounded by sabres and *Tartarian* picks, which are called *Copeies*.

The picket of the army having heard the fire, advanced with great haste; but the *Valoches* had the prudence to retreat at their arrival, and to carry their prisoners away with them. The King returned safely to the camp, without having received the least hurt, tho' he had never been in greater danger, his horse having twice fallen under him in the middle of his enemies.

The King having lost all hopes of bringing the enemy to a battle, turned towards *Cracovia*, to stay for the arrival of General *Gyllenstierna*, who came from *Pomerania* with 12000 men to reinforce him. The army staid some days on the road near the Convent of *Stauenko*, three leagues from *Bochnia*, where the Duke of *Mecklenbourg-Swerin* arrived, and had an immediate audience of the King. At the same time two Deputies from the Palatinate of *Cracovia* came to beseech
his

his Majesty to have pity on their country, which had already suffer'd much by the *Saxon* army that had staid some time amongst them. They offered to furnish his Majesty with provision and whatever he would exact for the subsistence of his troops. This submission was very well received, and they departed well satisfied with the promises which were delivered him in writing on the behalf of his Majesty by Mr. *Hermelin*, Secretary of the Chancery, which assured them of his protection, and that he would take care to make his troops observe a most exact discipline.

From thence the army marched directly to *Cracovia*, a large and fine city situated on the *Vistula*, where the Kings of *Poland* are commonly crowned, and where they often fix their residence. It is surrounded by an old wall, with a mote, and has very large and beautiful suburbs. The castle is sufficiently strong to make some resistance in case of an attack, and by that means to obtain an honourable capitulation.

When our army presented itself before *Cracovia*, the Starost *Francis Vielopolski*, who commanded there, caused all the gates to be shut, as well of the town as the castle, making a shew of pretending to defend himself with the small garrison of the crown, which he had under his command. The King, incensed at seeing a place of so little consequence dare to dispute the entrance of a victorious army, embarked a detachment of 400 men under the command of Count *Stenbock*, on several boats which we found on the *Vistula*, and made them pass over to the other side, the *Saxons* having taken the precaution to break down the bridge which usually stood in that place.

This detachment having found the gates of the suburb of *Casimir* open, enter'd them without any opposition, and advanced up to the gates of the town, which were shut, and provided with guards. The Count caused them immediately to be summon'd in his Majesty's name to surrender; and having had no other answer, than that *they had lost the keys*, he desired to speak with the Governor; who, after much difficulty, came to confer with him in an out-work, which was only of wood armed with palisades and an iron gate. The Count summoned him again to open the gates to the King, shewing him the danger to which he exposed himself and the town by a longer resistance: He represented to him especially the good intelligence which subsisted between his Majesty and the Republick, and that they had every where opened the gates to the *Swedes*. The Governor's answer was, that the town and castle had been intrusted to him by the King his master, and that he could not surrender them without making a defence.

In the middle of this dispute, and whilst the Count was beginning to threaten the Governor, that if he did not open the gates immediately, they would be all put to the sword without having any favour to expect, the King, impatient for the event of this affair, and who had passed the river, came up to the Governor without making himself known to him, and ordered him in *French* to open the gates instantly, saying to him, *Ouvre la porte*. The Governor, who knew not the King, made him no answer; at which he being to the last degree enraged, order'd the gates to be instantly attacked and forced; which orders were executed with such vigour, that the Governor had scarce time to regain the great

gate

gate of the town, which the King entered at the same time. As his Majesty had forbid them to fire, they forced the guards with their swords, bayonets, and canes to throw down their arms. The King, pursuing his point, detached presently some platoons to secure the streets, which were all full of Gentry on horseback, and to disarm the main-guard in the market-place. *Charles* himself with a small party pursued the Governor so briskly, who fled towards the castle to defend himself, that he enter'd at the same time with him with his sword in his hand; 200 men being the guard were so disconcerted, that they presently threw down their arms.

At this instant a Lieutenant of the artillery had the boldness to attempt to give fire to a cannon which was pointed at the gate against the *Swedes*, who crowded in to follow the King. His Majesty perceiving him caught him by the throat, threw him down, and snatched the match out of his hand. The Governor now perceiving himself in the hands of the *Swedes*, and knowing that the King was there in person, approached his Majesty, and threw down his arms, desiring his favour; but it was now too late, so that he was arrested and made prisoner. The Deputies of the Palatinate in vain interceded on his behalf; he was kept prisoner till he had paid a large sum of money for his ransom.

The conduct of *Vielopolski* on this occasion was condemned by his own countrymen; for when he should have either taken measures to have defended himself, or have surrendered the town and castle with a good grace, he did neither the one nor the other, and by his false bravery incensed a Prince who was inured to conquest, and whom he could not resist. Count *Stenbock*
was

1702. was made Governor of the town, which paid very dear for the rash resistance of their late Governor; and the inhabitants were condemned in 100,000 crowns contribution, besides the provisions which they were obliged to furnish the garrison with, which consisted of three regiments of foot, which the King placed here to keep the town and suburbs in order.

To open a free communication, they began at the same time to throw a bridge over the *Vistula*, which was finished the next day, but was carried away a few days afterwards by a great overflowing of the river, occasioned by the rains which fell on the *Hungarian* mountains, where this river rises. These waters likewise overflowed the quarters of some regiments of horse, which were encamped on the banks of the *Vistula*. The bridge was however soon repaired, and the King brought all the sick into the town, for their better accommodation.

All this while the *Valoches*, who from *Clifchow* had never ceased to attend our army, continually harassed those parties which we were obliged to detach for forage and contributions, and who sometimes brought off some soldiers, victuals, and servants from the enemy: The 7th the *Valoches*, to the number of 3 or 4000 men, attacked, a quarter of a league from the camp, Mr. *Ornstedt*, who was made Lieutenant-Colonel to the regiment of *Scania*, which had been detached to cover the foragers. This officer with his small party overthrew them, and push'd them into the wood, before the picket, which hastened to his assistance, was come up. The King, to prevent these frequent disturbances from the *Valoches*, ordered the foot always to accompany the horse on the foraging-days, and to lye in
ambuscades

ambuscades to surprize them. This precaution obliged the *Valoches* to keep on their guard, and not to return but with a good force.

The King now caused them to make a brass-coffin at *Cracovia* for the corps of the Duke of *Holstein*, which they had always carried in the rear of the army, and which had been embalmed the day after his death at the battle of *Clissowa*. *Charles*, according to the established custom of *Sweden*, repaired in company of the Duke of *Mecklenbourg*, Count *Piper*, and his principal Generals, into the hall, which was all illuminated, where they had deposited the body of the Prince, which they had laid on a bed three foot high under a canopy of black velvet, laced and fringed with silver. His Majesty and the Lords of his train laid the lid on the coffin, on which they afterwards spread a long velvet pall edged with silver.

After this ceremony the King retired, much afflicted with the loss of a brother-in-law, whom he very tenderly loved. The Duke of *Mecklenbourg* appeared no less afflicted, having been a great friend of his late Highness, who when the King was at *Warsovia* had sent Mr. *Birckholtz*, a Gentleman of his Chamber, to the Duke, to assure him of his desire to make a campaign with him under his Majesty. Perhaps he had likewise another secret reason for this, namely, to marry the younger Princess of *Sweden*, sister to his Majesty and the Dutchess Dowager of *Holstein*. He was already come as far as *Breslaw*, when he heard of the Duke of *Holstein*'s death; and being unwilling to return before he had seen the King, repaired afterwards to his Majesty, who gave him a very good reception.

He

1704. He returned post as soon as he had paid his last respects to the Duke of *Holstein*.

The 11th the King caused the whole army to defile through *Cracovia*, and encamp on the other side of it, where the ground was higher and the forage better. *Augustus*, after his retreat from *Bochnia*, was come to *Sendomir*, to convene the Nobility and Grandees of his kingdom. After they had deliberated on the present conjuncture, which appeared very dangerous to this King, they resolved to send a new embassy to the King of *Sweden*, ' to offer him the mediation ' in the name of the Republick; and, if he ' would not consent to it, that the Nobility, or ' *Pospolite*, should confederate themselves in fa- ' vour of King *Augustus*, and assure him of an ' inviolable fidelity, with a promise never to ' consent that this Prince should be dethroned.

But as the greatest part of the Nobility, especially those of *Great Poland*, were not herein comprized, nor present, and consequently the Republick was not complete, the resolutions of this assembly were looked on as null, and produced no effect. Mr. *Lipski*, Waiwode of *Calis*, who had been a Deputy to his *Swedish* Majesty at *Dlougowitz*, in quality of first Ambassador from the Republick, had the misfortune to lose his life on this occasion. The Nobility, who knew very well that he had been gained by the presents of King *Augustus*, and who likewise knew with what haughtiness he had spoken to the King of *Sweden*'s Ministers, reproaching him with having been the cause of the war, by an ill-taken pride, which had incensed that Prince; so that after having resolved on his destruction, they gave him some cuts with a sabre, of which he died a few days afterwards.

As

As trouble and division encreased every day, and the Diet was on the point of breaking up, *Augustus* abandoned *Sendomir*, passed the *Vistula* at *Casimir*, with his *Saxon* army; and after having settled his march, he went before to *Warsovia*, with 4000 horse. But before he quitted the first of these places, he sent back to the King of *Sweden* thirty-eight soldiers and valets, made prisoners by the *Valoches* since the last battle, with a Lieutenant, who was to present them to the King, and an escort of thirty troopers. *Charles* took this very well of *Augustus*, treated the Officer at his Court, and ordered the escort to be well entertained till their departure. He likewise made the Officer a present of fifty ducats, ten to each non-commission Officer, two to every trooper; and not contenting himself with all this return of civility, he sent back at the same time a Major, named *Opeln*, to whom he presented a fine horse out of his own stable, with all his caparison, and a sword of the *Swedish* fashion: he likewise permitted the officer to retake with him from *Pinschow* all the *Saxon* officers who were recovered, and in a condition of travelling: and likewise gave leave to 400 *Saxon* soldiers, who were sick at *Cracovia*, to return into their native country.

In the mean while, General *Brandt* joined the Crown Army at *Sendomir*, with a regiment of dragoons which he brought with him from *Prussia*; he likewise gave them to understand, that he had formed some design on the castle of *Pinschow*. He was a man of fortune, but an old soldier, and a famous partizan, and had acquitted himself with great reputation in the last war in *Poland*. The King being apprized of his design by Lieutenant-colonel *Feilitz*, who commanded

manded at *Pinfchow*, and knowing likewife that he haraffed the parties detached from the caftle to raife contributions, fent Colonel *Meyerfelt*, at the head of 600 troopers, who having laid all the neighbourhood under contribution, fupplied *Pinfchow* with a great quantity of provifions, and burnt the town of *Noviomafta*, which had refufed to contribute. By which example of feverity, he defigned to infpire terror into all places which might be inclined to refiftance.

The fame day Count *Zinzendorff*, the Emperor's Envoy, had his firft audience. He began with congratulating his Majefty, in the name of the Emperor his mafter, ' on the victories which ' he had gained; affuring him of the unalterable ' friendfhip of his Imperial Majefty: laftly, en- ' treating him to have at heart the deplorable ' ftate of affairs in *Europe*, and to apply a re- ' medy to them, by a firm peace with *Auguftus*, ' and by accepting the mediation of all the con- ' tending parties, as he had formerly done at ' *Ryfwick*. He concluded with complimenting ' his Majefty, in high *Dutch*, in a very high ' ftrain, on the laft battle of *Cliffowa*.' The King thanked him very gracioufly, in the fame language; and appeared very well fatisfied with this Ambaffador.

We have already obferved, that this Minifter not being able to obtain audience at *Kielce*, had followed the army to *Pinfchow*; where his Majefty, who was weary of feeing him always at his heels, fent Mr. *Duker*, his Aid-de-camp-general, to make him a compliment, and defire him to abfent himfelf from the army, till he could find fome place more commodious; reprefenting to him at the fame time, that his Majefty could not allow him a liberty which he refufed all other Minifters.

King Charles XII. of Sweden.

Ministers. Count *Zinzendorff* repaired then to *Cracovia*, where he was at last admitted to an audience of the King, whose gracious reception made him amends for all the time which he had lost in solicitation.

This Minister had, however, little reason to be pleased at the success of his negotiation. He was charged to neglect nothing to effect a reconciliation between the two Kings; with which view he offered the mediation of the Emperor his master. And observing the civilities which mutually passed between these Princes, in sending back prisoners to each other without ransom, he thought he could not make use of a more favourable conjuncture; flattering himself that the King of *Sweden* would at last comply, and be brought to a perfect reconciliation with the King, who was his relation, and who protested, that he wished for nothing more ardently than peace. To prevent any doubts of these good dispositions in *Augustus*, this Minister produced letters from Count *Stratman*, who was his Imperial Majesty's Envoy to the King of *Poland*; in which he asserted that this King was ready to give *Charles* the XIIth all the satisfaction which could be required of him. Lastly, to remove all suspicion, he gave assurances that King *Augustus* would, without delay, withdraw all his troops from *Poland*, to engage them in the Emperor's service. And, that he might not give the least room for any umbrage, he engaged, in no manner to oppose the march of those troops which Major-general *Maidel* was bringing to re-inforce his *Swedish* Majesty's army. Besides all these fine promises, Count *Zinzendorff* produced a letter, written with King *Augustus*'s own hand, by which his *Polish* Majesty left not any reason to suspect the sincerity of his intentions: but as this Minister feared that letter might remain unanswered, he excused himself at present from leaving it in his Majesty's hands.

Whilst Count *Zinzendorff* employed all his engines to make these fair propositions agreeable to the King of *Sweden*'s Ministers, *Augustus* laboured on his side to re-unite men's minds at *Warsovia*, where he had called a Diet, that he might animate them against the King of *Sweden*, and bring them heartily to espouse his cause. These proceedings, which did not at all agree with the fine promises of the Imperial Minister, broke all the measures which he had taken, and involved him in very great difficulties; till at last, not knowing which way to turn himself, he cast all the blame on the Cardinal Primate, and the family of *Sapieha*, whom he suspected to be always good *Frenchmen*, and publickly accused to be the cause of the continuation of all the troubles; in which opinion he was particularly confirmed, by the Cardinal sending Colonel *Sauerbre*, with a particular commission to Count *Piper*. In reality, Count *Stratman* knew so well how to infatuate King *Augustus*, that Mr. *Heron* the *French* Minister, as well as the Cardinal, afterwards very much resented this, as we shall see a little lower.

About this time Baron *Nils Gyllenstierna* arrived at *Cracovia*, and informed his Majesty that the *Pomeranian* Army, which had passed through the higher *Poland*, was but four leagues distant from this town. The King came hither the next day, and was highly pleased with the fine appearance of his troops, which amounted to near 12,000 men, all well disciplined, and well clothed. As it was very easy to find forage in these quarters, which indeed very much abounded

bounded with it, the King left here the main body of his army, and detached Lieutenant-colonel *Burenschild* on the other side, towards the *Hungarian* mountains, to lay all the country under contribution.

General *Gyllenstierna* remained not long with the army. As the King wanted a man of some capacity in the conquered provinces in *Germany*, he ordered that General to repair thither, as well to have an eye over the neighbouring powers, as to levy troops, and put those provinces in a posture of defence.

As soon as all the dispositions were made, the body of the late Duke of *Holstein* was carried, with a strong escort, to the frontiers of his dominions; where he was afterwards buried in the tomb of his ancestors at *Sleswick*, with great funeral pomp. About this time a great number of invalid soldiers, who were in no condition to serve, were sent back to *Sweden*; his Majesty having before their departure distributed twenty crowns to every one of them, to defray the expences of their journey.

Some days afterwards the King gave orders to the army to hold themselves ready to march. As he intended to conduct the sick and trophies by water on the *Vistula*, he detached Colonel *Axel Sparre*, with 300 foot, to get together as many boats or vitines as he could pick up along that river; at the same time ordering him to prepare floats, which might be used in case the boats should not be sufficient. The night before Colonel *Sparre*'s departure the castle of *Cracovia* took fire, without any one's being able to discover how it happened. This fire continued all the day, and reduced the castle to ashes; several persons being buried under its ruins.

The

1702. The news of Mr. *Sparre*'s departure being brought to the Crown army, which still remained at *Sendomir*, Prince *Lubomirski*, Chamberlain of the Crown, began his march immediately, with twenty-four companies, to attack him. The Colonel was posted in a Town called *Usia*, four leagues from *Cracovia*. The enemy arrived about noon, having with them a great number of peasants, to level the hedges, and remove every thing that might obstruct the attack. Mr. *Sparre*, who luckily had received timely information, drew up in the place in order of battle, and distributed platoons through all the streets, to divert the enemy, who entered with a dreadful outcry on all sides. Our platoons presently fired on these troops, being almost close to them; and as they were usually afraid of our foot, they soon gave ground, and contented themselves with having set fire to some wooden houses round the market-place. This enterprize not having succeeded according to the enemy's hopes, they now began to retreat in great confusion, and were briskly pursued by our people; some of them retreated into the Church-yard, and made a shew of intending to defend themselves there, others got into the Church, and climbed up into the bellfry, whence they fired incessantly on the *Swedes*. Mr. *Sparre* ordered *Gyllenstierna*, Captain of the Guards, to dislodge them. The Captain attacked them so gallantly, that he was in a little time master of the Church-yard, and put them to flight, with the loss of several both killed and wounded.

On the other side, General *Brand* gave continual disturbance to the garrison of *Pinschow*, which he made a shew of attacking by storm, to prevent which his Majesty gave immediate orders to the two Majors of foot and horse guards, *Gyllekrok*

Gyllenkrok and *Creutz*, to march with 2000 and some hundred men, who were also to bring away from *Pintzchow* all the sick, and the *Saxon* trophies, which they were to guard as far as the *Vistula*; and as this detachment was to use expedition, they mounted the foot on horseback, in order to hasten their march: as soon as the *Polish* General was informed hereof, he changed his resolution, and passing near *Pintzchow* with 1000 horse, went and posted himself at twelve leagues distance; he surprized at *Drbrokowa*, and near the castle of *Zarnowatz*, and in a third place, 200 horse, with two Captains and two Lieutenants, who were all made prisoners. Colonel *Crassau*, of the *Pomeranian* army, had sent that detachment toward *Peterkow*, to levy contributions. The Majors *Gyllenkrok* and *Creutz* finding no enemy at *Pintzchow*, contented themselves with withdrawing the sick and wounded, most of whom were already recovered, whom they conducted, with the cannon and trophies, to *Oparowitz*, some leagues from *Cracovia*, to wait the arrival of his Majesty.

Our troops subsisted every where at the enemy's expence. A large party which had been detached by Lieutenant-general *Stuart*, and which was commanded by Colonel *Adam Lowenhaupt*, made continual incursions into *Samogitia*, where they committed great ravages; the Colonel likewise made several prisoners, among which were Colonel *Korff*, the Constable *Pusina*, and Captain *Russel*, whom *Lowenhaupt* had sent to *Mittau*, as hostages for the contributions which were laid on the country. At his return he was beset near the pass of *Possuole*, by a large body of *Lithuanians*, whom he routed with half their number. This party returned to the charge with fresh troops, near the town of *Cheimen*, and attacked *Lowenhaupt* with all imaginable fury, both parties fighting with great obstinacy: the victory was sometime doubtful, till the *Lithuanians* having lost their commander, were put to flight; and *Lowenhaupt* pursuing them, they left great numbers dead and wounded behind them. We had on our side only one non-commissioned officer and sixteen soldiers killed, and two Lieutenants, some non-commissioned officers, and twenty-four soldiers wounded.

Every thing was now ready at *Cracovia* for the embarkation of the cannon and trophies on the vitines and floats, which they had there got together, when an express arrived with letters from the Cardinal Primate, and Mr. *Morstein*, who at the last diet at *Sendomir* had been picked out as an ambassador to the King. The former yet offered his mediation, and the latter brought advice of the commission with which he was charged. But Mr. *Morstein* having used some haughty expressions, and even such as were a little hard, in the letter which he writ to Count *Piper*, the express was presently sent back with an answer, purporting, ' That his Majesty would not admit
' *Morstein*, in case that he had any propositions
' to make, differing from those his Majesty had
' made on his part; that the Republic had be-
' sides shewn too much partiality for him to ac-
' cept of her mediation; that if she had desired
' to have had a share in determining the diffe-
' rences between the contending parties, she
' should not have interested herself either on one
' side or the other; that several of her mem-
' bers had committed many hostilities; and last-
' ly, if his Majesty should resolve on peace, and
' to accept of the Republic's mediation, she
' ought first to punish those who had disturbed
the

' the public tranquillity, and by their continual
' excursions had hindered his Majesty from ef-
' fecting his good designs.'

Mr. *Morstein* did not rest here; he writ back again, and once more desired his Majesty to allow him an audience; with assurances, that as soon as the negotiation should be on foot, the Republic would not fail to punish those who had the misfortune to displease him by their conduct. The King remained unmoveable on this article: he sent no answer to *Morstein*, and gave him sufficiently to understand, that he would not fail to execute the resolution he had taken.

An accident which happened to the King seemed likely to disappoint all his great projects, his Majesty having had the misfortune to break his left thigh; that unfortunate accident, which spread a consternation through the whole army, happened by the following means.

Count *Stenbock*, who was lately made Director-general of war, had formed a company of *Towarches*, which was composed of 150 men, all poor *Polish* Gentlemen, who were ordered to perform their exercises in his Majesty's presence. The Count putting himself at their head, to this purpose departed from *Cracovia* on a gallop, and passed by the King's tent at the instant he was sitting down to dinner; his Majesty, instead of dining, ordered his horse immediately to follow them; and being arrived at *Morner*'s regiment, his horse entangled himself in the lines of the tents, and falling on the King's left thigh, broke the bone quite off.

This unforeseen accident brought tears into the eyes of all who were present, he alone seemed not to feel it; and speaking to those who appeared the most frightened with wonderful resolution, he told them

them it was nothing, and would be eaſily cured; no one heard him complain, or give the leaſt token of that pain which he muſt neceſſarily endure.

As he could not ſupport himſelf on his leg, ſome Drabans carried him into Mr. *Morner's* tent, where the ſurgeons applied their firſt remedies; from thence the King was carried into a houſe in the ſuburbs. And as this misfortune neceſſarily retarded the departure of the army, they were ſent into quarters in the town and the ſuburbs, the ſeaſon of the year not permitting them any longer to keep the field.

The news of this fall ſoon became publick; nor were any pains omitted to ſpread abroad that *Charles* XII. was dead; his enemies cauſed that news to be put in the foreign gazettes. It is certain, that he appeared at firſt in extreme danger, which put all the army in a great conſternation. They were very much afraid of the coming on of a fever, which is common enough on ſuch occaſions; at leaſt they thought he muſt paſs his Winter at *Cracovia*. But the King's excellent habit of body ſoon gave them comfort; and in about eight days he began to talk of his departure.

To make the King's voyage more commodious, they had prepared ſome large vitines, in which they had built cabins for his Majeſty, and part of the court, in order to carry them by water; but the evening before his departure he changed his reſolution, and choſe forty-eight ſoldiers of the guards, which were to carry him by turns on a bed, and to whom he gave every day of their march a crown a-head. The King found this way of carriage more convenient than a litter, which would have ſhaken him too much.

Every

Every thing being ready for the departure of the army, and the floats which the Colonels *Axel Sparre* and *Rank* had taken care to provide being got ready, four regiments of horse were ordered to go before towards *Sendomir*, and the King himself began his march with the rest of the army.

They encamped at *Igolomia*, whence Count *Jaspar Sperling* was detached with some hundred men over the river, to take up provisions, and to cover on that side the boats which came down from *Cracovia*. Some days before the King had given Count *Zinzendorff*, who went to attend his Majesty's arrival at *Warsovia*, an escort of fifty troopers, under the command of a Captain, to secure him from the insults of the *Polish* parties; a regard, with which this Minister seemed highly delighted, and which he very publickly extolled.

The Princes *Lubomirski* were much alarmed at the rout of our army, on account of their large estates on the *Vistula*; and very far from continuing obstinate, as they had been, in the demand of 9000 ducats for the ransom of Mess. *Dahldorff* and *Rosenstierna*, who were taken by the *Valockes* at *Bocunia*, *Lubomirski*, the Great-chamberlain of the Crown, sent them hastily back to *Igolomia*, under an escort of some *Tartars* and his Aide-de-camp.

He took this resolution as soon as he saw the King's answer to Mr. *Dahldorff*, who informed his Majesty of the pretensions of the *Lubomirski* touching his ransom; the King signified to Mr. *Dahldorff*, that if the Great-chamberlain refused to set him and Mr. *Rosenstierna* at liberty, he would entirely destroy all his estates. *Lubomirski* endeavoured to make a merit with his Majesty of the liberty which he had granted these Gentlemen. He writ to Count *Piper*, that he had taken great care of the prisoners, and that he hoped they would shew the same tenderness to his estate; the rather, for those respectful sentiments, and that attachment, which he bore to his Majesty, and his interest. This declaration of *Lubomirski* carried no appearance of sincerity; and it was very easy to observe, that his present circumstances, and his own interest, had brought him to this language: his Majesty therefore contented himself with giving him for answer, that in sending back the prisoners he had done no more than his duty, and that he should see if his future actions would verify the desire which he expressed to gain his Majesty's good graces. About this time the *Cossacks* of the *Ucrain*, which were under a dependance on the *Poles*, having begun to stir up a great revolt, and kill their chiefs, who endeavoured to oppress them, entered, to the number of about 20,000 men, into *Podolia*, and cut off all those Lords who had the misfortune to fall into their hands. Some rich and powerful persons, who were enemies to the Gentlemen of the Country, were at the head of this revolt.

It was plain by those letters which we intercepted, that the Czar and King *Augustus* underhand fomented this rebellion, with hopes, by those means, to oblige the Nobility to mount their horses, and to bring them against the King of *Sweden*. This project had not the success which *Augustus* expected; nay, he had the mortification to see a resolution taken in his presence at *Warsovia*, to march a great part of the Crown Army, under the inferior General *Siniaffki*, to reduce those rebels.

In the mean time the King began visibly to recover; and the army having marched from *Igolomia* to *Pikari*, (two leagues) he caused himself to be carried from regiment to regiment, by that means to visit and encourage his Troops, who were yet alarmed with the danger to which his Majesty was exposed by his wound. The army remained at *Pikari* till the 29th of *October*; which time the King employed in settling the rout; and it was agreed, that the troops should march but slowly during the winter; and that they should always chuse the best places to repose themselves several days together.

Augustus, on his side, feeing the Diet which he had convened at *Warsovia* was like to produce him as little good as all the rest, the Senators and the greater part of the Nobility not coming thither, caused his army to march into *Polish Prussia*, in order to put them into winter quarters.

He soon followed them himself, and came to *Thorn*, where he was received with all the honours due to him. He knew so well how to gain on the Magistrates of that Town, by his eloquence and great civility, that they consented, against their privileges, to receive a strong garrison of *Saxons*, to reinforce, as he pretended, those of the town, in case of an attack. The Magistrates of *Dantzick* and *Elbin*, fearing to be surprized in the same manner, had the precaution humbly to offer their towns to that King; with a request, that he would come as Father of their country, and not as Sovereign. He, however, obtained, by his presence in these provinces, infinite advantages for his army, greater than he could have had in *Poland*, had he remained there. It must be, however, confessed, that they granted ed him all this more through fear, than any love they had for him. The Marquifs of *Heron*, the *French* Ambaffador, fuffered at that time a very fenfible affront. The Emperor's Minifter had a long time placed him in a bad light to King *Auguftus*, who fufpected that he had by his intrigues continued the war. Mr. *Heron* could not but obferve the difcontent of this Prince; and feeing himfelf treated with great coldnefs, he writ to the King of *Sweden*, defiring his leave to repair to him, which his Majefty would not grant, after having refufed it to other foreign Minifters. King *Auguftus* having been informed of this ftep which that Minifter had taken, forbid him the Court, and ordered him to depart from *Warfovia*. Mr. *Heron* anfwered, that he did not think himfelf obliged to obey him, without an exprefs order from the Republic, to whom he was as well fent by his mafter, as he was to his Majefty. *Auguftus* was extremely fhocked at the anfwer of this Minifter; and after having repaired from *Warfovia* to *Thorn*, he gave orders to have him arrefted: one evening, as this Ambaffador came out of the houfe of the Great-marfhal *Bielinfka*, where he had fupped, twelve of the Body-guards feized his perfon; and without giving him leave to return home to fettle his affairs, they carried him inftantly from *Warfovia* to *Thorn*, where he remained prifoner fome time, and was from thence conducted thro' all *Germany*, to the frontiers of *France*.

The Marquifs of *Bonac*, the *French* Envoy at the Court of *Sweden*, had at the fame time an accident of much the fame nature. This Minifter, after having ftopped at *Riga*, according to the orders of the King his mafter, had fet out for *Warfovia*,

King CHARLES XII. *of* SWEDEN.

Warſovia, without an eſcort, confiding in his character, which he thought would have protected him from all inſults. At his approach to *Kauro*, he fell into the hands of *Oginſki*, who, without paying any reſpect to the right of nations, killed his valet-de-chambre, treated him as a priſoner of war, and carried him about with him for ſome time.

The moſt Chriſtian King, incenſed to the laſt degree at the inſolence of the Republic, in ſuffering ſuch violences to be committed on two of his Miniſters, though both of them had been ſet at liberty, demanded a publick ſatisfaction; and at the ſame time impriſoned all the *Poles* of diſtinction who were found in the provinces of *France*.

After his *Swediſh* Majeſty had ſettled the march of our army, he cauſed them to decamp from *Pikari*, and march to *Przimakow*, where they remained eight days together.

The loſs of the battle of *Embach* had changed the face of affairs in *Livonia*, where Mr. *Schlippenbach* was no longer in a condition to keep the field, till he had received a new reinforcement, which he importunately ſolicited. The Czar, taking advantage of the weakneſs of the *Swedes*, cauſed his army to defile towards *Ingria*, to beſiege the little town of *Noteburg*, ſituated on the *Nieva*, at the mouth of the lake *Ladoga*, which is the key of *Sweden*, being her fartheſt fortreſs on that ſide. We had ſome ſmall veſſels which cruiſed thereabouts, but the enemy, whoſe forces were ſuperior to ours, obliged them to repaſs the *Nieva*, and to retreat towards *Wybourg*, ſo that the *Ruſſians* became entire Maſters of *Ladoga*.

Velt-

Velt-marshal *Scheremetof* having approached this place with the *Russian* army, detached on the 26th of *September*, 400 of the *Preobrasinski* guards to post themselves before the place. Two battalions of the same regiment followed the same evening, with all the army, and arrived there the next day. The *Russians* presently opened their trenches, and raised some forts, to prevent any succours being conveyed into the town. However, three vessels from *Carelia*, with some soldiers and provisions, found means to get in. But to shut up this place the closer, and to hinder it from receiving any future succours, the enemy caused 2000 men to pass the *Nieva* on the 30th, and take possession of a small redoubt, situated on the other side, which some few soldiers who were there had abandoned. In this manner the town was shut up on all sides.

The *Muscovites* at the same time raised three batteries, placing twelve mortars on the one, and mounting the two others with thirty-one pieces of cannon, the first with nineteen-pounders, the other with twelve twelve-pounders. From these batteries they made a continual discharge, which set the town on fire in several places. The Velt-marshal afterwards having summoned Governor *Sclippenbach* to surrender, he demanded a four days truce, to send to Major-general *Horn* at *Nerva*, from whom he was to receive his orders. *Sclippenback* not being able to obtain this favour, hoisted the royal flag, as a signal of the extreme distress to which the place was reduced, and the necessity he had of immediate succours.

Major *Sion* was presently detached with 400 horse, and four field-pieces, to attack the besiegers on the side of *Carelia*, and make his way

way into the town. In which attempt he at first succeeded well enough, having beat the enemy, who encountered him, back into their entrenchments: but at the instant that he entered them, with a design of making himself master of them, he was attacked by all the forces of the besiegers, with Colonel *Konigseck*, whom the King of *Poland* had sent to the Czar, at their head. The *Swedes* now found themselves obliged to retreat, with the loss of their cannon, having had twenty men killed, several wounded, and a Corporal, with seven men, taken prisoners. A new battery of six pieces of cannon and two mortars, which was in readiness some days after, was appointed to fire on our vessels, which lay at anchor under the cannon of the town, but they did us no damage.

The breach being now made, the enemy on the 10th of *October*, being *Sunday*, caused their troops to give us an assault, at a time when a fire raged in several quarters of the town. The attack was carried on with all the vigour imaginable; notwithstanding which, the besiegers were repulsed with wonderful valour. So after a fight which lasted, without any discontinuance, from two in the morning till five in the evening, they were obliged to give us some rest, after a very considerable loss. We now thought that they would return no more to the charge; but soon after, seeing them make dispositions for a new attempt, the Governor determined to beat a parly. He obtained an honourable capitulation, and was permitted to march out through the breach with forty men, which were all he had left, drums beating, colours flying, and to retire with four field-pieces to *Nerva*, whither he transported himself by water, with all his men, after having

having sustained a siege of more than fifteen days (*).

In *Courland* continual skirmishes passed between our troops and the *Lithuanians*. Major *Sass*, whom Colonel *Poss* had detached from *Raufkenburg*, surprized, at some distance from *Pomusk*, four companies of *Lithuanians*, commanded by one *Goes*, a Gentleman of *Courland*, whom he attacked, and entirely defeated.

The enemy having posted themselves some days afterwards in the castle of *Dobeln*, whence they made excursions into all the adjacent parts, Lieutenant-colonel *Wennerstedt* was ordered to dislodge them, with a considerable detachment, with some cannon and mortars. He departed from *Mittau* on the 17th in the evening, and the next day presented himself before *Dobeln*. On his arrival he found the enemy were retreated, having left some few of their men behind them, whom he made prisoners.

On the other side, the Regimentaries *Wasinski* and *Knesiewitz*, after having burnt the Lordships of the *Sapieha* in *Samogitia*, made an excursion into *Courland*, taking their way through *Schrunden*. They invested *Goldingen* with 2000 men, 600 of which made themselves masters of the town, and took there Lieutenant *Deston*, who, however, escaped from them by means of a sally which Captain *Aderkass* made from the castle with 30 horse. The Captain dispersed them, and forced them to retreat, after leaving several killed and wounded on the spot. The next day, on an account that Colonel *Patkul* was approaching from

(*) The articles of this capitulation are inserted in the Memoirs of the Reign of *Peter* the Great; together with the particulars of the triumphal entry which the Czar made into *Moscow* on this occasion.

Mittau,

Mittau, they entirely abandoned thofe parts, and repaffed their frontiers. But we will enter into no farther detail of all the rencounters, and other particulars which paffed amongft thofe little parties, fince it is now time to follow the King into *Poland*.

The *Swedifh* army decamped on the 20th of *October* from *Przimakow*, and advanced two leagues and a half, which is a little diftance from the town of *Viflicza*, formerly famous in the laft *Polifh* war, in the time of *Charles Guftavus*. Two days afterwards the King detached Count *Stenbock*, with 2200 horfe and foot, to pafs the *Viftula*, and levy contributions in the adjacent parts. He advanced as far as *Lemberg*, and taxed the lands in grievous fums, efpecially thofe of the Princes *Lubomirfki*, and their adherents, to force them to give the King fatisfaction, and quit *Auguftus's* party.

Thefe Lords were the more alarmed, as the Count threatened, in cafe of refufal, to put all to fire and fword. Thefe menaces brought from them all kind of fubmiffions, by which they hoped to foften his Majefty.

Mr. *Stenbock* neglected nothing to gain over the Nobility of the country, ufing gentle methods with fome, and rigorous with others. The methods which he took produced all the effects which he could defire. The Nobility, on all fides, fent back the *Swedifh* prifoners which they had taken in feveral rencounters; the whole, including thofe which General *Brand* had made, amounting to upward of 400 men.

The better to fubfift the army, the King made them take different routs, keeping no more than the Drabans, and the regiment of Foot-guards, near his perfon. He made the army march in columns,

columns, himself marching to *Pierzicz* (three leagues.) Here Mr. *Meyerfeld*, who commanded the party which had hitherto remained at *Opatowitz*, joined us, with those other officers and *Saxon* soldiers, which had been taken prisoners at *Pinfchow*, and which were entirely cured of their wounds. The King gave them money for their journey, and sent them all back to *Saxony*.

As to the other wounded *Saxons*, who were not yet recovered, his Majesty had the goodness to put them with our own wounded men, on the vetines commanded by Mr. *Sparre*; and which were yet but a few leagues from *Cracovia*, because the waters of the *Vistula* were very low. The Colonel, the better to subsist his sick and his detachment, sent out parties on every side to raise contributions. He also sold to that purpose, at a very moderate price, a great quantity of salt, which he had taken from the salt-pits of *Bochnia*, belonging to the demesns of the King of *Poland*. As soon as the water began to rise he continued his voyage for *Casimir*, where he placed both the *Swedes* and *Saxons* in the town, to be there kept till they were entirely cured.

Augustus, who remained still in *Prussia*, had little reason to be pleased with what now passed in his kingdom. This King, enraged that the Nobility of *Great Poland* appeared so attached to the King of *Sweden*, especially the Count *Leszinski*, who, after the battle of *Cliffow*, had openly declared for his *Swedish* Majesty, detached 8000 men to bring these nobles back to their duty.

These troops lived at discretion on the lands of the nobility, in which they committed terrible disorders, and unheard-of violences, by that means

means so incensed them, that Count *Leszinski*, putting himself at the head of some tooops, fell on several *Saxon* parties, in different places, and defeated them. On the other side, the Starost *Gembiski* surprized *Ægidii*, a *Saxon* Colonel, defeated all his party, and killed him with his own hand, because he had put his brother under arrest.

The Cardinal, who had long displeased King *Augustus*, felt, with several others, the effect of his anger. That King having raised more than 60,000 crowns of contribution on his estate, he complained bitterly; but finding that did him no service, he writ the King a very severe letter, which was all the revenge he could get. In the mean time the King of *Sweden* was entirely cured of his hurt, so that he could walk in his chamber, by the assistance of his staff. When the army decamped from *Pierszicz*, he would try to mount his horse, but was soon obliged to dismount. The army marched thence (two leagues) to *Olesniga*, where they rested some time.

On the 4th of *November* Captain *Funk* was detached from the army, with 200 dragoons, towards *Sendomir*, to establish a magazine there; and the King following with his column, arrived the 21st of the same month at *Sczeka* (two leagues,) and the next day marched two leagues farther to *Nawodzic*.

Here General *Maidel* joined his Majesty. He came from *Riga* through *Lithuania*, with his regiment of dragoons, a great number of recruits for the army, and three regiments of horse, *viz.* that of the *Swedish* Nobility, and those of *Craus* and *Patkul*. The two last had remained continually in *Samogitia* and *Lithuania*, to cover the territories of the *Sapieha*; but being now ordered to join the army, the Great-general *Sapieha* thought

1702. thought himself no longer secure; and therefore that he might not live at the mercy of *Oginski* and *Wisniowiski*, he followed these regiments with a small body of two or three thousand men, and arrived at the same time with them at the King's quarters, whom he attended ever afterwards, throwing his fortune entirely upon his august protector.

In the mean time Count *Stenbock* had several disputes with the nobility of *Russia* and *Volhinia*. He arrested the Waivode of this latter province, who having refused to pay contributions, was afterwards obliged to buy his liberty with a very large ransom.

As the nobility were very turbulent, the Count asked them, whether they intended to declare for the King of *Sweden*, or against him, and insisted on a categorical answer. They were very much perplexed with this question, especially the *Lubomirski*, who were in great fears for their estates, which they incessantly entreated might be spared. They assembled at *Reisna* to debate on an answer, the result of which we shall see hereafter.

The King continuing his march, arrived the 4th of *December* at *Gorciczani*, half a league from *Sendomir*, the capital of the Palatinate of that name, situated on the *Vistula*, where there had been a castle, which *Charles Gustavus* blew up, and of which, at this day, there remains nothing but the ruins. The King, after a short stay here, gave orders to Baron *Rheinschild*, a Lieutenant-general, to march, with part of his army, towards *Warsovia*, to cover the assembly of the nobility, which the Cardinal had convened there, and to be ready to assist that of *Great-Poland* against the *Saxons*.

Some

Some days afterwards his Majesty passed by Sendomir, and marched towards *Zavigost*, where finding himself entirely recovered of his fall, he threw away his crutches, mounted his horse, and began as usual to fatigue himself, and visit the quarters of his troops. All the army shewed an inexpressible joy, at the dissipation of that long fear in which the accident that happened to that illustrious hero had held them.

Neither the bad weather, nor the frequent storms, attended with hail and snow, which fell in abundance, nor, in a word, the severe and sharp winter, could hinder the King, who was but just recovered from his fall, from paying regular visits every day to the several quarters of the army. The troops were now encamped about *Zavigost*, which is situated on the *Vistula*, and where *Charles Gustavus*, King of *Sweden*, the Grand-father of our hero, was joined, in 1657, by *Ragotski*, the Prince of *Transilvania*, at the head of a numerous army of *Hungarians* and *Cossacks*. Here we remained during the *Christmas*; after which his Majesty passed the *Vistula* with the rest of his army; leaving behind him only some regiments, which afterwards passed the river about *Casimir*.

About this time our troops were much harassed in different places by the *Lithuanians*. Mr. *Stuart* detached several parties to give them chace. Captain *Hammelstierna*, who was posted at *Dobeln*, being joined by Cornet *Anrep*, encountered them near *Schagern*, killed 50, and made 161 prisoners. Some days afterwards, the *Lithuanians* having shut up, at *Lamberts-hoff* near *Baufke*, Lieutenant-colonel *Bruchner*, who was raising contributions, he repulsed them with great bravery,

put

702. put them to flight, and safely joined our detachment from *Baufkenburg*.

On another side, Major *Mentzer* surprized a great number in a place, where they had got together a magazine, put all whom he met with to the sword, and carried off their whole magazine of provision. Major *Meyerfelt*, brother to the Colonel of that name, and who was in garrison at *Seelburg*, performed such another exploit a few days afterwards, having beat a *Lithuanian* party from *Bandomir*, who were returning to *Livonia* with a great booty, which he took from them, after having routed them.

Livonia after this was quiet enough for some months, whilst *Ingria*, on the contrary, became the bloody theatre of the most barbarous tragedies, which were there acted by the *Ruffians*. After having burnt the villages of *Zola*, *Kulla*, *Allekulla*, *Onekulla*, and *Kleinbulla*, several mills, and the garden of the senate of *Narva* or *Rathfhoff*, they surprized, with some thousand horse, on the 4th of *January*, a little after midnight, the advanced posts at *Narva*, and penetrated quite into the suburbs. To bring the inhabitants out of their houses, they made use of a stratagem, crying out in the *French* tongue, *Let us save ourselves, my friends, the Ruffians are a-coming*; which expedient had such success, that these poor people having opened their gates, were all inhumanly massacred, without any distinction of age or sex. The few troops which were in the suburbs made all the resistance they could, but were with great violence driven back to the counterscarp, after a very stout fight.

The *Ruffians*, as soon as this expedition was over, seeing the whole garrison ready to attack them, retreated, with all their dead, after having

ing for six hours together done a great deal of mischief, and exercised all sorts of cruelties.

The King continued his march the 3d of *January*, on the road of *Lublin* towards *Dzircowizza* (four leagues.) Here his Majesty met the two *Potocki*, sons of the Great-general of the Crown, who had audience of his Majesty, and very humbly begged his protection. His Majesty received them very graciously, and made them a very considerable present of money; which they so ill requited, that instead of employing it, as they had promised, in raising men for his Majesty's service, they put it to a quite contrary use.

At this time Count *Stenbock* returned from his expedition, with advice that the assembly at *Wisnia* had at last declared for his Majesty, and had already named Deputies to demand his protection, in the names of the nobility of *Volhinia* and of *Russia*. Count *Stenbock* was now ordered to write to the Magistrates of the town of *Lublin*, to signify to them his Majesty's dissatisfaction, at the injustice the inhabitants had done the year before to General *Morner*, as he was passing with his body of the army near the town; for which they were taxed at 50,000 crowns as a penalty; and Colonel *Meyerfelt*, with some foot and dragoons, were sent to raise it.

The army decamped on the 12th, and marched to *Krezniza*, a Gentleman's house, near the little town of *Belziz* (three leagues;) from thence to *Wotgechow* (one league,) afterwards to *Lublin*, where the Magistrates came out to meet the King. He marched through the town with his army, and encamped at *Jacobowitz*, a castle situated half a league from *Lublin*, and which belongs to Prince *Lubomirski*. Here the King fixed his head quarters, and distributed the Drabans, with the regiment of guards, among the villages and neighbouring houses.

Some days afterwards his Majesty dispatched an express, with a Letter to the Cardinal, in the following terms.

CHARLES, &c.

'AFter our long expectation, we do not see any remedy proposed capable of putting an end to those troubles, which have so unprofitably retained our armies in this kingdom; whereas we have nothing more at heart, than to find out measures proper for that purpose. For though there be no rupture between the Republic of *Poland* and ourselves, this delay is however attended with inconveniences which must be very pernicious to both kingdoms, unless speedily prevented.

' In reality, we are not so jealous of the glory of our arms, as we are desirous to give repose to the people whom we love. For this reason we wish that expedients might be found to procure, as well tranquillity for the people of *Poland*, as advantage and security for those of *Sweden*. But as we cannot hope for success in a place where the hatred, envy, hope, fear, and animosity of the parties, have entirely taken away all freedom of debate, we think it may be very wholesom, in so important an affair, to convene an assembly, in which the nation, being entirely at her liberty and without any constraint, may freely, and without constraint, speak her sentiments, take proper measures for a lasting safety and repose, and provide for the common good.

' We

'We have therefore thought proper to acquaint your Eminence with our intention, as being the first Minister of the Republick; and to put it into your power, not only to deliver this country from the danger of utter ruin, which threatens it, but likewise considerably to encrease her power, by a conjunction of arms, to recover those provinces which the common enemy hath taken from her, and is now in possession of. Lastly, after recommending your Eminence to the divine protection, we wish you long prosperity. Given at *Jacobowitz*, the 24th of *January*, 1703.

Your Eminence's most affectionate friend,

CHARLES.

And underneath,

PIPER.

The Cardinal, who arrived the 26th of *January* at *Warsovia*, having received this letter, and being incensed, as we have already seen, against King *Augustus*, published an order, convening the Convocation on the 5th of *February*: which order contained in substance what follows.

' That he lamented the negligence and insensibility of the *Poles*, who looked without emotion on the ruin of their country, which was become a prey to foreign troops, and a jest to her neighbours. That they appeared to have neither the laws, nor the justice, nor the liberty, nor the courage, nor, indeed, any of the virtues of their ancestors. That nothing was to be found among them but weakness and dejection; they being all dispersed, and keeping
' themselves

'themselves at a distance, as if they had no con-
'cern in the destruction of the Kingdom.
  'That he had repaired to *Warsovia* to con-
'sult with the Pope's Nuncio, and the other fo-
'reign Ministers, on some means to remedy such
'pressing evils; but they had all assured him
'that it was impossible to find any, unless the
'*Poles* themselves would set their hands to the
'work. That therefore, for the discharge of
'his conscience, and by the authority inherent
'in his dignity, he convened all the Senators,
'and those who had been Deputies to treat of a
'peace, to *Warsovia*, on the 5th of *February*,
'that they might deliberate on the best means
'of saving the Republic, and appeasing the tu-
'mults with which she was agitated, &c.'

Very few, however, of the Grandees repaired to *Warsovia*. The Great-treasurer Count *Etienn Lefzinski*, and *Sapieha* the Great-treasurer of *Lithuania*, were almost the only persons there: so that the Cardinal was obliged to adjourn the assembly to the 27th of *March*, and thence to the 16th of *April*.

The cause that the convocation came to so little was, the *Senatus Concilium*, which King *Augustus* had appointed at *Thorn* the 16th of *March*, and which he removed to *Marienburg*, for the conveniency of the quarters. This King, being dissatisfied with the Cardinal's conduct, taxed him in his turn with partiality to the *Swedes*, and accused him of being the cause, by his obstinacy, of all the confusion and troubles which had raged in *Poland*. He concluded with saying, that it did not belong to the Cardinal to call a congress; and that the assembly at *Warsovia* was contrary to his rights, and the direct way to overturn the state.

Towards

Towards the end of the month the Deputies of the Palatinate of *Ruffia*, in conformity with the decree of the affembly at *Wifnia*, fearing to be facked, as they were threatened, came to *Jacobowitz*, and had an audience of the King, who took them under his protection; and after a gracious reception, fent them back with a very favourable anfwer.

Hoftilities continued daily between the parties of the two armies. In *Courland*, General *Stuart* detached Lieutenant-colonel *Bruchner*, with fome troops, to oppofe *Oginfki*'s party. He met with fix companies at *Janifka*, put 100 of their men to the fword, made nine prifoners, took two ftandards, twenty-four lances or *Copies*, three pair of kettle-drums, two trumpets, and above 300 horfes, with fome other booty.

A few days afterwards Count *Adam Lowenhaupt*, entring *Lithuania* with a detachment, furprifed, under the favour of a thick mift, four companies of *Lithuanians*, which guarded an advanced poft before *Janifka*; he killed forty, made feveral prifoners, and carried off a ftandard, with two pair of kettle-drums. Thofe who efcaped having carried the alarm to *Oginfki*, that commander retreated haftily, without drawing far, however, from *Janifka*, which was in the poffeffion of *Lowenhaupt*. The enemy, on their fide, fome days afterwards attacked a fmall party detached from *Janifka* to raife provifions, but were repulfed, with the lofs of two Captains, and fome foldiers killed.

Whilft thefe were haraffing each other, King *Auguftus* fet all his engines to work to gain over the Nobility and Senators affembled at *Marienburg*. This affembly was very numerous; nor were King *Auguftus*'s endeavours abfolutely vain.

The

The Crown-army under Prince *Lubomirski* the Great General, who remained faithful to him, notwithstanding the desolation of his territories, sent Deputies to assure his *Polish* Majesty, that they were resolved to sacrifice under him their lives and fortunes for the maintenance of the Republick and their religion. The whole army then took an oath of fealty, according to a formulary which King *Augustus* drew up, as well for the Generals of the Crown, as the subalterns and soldiers.

At the same time Prince *Lubomirski* published with the sound of trumpets in the city of *Leopold*, at *Reschow*, and other places, that the Nobility should mount their horses within a month's time, in order to join the Crown-army against the *Swedes*, under pain of being declared guilty of high treason, traitors to their country, and punished accordingly.

This affair was brought on the tapis in the Diets of all the Palatinates, where they deliberated on the choice of Deputies, which were to be sent to *Marienburg*. The Palatinate of *Lublin* did not dare to declare herself openly, on account of the *Swedish* garrison which was in that capital, and the near neighbourhood of our army. They however assembled some of the Nobility, who demanded an audience of the King of *Sweden*, which favour his Majesty willingly granted them, and promised them his protection, which they desired.

Count *Stenbock* having finished his levy of contributions, followed his Majesty with his troops; and passing near *Zamosk*, a town included in the number of the fortresses of *Poland*, a great many of the Nobility, who were fled hither with all their effects, were strangely alarm'd with the apprehension

King CHARLES XII. of SWEDEN.

prehenfion of an attack by the Count; which fear carried them to fet fire to the fuburbs, and to rely entirely on the defence of the place, which they were refolved to make in the beft manner poffible. But the Count paffed by them, contenting himfelf with laying all the country under contribution, which he continued to do till he at length joined his Majefty's army.

Some days afterwards the King detached Lieutenant-Colonel *Charles-Gabriel Horn*, with the regiment of foot of *Pomerania*, towards *Brefzifzi*, to fecure that important pafs, which is fituated on the confines of *Poland* and *Lithuania*; and the fame day his Majefty, after a ftay of fix weeks at *Jacobowitz*, marched (3 leagues) to *Lewarthoff*.

Mr. *Robinfon*, the *Englifh* Envoy, who came to fpeak with the King, met him half way, attended by feveral Generals. This Minifter had no fooner faluted his Majefty, but he demanded his permiffion immediately to difclofe the orders of the Queen his Miftrefs; to which the King confented, and remained uncover'd while Mr. *Robinfon* made his fpeech in the *Swedifh* language, which he fpoke perfectly well, having been a long time a Refident at the Court of *Sweden*. As the King well knew this Minifter, he gave him a very gracious anfwer; nor could he keep himfelf from laughing at the pleafant figure which he made, having turned the fur of his *Peliffe**, as well as his cap, on the out-fide, which, joined to the great high road where this fudden audience was given, put the King into a very good humour.

The day after his Majefty's arrival at *Lewarthoff* he perceived in himfelf fome fymptoms of a fever; but as this flight indifpofition produced

no

---
* A fur or leather jacket.

no ill confequence, the army continued their march, and encamped at *Czermenick* (3 leagues,) after having pafs'd the little river *Wieper*, which empties itfelf into the *Viftula*.

The fame day the council of *Marienburg* was opened; it was in fome refpects imperfect, as well through the abfence of the Primate, as of feveral other Senators, who excufed themfelves from coming, on account of the *Saxon* garrifon, which hindered the freedom of their debates. *Auguftus* however propofed to them feven articles, of which the following is the fubftance.

1. What was to be done for the defence of the Kingdom and the Republick, fince there was no longer appearance of peace.

2. What means were to be employed to oppofe the Diet which had been convened at *Warfovia* to the prejudice of his Majefty's rights, and to the fubverfion of the State.

3. What method they fhould take to punifh the adherents to and fupporters of the *Swedifh* party, who ftubbornly perfifted in their defigns.

4. If any regard fhould be had to the demand of fome of the Palatinates, who defired the calling of a general Diet.

5. How to encourage more and more the army of the Crown, and accommodate their Generals.

6. If alliances fhould be made with the neighbouring powers who mediated them, offering fuccours of troops and money, and in what manner their offers fhould be accepted.

7. It was propofed to fettle their limits with the *Turks*.

After eight days deliberation on what was to be done in the prefent unhappy conjuncture, the council

council agreed provisionally on the following articles:

1st, That by virtue of the convention of *Sendomir*, of *Great Poland*, and *Lithuania*, the whole Republick ought to oblige themselves by oath to concur in their defence of Religion and Liberty, and the safety of the Republick and the Kingdom.

2. That the *Russia* Pospolite should be assembled.

3. That they would in the mean time agree on a general Diet for fiftteen days.

4. That the *Swedish* partizans should be declared enemies of their country, and their effects confiscated towards paying the army.

5. That the assembly called by the Cardinal should be deemed unlawful.

6. That in order to neglect nothing which might advance peace, the embassy, which had been named a long time ago for that purpose, should have fresh orders to sound the King of *Sweden*'s dispositions, and endeavour speedily to procure peace, without engaging, themselves however in any projects which may cause a dismembering of the Republick, or the plunging her into a foreign war.

7. That they would debate farther on the alliances to be made with foreign powers, in order to extricate the Republick out of the perplexity in which she was entangled.

This convention was signed by all the assembly, except the Bishop and the Palatine of *Culm*, who refused it; and they afterwards dispatched the Commissaries of *Poland* to the King of *Sweden*, as we shall see presently.

1703. This King, who continued to advance towards *Warfovia*, marched through *Razin* (1 ½ league) to *Lukow* (3 leagues,) thence to *Wifniow* (1 ½ league.) But fcarce had he quitted *Lublin*, when *Potocki*, who had made him fuch fine promifes began his hoftilities, by difturbing the *Swedifh* pofts in the very fuburbs of that town, where Colonel *Meyerfeld* had remained with fome troops ; and as this Colonel was efcorting the contributions which that town had been obliged to furnifh, *Potocki*, whofe courage was perhaps fomething elevated with the hopes of carrying off that fum, continually haraffed this detachment in their long marches towards *Cazimir*, but that in fo weak a manner, that, through the great care and vigilance of Mr. *Meyerfeld*, they arrived fafely at *Cazimir* with all the baggage, and without the lofs of a fingle man.

At *Cazimir* they met the *Vitines* which had carried the trophies and fick upon the *Viftula*; Mr. *Meyerfeld* joined them, and continuing his march along the river fide for their fecurity, they all arrived fafe at *Warfovia*, without having loft the leaft thing by all the efforts of *Potocki* to traverfe them and give them difturbance.

On the 13th of *March* the King decamped from *Wifniow*, and marched to *Zelifchow* (three leagues,) where the army remained fome days ; and afterwards to *Ceglow* (2 ½ leagues,) and thence through the town of *Mincko* to *Okniow*, which is three leagues from *Warfovia*.

The Nobility of *Samogitia* began now to difband, and retire in whole companies, being weary of making war with fo little fuccefs, and in which they got nothing but blows. *Oginfki*, who was in defpair at feeing them take a refolution to make no farther head againft our troops,

did

did all he could to prevent them; but when he found that all his efforts were in vain, and fearing that after this desertion he should be inclosed by the *Swedes*, who would not fail to make their advantage of this conjuncture, he thought the best measures he could take were to procure himself an advantageous retreat.

With this view he took with him his best troops, and went directly to *Birsen*, which he took possession of, tho' that town belonged to the house of *Neuburg*. He resolved at the same time to draw thither a body of 3000 *Russian* foot, which had been in winter-quarters at *Drugen* near the *Duna*, flattering himself, that with this reinforcement he should be able to form a good garrison, and to assure himself a retreat, where he should be able to resist all our efforts.

As this neighbourhood must have given great disturbance to our troops in *Courland*, Baron *Stuart*, their Governor-General, being desirous to prevent the *Russians* who were on their march towards *Birsen*, took a resolution to send thither a large detachment, which were to make themselves masters of that town before their arrival. To this purpose Count *Adam Lowenhaupt*, a Colonel, who was posted in *Samogitia*, ten leagues only from *Birsen*, received orders to march thither with all expedition, and in case he should find the *Russians* already entered, to endeavour to bring them to a general engagement. Colonel *Cloot* was sent at the same time to reinforce him; he was to join him without delay with some artillery and 400 foot, which Count *Frolich* had drawn out of the garrisons of *Riga* and *Mittau*.

Colonel *Lowenhaupt*, with 900 foot and horse of his detachment, having joined Mr. *Cloot* at *Janiska*, turned towards *Birsen*, and was attended

1703. ed the whole way by fourteen companies of *Lithuanians*, who only haraſſed him from time to time, without ever daring to come to a formal attack. But nothing retarded ſo much the Count's march, as the horrible defiles and almoſt impaſſable roads through which he was obliged to paſs, which gave the *Ruſſians* time to get into *Birſen* when our troops were about 4 leagues off.

Mr. *Stuart* having received advice, and knowing likewiſe ſomewhat of himſelf, that theſe were ſome of the *Czar*'s beſt troops, being old *Strelizes*, which were very full of bravery, and who had ſerved in the laſt war againſt the *Turks*, ſent the Count orders to return the ſame way he came, the rather, as ſeveral of our men were ſick through the fatigue of their tireſome march.

The enemy looking on this retreat as a flight, marched out of *Birſen* to the number of 6000 and odd hundred men, both *Ruſſians* and *Lithuanians*, with ſome artillery, to cut off the Count's paſſage, whom they encountered near *Salat*. They preſently poſſeſſed themſelves of all ſides of the wood through which he was to paſs, and ſhewed themſelves only in platoons, to make him quit his advantage, and draw him to an engagement. *Lowenhaupt* obſerving their deſign, preſently recalled all his detached parties, and that night lodged himſelf with his men in the beſt manner he could in the little village of *Salat*, and held himſelf ready againſt all events. The enemy, tho' much his ſuperior in ſtrength, made no motion, but contented themſelves with kindling large fires, to preſerve themſelves from the cold, which was then very piercing. The next day the *Poles* appeared in greater numbers. The Count on his ſide drew up his men, and, after he had cauſed prayers to be ſaid, he exhorted

horted them to conquer, or die. He then marched boldly up to the enemy, and, under the favour of a very thick mist, made himself master of a defile which the *Ruffians* had neglected to possess themselves of. These, believing they might easily repair the fault which they had committed, passed a small river, and ranged themselves in battalia on the other side, where they stood expecting us. The Count, who had with him about 1000 men only in a condition of fighting, pass'd the river likewise, and drew up in one line, mixing his foot with his horse. The baggage was placed in the rear, and formed the second line. The *Ruffians* under the command of the two Colonels *Nizefchof* and *Protopon* had the precaution to barricade themselves with their waggons, which they guarded on the outside with *Chevaux de frife*, and within by their artillery. The *Poles* were on the two wings, commanded by the Regimentary *Gordon* and two Gentlemen, whose names were *Karper*.

Count *Lowenhaupt*, being advanced within cannon-shot, gave orders to attack the *Ruffians* in their intrenchments. At the same instant the *Poles* began to charge our left wing under Colonel *Cloot*, who received them so briskly, and gave them so many home charges, that they were obliged to retreat in confusion. Whilst our left wing under the command of Count *Lowenhaupt* continued advancing, 6 or 700 *Poles*, who were in the dress of *German* dragoons, and who attempted to take us on our flank, were likewise repulsed with loss by our cannons and granades.

Lieutenant-Colonel *Baneer*, having had two horses killed under him, put himself at the head of the infantry with Major *Wrangel*, who was killed

killed soon afterwards, and marched sword in hand towards the *Russians*, who were intrenched up to their teeth behind their waggons. As there were a great number of them, they made a terrible fire, but without effect, most of their shots flying over the *Swedes*, who were now ascending a hill, at the top of which the enemy was barricaded. Our fire, on the contrary, did great execution, very few shots miscarrying; and our foot, having at last broke through and forced their intrenchments, began to make a dreadful execution, in spite of all the vigorous resistance of the *Russians*, who, seeing themselves pressed and lost, fought with the but-ends of their musquets, halberds, and pikes, and at last threw themselves under the waggons, where they made a most desperate defence.

The long pikes of our foot were now so extremely useful, that the *Russians*, seeing themselves unable to make any longer resistance, took to their heels in the rear of their intrenchments, and fled in great confusion through the village of *Ziaggerini*, which is situated some miles off towards *Birsen*. Great numbers of them were killed in their flight; and it is certain, that not one would have escaped if the Count had had more horse, the whole complement which he had with him amounting only to 300 men.

As to the *Poles*, they made not the least motion during the whole action, contenting themselves with very quietly looking on; but as the Count did not know what might be their intention, he called back those who had pursued the enemy, and presently drew up all his men in order, that he might be ready in case they should think proper to attack him a second time. But as they thought of nothing less than so rash an enterprize,

enterprize, after they had obferved our difpofition, and gather'd together thofe *Ruffians* who had had the good fortune not to fall into our hands, they ran away full fpeed, and by that means about noon put an end to a very obftinate and bloody battle.

The Count now ordered a double difcharge of 16 pieces of cannon, as a fignal of his victory, and then commanded his men to conduct all the wounded to *Ziaggerini*, together with all the cannon and the trophies, which confifted of 12 brafs culverins and field-pieces, 1058 fmall banners of taffety or damafk, embroider'd with gold, filver, and filk, and 33 drums, without reckoning the reft of the booty, which was confiderable.

Six hundred *Mufcovites* were flain on the fpot, befides thofe killed in the flight; fo that of all this body, 1200 *Ruffians* only returned to *Birfen*, having loft in this rencounter a Colonel, a Lieutenant-Colonel, and feveral other officers. Of all the prifoners we fpared only eight. On our fide 2 Majors and 40 men were killed, and about 100 officers and foldiers wounded.

The night after the battle the Count remained in the village, and gathered together his dead and wounded; the next day he decamped on his return through *Baufk* to *Mittau*.

This victory, gained over an enemy fix times our fuperior, and intrenched, was much applauded, and pleafed his Majefty fo greatly, that he fent Count *Lowenhaupt* a commiffion of Major-General, and a little while afterwards that of Vice-Governor of *Courland*, in the abfence of Mr. *Stuart*, who was gone to drink the waters in *Germany*.

The LIFE and HISTORY of

The King was now at *Okniow*; but being desirous to speak with the Cardinal, he set out with a few attendants for *Warsovia*, and had an interview with that Prelate at *Villanova*, where the conference lasted three hours, namely, from four in the afternoon till seven.

Immediately after this interview, General *Rheinschild* was ordered to march with his army towards *Rava* and *Lenzici*. We have already remarked, that this General, when he quitted the King at *Sendomir*, had set out to cover the assembly of the Nobility, convened at *Warsovia*. He had passed through *Janowitz* by *Radom*, and came to *Blonia* the 9th of *January*, where he had canton'd his army in the adjacent houses and villages. The 16th of the same month he detached Lieutenant-Colonel *Rotblieb* with 200 horse towards *Zukazow*, who defeated a party of *Poles* and *Saxons* in a little town called *Clodowa*, and took a Captain and two Lieutenants, with 22 Pancernes.

Rheinschild having received orders to march towards *Rava*, decamped from *Blonia*, and arriving at *Rava* the 24th of *March*, he quartered his troops in the neigbourhood of that town; and judging that it would be convenient to prepare a magazine at *Wladiflaw*, situated on the *Vistula* and on the road to *Thorn*, he detached Major *Laurence Creutz* with 270 horse to possess himself of that place, and presently to get together whatever might be necessary for the subsistence of the troops, in case his Majesty should take that road; and as he apprehended a surprize from the enemy, Colonel *Lilliehock* was ordered some days afterwards to reinforce him with his regiment of foot.

As

As soon as the floats were arrived at *Warsovia*, the King went to *Prague* to see them, and caused a bridge to be thrown over the *Vistula*, at the same place where he had passed before, which was perfected in a few days. His Majesty was now again attacked with some feverish symptoms, which did not however prevent him from continuing his exercises, which, joined to his excellent habit of body, contributed much to the entire re-establishment of his health.

The King, having decamped from *Okniow* on the 7th of *April* with the Court and Drabans, took up the same quarters at *Prague* which he had been in the preceding year, and gave some days afterwards a publick audience to the Imperial, *French*, *English*, and *Dutch* Ministers.

The army having followed his Majesty, all the regiments were distributed near the town and in the suburbs of *Warsovia*, the better to guard against the insults of *Potocki*, whose parties continually scoured the country, and had lately carried off some of the horse belonging to the regiment of *Smoland*, and some foot from another regiment: They were desirous of doing the same by the regiment of horse-guards, whom they closely attended in their march, but had not the courage to attack them.

Lieutenant-Colonel *Charles Horn* was ordered at the same time to return to *Breszizi* with the regiment of *Pomeranian* foot, that the army might not be too much scattered, since we had entirely changed the plan of operations for the campaign. We had however so well succeeded in all our marches, that the river *Bug* only separated our army from that of *Saxony*, the latter being encamped near *Pultowck* along that river,

1703. while ours was posted between that and the *Vistula*.

The King, burning with impatience to come to blows with the enemy, thought on all imaginable methods to oblige them to defend themselves and stand their ground: To this purpose commanding Prince *Wurtemburg* and some others to follow him, he repaired to the *Bug*, from whence he could *reconnoitre* the *Saxon* camp, the sight of which extremely animated him; but whilst he was riding backwards and forwards, the better to remark their situation and the ground thereabouts, he perceived at a distance a *Saxon* Corporal with some Dragoons, who had passed the river in quest of some provisions in a neighbouring village. The King presently pursued them, but could take no more than two, the Corporal with the rest having had time to recover their boat and save themselves. His Majesty, on his return to *Warsovia*, being firmly resolved to attack the enemy, set his men to work about a bridge which was to be thrown over the *Bug*, and at the same time gave private orders to get together all the boats which they could find, small and great, to place them on waggons, and, when every thing was ready, to carry them to *Nowodwor*, a village where the *Bug* discharges itself into the *Vistula*, and where *Charles Gustavus* King of *Sweden* had formerly passed that river, and defeated his enemies.

Whilst these preparations were carrying on, his Majesty made a promotion of General-Officers. Lieutenant-General *Rheinschild* was made General of horse; Lieutenant-General *Liewen*, General of foot; and the Major-Generals *Meidel*, *Stuart*, and *Stromberg*, were made Lieutenant-Generals. Some days afterwards Count *Morstein*,

Morstein, who had been deputed by the assembly at *Sendomir* in the quality of first Ambassador to his Majesty from the Republick, arrived at *Marienburg* with two other of our Commissaries, namely, *Zudowsky*, Ensign of *Cracovia*, and *Stephen* Count of *Leznic Lescinsky*, according to the sixth article of the result of the council which they had held. They demanded an audience of his Majesty, which was granted them; but as their propositions were by no means agreeable to that satisfaction and security which he required, they received the next day a very short answer, by which they were given to understand that his Majesty apprehended, that the Orders or Members of the Republick would have immediately entered on such measures as might have produced a firm peace, and that his Majesty might, in consequence thereof, have regulated his proceedings, and taken such steps as he should have thought proper. As to the rest, they were referred to a declaration made in the King's name by Count *Piper*, to the Cardinal Primate, of the same date with the day of their audience, and which laid down the deposition of King *Augustus* as a preliminary article.

This embassy having incensed, instead of appeased his Majesty, he now resolved to push his enemy to the utmost. As soon as the necessary preparations were made for the expedition in question, the King departed from *Prague* on the 18th of *April* at four in the morning, without speaking to the Cardinal, to whom Count *Piper* afterwards sent a letter, when the battle of *Pultowck* was gloriously determined.

The King took with him all the horse and foot, except the regiment of *Upland*, which remained at *Prague*, to cover the Court, the Chancery,

1703. cery, and the Artillery. The Colonels *Axel Sparr* and *Clerk* were likewise ordered to stay at *Warsovia*, to take care of the sick, and have an eye on the conduct of the *Poles*. The *Vitines* began in the night to fall down the *Vistula* under the command of Colonel *Rank*; and the waggons, which carried the boats for the bridge, took the same road with his Majesty, and with the horse being all arrived at *Nowodwor*, which is four leagues from *Warsovia*, they began in the evening to work upon the bridge, under the direction of Count *Stenbock*.

The 19th the *Saxons* having appeared in the morning on the other side opposite to the bridge, where they threw up some breast-works with a shew of intrenching themselves, his Majesty caused 16 pieces of cannon to be brought down to the banks of the *Bug*, which played so well on the other side, that the enemy were obliged to abandon their works, which were just begun. This determined the King immediately to pass over 1500 men to take possession of them. Lieutenant-Colonel *Poss* pass'd the river in front with 500 of the foot-guards on boats which they had tied together, and on the floats. *Poss* was supported by Count *Jasper Sperling*, a Lieutenant-Colonel at the head of 1000 men of the same regiment, who all landed safely, without any opposition from the *Saxons*, who, tho' they were all horse and dragoons, had no disposition to engage, and retreated out of musket shot to at least 150 paces distance.

The King, who plainly saw by this, that the enemy were afraid to try the fortune of a battle, passed hastily over the river, followed by the Princes of *Wurtemberg* and *Saxe-Gotha*, several Generals and Officers; but as the boats could

not

not be pushed fast enough to the shore, his Majesty threw himself into the water some distance from the bank, and led his troops after him, who were all up to their middle.

This bold action so intimidated the *Saxons*, that they ran away full speed without a single discharge, nor were we able to overtake one of them, except a few *Poles*, for want of horse. The King however pursued them half a league home to the village *Ponikowa*, where he left the detachment, which posted itself there, and returned the same evening on foot to *Nowodwor* with the Princes and other officers.

The next day the King passed the bridge, in order to find out the enemy. His Majesty was attended by the Princes, Generals, Officers, and Voluntiers, and followed by his Drabans, his regiment of horse-guards, with the regiments of horse of *Smoland* and *Scania*, and 200 of Colonel *Buchwald*'s dragoons. He knew the chief forces of the enemy were posted at *Pultowsk*, under the command of Veldt-Marshal *Steinau*.

He took the road of *Ponikowa*, where our detachment had passed the night. Before this village runs a little river, not wide, but deep, over which was a bridge, which the *Saxons* had broke down in their retreat. The King, who saw their advanced-guards on the other side, was so animated, that he resolved to pass it instantly, whatever price it cost him. A *Polander*, who offered to sound the depth, had all the difficulty in the world to get over to the other side, where, as some *Saxons* were approaching to lay hold of him, the King ordered some of his men to make ready to fire on them, which checked them, and gave our people time to fetch him back in a small boat which they had at last found in a little village.

1703. village. His Majesty ordered 30 ducats in gold to be immediately paid down to the *Polander* on his return.

The King, seeing the impossibility of passing at this place, went half a league farther to find out another near a mill, where having sounded the ground himself, he found it firm, and threw himself the first into the water, whose example was presently followed by all his men, only one of whom was drowned, notwithstanding the rapidity of the current, and that a great number of our cavalry were obliged to swim over their horses.

His Majesty then marched through a neighbouring wood without the enemy's having the least suspicion. We took some *Valoches* with a kettle-drummer prisoners, who were far from believing us so near. At last, after a moment's halt, we arrived at a little village, where a *Saxon* officer was posted with some dragoons, who were all taken, except a very few that escaped and carried the first news to Mr. *Steinau* of the approach of a large body of *Swedes*. The King, who followed on a full trot at their heels, arrived at *Pultowsk* before break of day, without having stopt a single moment during the whole night, after having surprised several advanced guards who were posted on that road.

Steinau, at the first news of our approach, came forth at the beginning of the night to *reconnoitre* us, but he thought us not so strong as we were; nor did he imagine that we intended to attack him, much less had he the least suspicion that the King was there in person. However, at his return he drew out his squadrons in battalia on a hill before the town, and gave orders out of precaution, that all those who were posted

posted in different places should mount their horses, and come immediately to his assistance; which they did, but it was now too late.

The King being arrived in sight of the enemy found them busy in making the proper dispositions to receive us. His Majesty presently examined the ground and the defile which led to the town, as much as the darkness would permit him, and afterwards ranged his horse in several lines.

Steinau, whom the break of day now undeceived, surprized at the number of our horse, which were superior to his own, thought of taking the necessary measures for a retreat. With this view he gave his men orders to return to the town, which is surrounded with water, intending to defend himself by pulling up the draw-bridges on all sides; but the King, who presently suspected his intention, detached the dragoons to cut off his passage, who attacked him so briskly, that Colonel *Buchwald* was with his squadron on the bridge at the same instant as the last *Saxons* were pressing to pass. *Buchwald* made himself immediately master of the gates of the town after a very slight resistance.

The *Saxons* now fled full speed through the town, passing near the castle to save themselves over the bridge on the river *Narewa*; but they were so smartly pursued by the dragoons, that falling over one another, those who were once passed broke down the bridge, and abandoned such as remain'd in the town to the mercy of the conqueror; these now made no longer resistance, and throwing down their arms begged humbly for quarter, which was presently granted them by his Majesty himself, who was now come up with the Drabans and the other regiments. We afterwards

1703. afterwards refitted the bridge, and Colonel *Buchwald* purſued the enemy half a league farther, but was not able to overtake them.

The King having poſted himſelf with a ſmall number attacked Lieutenant-General *Beuſt*, who ſeeing no poſſibility of eſcaping had hid himſelf with ſome dragoons in a water-mill. His Majeſty took him priſoner himſelf, and without making himſelf known to him, left him his ſword on his parole; and hearing a new fire on that ſide where we had entered, he haſtened up to us, where he found a party of our horſe, which had ſtood to obſerve the enemy, engaged with a *Saxon* regiment which was juſt come from their quarters, and knew nothing of what had paſſed. Our horſe received them ſo gallantly, that after having loſt many of their men both killed and wounded, they were utterly broken, and put to flight in great diſorder.

As to Mr. *Steinau*, he had the good luck to ſave himſelf over a little bridge, and thence through a convent of *Jeſuits*; but all his baggage, with that of his officers, a great number of horſes, two pair of kettle-drums, and five ſtandards were taken by the *Swedes*.

Amongſt the priſoners were the Count *de St. Paul*, three Majors, ſeveral other officers, and between 6 and 700 men, who were all conducted under a guard to the caſtle. Several officers were killed on the ſpot; but the place where the enemy ſuffered the greateſt loſs was in their paſſage over the laſt bridge, where, ruſhing one upon another, more than 1000 of them were drowned. It is almoſt incredible, tho' it be a certain and well-known truth, that we had but eleven men in all either killed or wounded.

In the evening Mr. *Beuſt* being conducted to pay his reſpects to the King, was very much ſurprized to ſee the auguſt perſon who had taken him priſoner. He had the honour to ſup with his Majeſty, who ever afterwards gave him many inſtances of his goodneſs.

The next morning early the King commanded Colonel *Wrangel* with the Drabans, 100 of *Buchwald*'s Dragoons, and four troops of the horſe-guards, to go and look after the enemy. His Majeſty, attended by the Princes and ſeveral officers and troopers, ſoon after followed this detachment, after having given his orders, and left the reſt of the horſe at *Pultowſk* under the command of Major-General *Ridderhielm*, they marched all that day without hearing any other news of the enemy, than that they had abandoned all the places where we came.

We continued our march on the 23d, and his Majeſty about noon being informed that the enemy was at *Oſtrolenka*, preſently took that road. After having marched all day, we arrived in the evening at a village one league diſtant from that town, where the King himſelf made an officer and ſome *Saxons* priſoners, who informed his Majeſty that 3000 *Saxons* were advantageouſly intrenched at *Olinka* with the *Lithuanian* army.

As it was dangerous for ſo ſmall a number to give an enemy battle, who was ſo much their ſuperior, and reduced to defend themſelves in deſpair, and beſides that the perſon of his Majeſty would run too much riſque, where the loſs appeared inevitable; the Princes, the Counts *Wrangel* and *Stenbock*, and all the other perſons of diſtinction, joined in their intreaties to diſſuade his Majeſty, who at laſt, on their lively

inſtances

instances resolved, tho' with some regret, to return back again.

We retreated two leagues that evening, to a village which is five leagues from *Pultowsk*, and where his Majesty caused the detachment, which had great need of repose, to halt. We placed however very strong guards on all sides, to prevent a surprize from the enemy, who thought of nothing less than attacking us. The next day at 9 in the morning, after prayers, his Majesty continued his march, and arrived in the evening at *Pultowsk*.

The Cardinal took this opportunity to answer Count *Piper*'s letter, in which he had acquainted him of the King of *Sweden*'s departure. This answer was very moving, and is a lively picture of the extremity to which the affairs of *Poland* were at this time reduced. It was written in the following words:

'I Flatter'd my self with the return of his Ma-
' jesty from his glorious expedition, till the
' moment that I received the honour of that
' letter, which your Excellency writ me when
' you set out to join him. So sudden a farewell
' could not be otherwise than very afflicting to
' me, as it deprived me of the pleasure of em-
' bracing you in a closer manner, and at the
' same time threw me into a very great anxiety
' on the present posture of our affairs, which
' seem to be entirely abandoned to the mercy of
' fortune.

' I have waited patiently five months at *War-
' sovia*, in order to obtain a more agreeable sepa-
' ration, and which might yield a greater conso-
' lation to the two kingdoms: nor will I yet
' despair of the piety of a Prince, who, con-
' forming

King CHARLES XII. *of* SWEDEN.

'forming his actions to the will of God, will
'not difdain to hearken to the voice of one,
'who neither ought to have, nor can have any
'other view than the glory and the intereft of
'his people. The angels were the firft that
'proclaimed Peace at the birth of our Saviour.
'The firft word which he fpake to his Apoftles
'after his glorious refurrection was Peace; it
'is this we are ordered to preach; a cir-
'cumftance which muft excufe me before his
'Majefty, if I always talk to him in that lan-
'guage. I doubt not but your Excellency will
'affift me with your authority, and fupport that
'little credit which I have always endeavoured
'to merit of his Majefty; and that your Excel-
'lency will on your part give me reafon in all
'places in a real, not a ceremonial manner, to
'exprefs with how much efteem and tendernefs
'I am, &c.
Warfovia, May 4, 1703.

Some days afterwards the affembly came to an end, and the King of *Sweden* appeared as little fatisfied as the enemy, who had fo loudly cried out againft the Cardinal on the account of their meeting. His Majefty particularly expreffed great impatience on their continual delays touching the propofition which had been made them of dethroning King *Auguftus*. In a letter dated the 5th of *May*, in which the Cardinal anfwer'd the King of *Sweden*'s declaration, he avoided even the mention of this article; which filence determined his Majefty to have the Cardinal written to on this fubject a few days before his arrival at *Thorn*. Count *Piper* therefore writ to him in fubftance as follows: 'That the Repub-
'lick would do well to declare themfelves as
'foon

'soon as possible by his Eminence, and positively to represent what satisfaction she intended to give his Majesty, to procure from him a firm and solid peace. That as his Majesty was always inclined to a strict friendship with the Republick, so he would take measures to prevent any future disturbance being given to the troops of *Sweden*, and to punish such as had had the boldness to give them any hitherto.'

As the King never lost sight of the great object which he had constantly proposed for the determination of the war, he applied himself, immediately on his return to *Pultowsk*, to put the army in a condition of undertaking the siege of *Thorn*, where the best foot of the enemy were shut up, and to penetrate afterwards into the heart of their estates. His Majesty had the goodness the day after his return, after having made Mr. *Beust* dine with him, to take that General alone with him into his chamber, where he conversed with him several hours in the most gracious manner in the world.

The day following a *Polish* Count arrived on the part of the Commissaries of the Republick with letters for Count *Piper*, whom he expected to find at *Pultowsk*; this Count was very well entertained at Court.

The King having permitted Count *St. Paul*, who was a Colonel, and another Captain of Dragoons, to go on their parole to *Warsovia* to be cured of their wounds, gave orders to Mr. *Creutz*, Major of the horse-guards, to escort all the rest of the prisoners with 500 horse and a squadron of dragoons, and sent them on before; but his Majesty kept Lieutenant-General *Beust* near his own person,

person, and would have him always eat at his own table.

The same day in the afternoon the King decamped from *Pultowsk* and marched (2 leagues) to *Szirotozin*. All the regiments that had remained on the *Bug*, as well as that of *Upland*, being foot, which was at *Prague*, had already received orders to join his Majesty's detachment. All these troops were immediately put in full march. As to the floats and *vitines*, which were under the command of *Ranck* and *Clerck*, they fell down the *Vistula*, keeping themselves always opposite to our army in their march.

The 29th his Majesty proceeded through *Novamiasto* towards a place where General *Welling* waited for him with a party of foot. They repaired through *Plensko* to *Razimino*, where they halted the next day, on which Count *Piper* joined the King. The army marched hence to a little town called *Bodzenow*, being two leagues distant, where we waited some days for the entire conjunction of all the regiments.

Whilst the King was every day thus gathering fresh laurels in *Poland*, our poor frontiers of *Livonia* lay exposed to the plunder and barbarity of the *Russians*, who, as soon as they had opened themselves a free passage by the taking of *Noteburg*, exercised the most horrible cruelties. They likewise laid siege to the little fort of *Nyenschantz*, a very bad fortification, and very weakly maintained; which nevertheless defended itself so well, that they could not carry it but after a long siege and three subsequent assaults. They allowed the Governor, upon beating a parley, very honourable conditions, which the enemy however did not think proper to keep, but made all the garrison prisoners of war.

1703. Some days afterwards they laid siege to *Jama*, an old castle two leagues from *Narva*. They began to bombard it the 12th of *May*, and took it the 14th by composition, the Governor retiring with his arms and baggage to *Narva*.

In this manner the *Czar* made himself master of all this desolate country, whence he was afterwards able to make continual irruptions into *Livonia*.

The King's army having decamped from *Bodzenow*, passed by *Ploczko* towards *Tschurs* on the road to *Thorn*. As 7000 of the best foot of King *Augustus* were here in garrison under the command of General *Robel* and Major-General *Canitz*, the same who had commanded the year before in the fort of *Dunamund*, we hastened our march to shut them up, and prevent them from any possibility of escaping.

We came then to *Camin* near the town *Drobrozin*, where some Gentlemen being got together fell on our baggage, but without success; for instead of the booty which they were in hopes of carrying off, they got nothing but blows, and, for a punishment of their bravado, they had the vexation to see all those houses and villages, where they retired, set on fire.

The army continued its march towards *Salmetz*, and the next day came to *Bobrownika*, five leagues from *Thorn*, where Count *Stenbock* was detached a few days afterwards with some horse and foot to post himself a league from the town on the river of *Dribentz*, and there to build a bridge.

The *Saxons* had no sooner received information of the King's approach, than they gathered up all the peasants of the country, whom they employed together with the garrison, which was

very

very numerous, to repair the old fortifications and add new ones. The day following, his Majesty coming with the army to *Slotoriza* on the *Dribentz*, found the bridge almost finished, as it was effectually a few hours afterwards.

In the mean time the advanced guards of the enemy were retreated under the cannon of the town. The Governor caused all the houses of the suburbs, which were nearest the fortifications, to be burnt; nor did he even spare the church itself.

The King seeing this fire afar off, without waiting till the bridge was finished, pass'd the river at a ford with his ordinary retinue and some Dragoons, and approaching within a quarter of a league of the town, he attacked an advanced guard, and forced them to a hasty retreat. The same night 500 horse were ordered to post themselves where the King had advanced the evening before. They were reinforced the next day by another detachment; so that the enemy being obliged to quit all their avenues, and shut themselves up within the walls, his Majesty pass'd all his foot over the *Dribentz*, and brought them to an encampment almost under the cannon of the town.

His Majesty rode round the town to *reconnoitre* it, and advanced up to the glacis of the counterscarp. To keep the town block'd up, we posted a guard on the *Vistula* on the side of St. *James*'s gate, amongst the ruins of those houses which had been burnt, under the command of a Major. We likewise placed another guard on the other side of the town opposite to the gate of *Culm*, in a garden near the church which they had burnt, under the command of a Colonel.

Several

1703.

Several other guards of less consequence were distributed in several other places, so near to each other, that they could soon join for their mutual support. They were relieved every day by the two first; so that on the side of the *Vistula* and the Palatinate of *Culm* nothing could either enter or go out of the town.

To hinder likewise all communication on the side of the city *Dantzick*, all avenues to the town on that quarter were possessed by the horse, reinforced by a regiment of foot. In the monastery of the village of *Putgarse*, opposite to the town, his Majesty placed *Albedhyl*'s Dragoons, under the command of Major *Trautfetter*. As to the floats, the *vitines*, and the other boats which were on the *Vistula*, they were placed near the quarters where the horse were posted on the road to *Dantzick*, and were covered by the two regiments of foot of *Smoland* and *Calmar*. The *Saxons*, who were taken prisoners at *Pultowsk*, were conducted into an island of the *Vistula* under a strong guard of foot.

The town being thus blocked up, the King repaired with the Princes of *Saxe* and *Wurtemberg* to the Colonel's quarters, who was posted before the gate of *Culm*, and beheld over a garden-wall the manner in which the *Saxons* carried on their new ravelin. General *Liewen* being now come up, and standing by the side of his Majesty [1] a little too openly, a *Saxon* gunner perceiving

---

[1] *Liewen* had impolitickly distinguished himself by the richness of his dress, which the King perceiving, and imagining he might on that account be picked out by the enemy, he ordered him to stand behind himself; and *Liewen*, who was afraid of endangering his Majesty, hesitated on obeying him. The King then took him by the arm, and pulled the General behind him, at which instant

ceiving him, pointed his cannon that way, and took off one of his legs, of which wound he died the same evening much lamented on account of his bravery and experience in the art of war.

The same day twenty soldiers, with a Captain, having been detached towards *Slotoriza* on the *Dribentz*, to bring up the timber which was to be employed in building a bridge over the *Vistula*, were attacked by 16 *Lithuanian* companies, against whom they defended themselves with so much bravery, that, after a continual fire, they had the happiness to gain the bridge, and repulse the enemy with the loss of a great many both killed and wounded. This action so extremely pleased the King, that he rewarded the officer very liberally, and gave ten golden ducats to every soldier. These 16 companies had been lately detached from the town of *Pultowsk*, where the *Lithuanian* army was posted after the departure of the King of *Sweden*, in order to procure intelligence.

Some days after this skirmish, 16 other companies having passed the *Vistula* partly on prames and partly by swimming, near *Bobrownika*, to have an eye on General *Rheinschild*'s army, which was collecting a magazine at *Wladislaw*, as we have said above, and where Colonel *Liellieboek* was in garrison with his regiment, they took it in their heads to attack them, which design they executed at day-break under the favour of a thick mist with all imaginable fury, and at stant he received the mortal wound from a cannon which was fired on his flank. This accident, says *Voltaire*, confirmed the King in his opinion of an absolute Predestination, and that his destiny had so singularly preserved him for the execution of very great actions.

first killed some soldiers whom they met in the streets; but the rest of the garrison presently getting together, soon repulsed them out of the town with loss, without giving them time to set fire to a single house, much less to the magazine, as they had proposed. At last, to complete their misfortune, as they were reposing themselves in a neighbouring wood, one *Vitting*, a Captain of horse, who had been sent out to levy contributions, by accident surprized them on his return, and entirely defeated them: He killed above a hundred of their men, and took from them almost as many horses, and all the booty as they had plundered in so many different places.

As to General *Rheinschild*, who commanded this army, he went from *Rava* on the 4th of *April*, where we left him, and having passed through the town of *Gezew*, *Glowno*, and *Piontek*, he came on the 7th to *Lencici*, where he staid till the 14th of *May*, when he took the road of *Zoravice*. The 15th he passed through the town of *Britzia*, whence he departed for *Mievice*, and marched on the 16th to *Radzieuf*, whence he came to pay his respects to his Majesty before the town of *Thorn*; he afterwards rejoined his troops, with whom on the 25th he took the road of *Konari*, as we shall see hereafter.

King *Augustus*, who had staid all this time at *Elbing*, now set out for *Warsovia*, making his tour through the bishoprick of *Worms*, with design of being at the Diet which he had convened at *Lublin*. He lodged in the suburbs of *Prague*, in the same house which his formidable enemy had quitted, not being willing to venture within the town itself.

But

But the better to decry the *Swedes* as a nation which trampled all laws under their feet, he complained to the foreign Ministers, and in all their Courts, on the subject of the battle of *Pultowsk*, which he would have looked upon to have been a breach of a suspension of arms, which he supposed to have been concluded between the two armies. This affair made so much noise, that as the Cardinal had writ to *Sapieha*, the Great Treasurer of *Lithuania*, the King was so enraged, that he ordered Count *Piper* to write to the Cardinal, which he did on the 15th of *May* in pretty sharp terms. This letter from Count *Piper* entirely undeceived the Cardinal, giving him very plainly to understand the falsity of the above-mentioned imputation.

While all this passed, the *Saxons* completed a new ravelin at *Thorn*, on which they had worked with so much diligence, without any interruption from the King. For as he had resolved to keep this town closely blocked up, he was well persuaded, that such laborious work, joined to the want of provisions for so strong a garrison, and the distempers which raged among them, would not fail to reduce them in a little time, without any necessity of using force, or exposing the troops. We therefore suffered them to carry on their works; and they had all the liberty they could desire to strengthen them with as many gabions and guns as they pleased.

They fired incessantly on all our quarters, especially those of the King and his Drabans near the village of *Mockre*. Those of the town discharged their artillery at the same time. They did us not however any great mischief; and, except some horses which they killed, with an old suttler, who had his head carried off, and a scullion,

scullion, who was divided in two by a cannon-ball, none of our men were much hurt. The King would never permit the least breast-work to be raised before his tent for the security of his person.

The day following the bridge was finished, which the King had caused to be built over the *Vistula*, out of cannon-shot from the town, to open a free communication with the troops encamped on the opposite side.

At the same time the Major-Generals *Ridderbielm* and *Nieroth* were detached with their regiments of horse, in order to penetrate farther up into the country, as well to furnish us with necessary forage, as to escort the provisions which should be brought to the camp, and above all, to have an eye on the *Lithuanian* army, which pretended that they would march towards *Thorn* and attack us.

Some time afterwards the regiment of horse-guards, with Colonel *Axel Sparr* at the head of some hundred foot, were ordered to join the Major-Generals, which they did without delay, and posted themselves all together in the little town of *Strasburg* on the *Dribentz*, whence they laid all the neighbourhood under contribution; and in order to have always a free communication with the army, they put a garrison into *Gollup*, which is on the *Dribentz* half way, or thereabouts.

At length, as the time approached for the opening of the General Diet, convened at *Lublin* on the 9th of *June*, King *Augustus* came thither from *Warsovia*, where he had remained some weeks. He arrived on the 7th, and was follow'd by the *English* and *Dutch* Ministers, who presented him with their credentials on the road, without

without being able however to give him the least hope of any accommodation.

The Diet being assembled on the 9th, while the *Russian* Pospolite met likewise some leagues from thence, the first thing they did was to elect a Marshal of the Chamber of the Provincial Deputies; and the choice fell on Prince *Wisniowiski* the younger, a *Lithuanian*, and consequently of King *Augustus*'s party.

The King then proposed to them 16 articles, which all turned on this question: *Whether the Republick ought to prefer the friendship of* Muscovy *to that of* Sweden, *in order to arrive at a firm and immediate peace?* It is easy to imagine to which side their inclinations leaned. The exclusion of the Deputies of the higher *Poland* came next on the carpet. It was alledged as a pretence, that their Provincial Diet had been broken; but the true reason was, that this part of the kingdom had always vehemently opposed the war with *Sweden*, and they feared lest those Deputies should be sent, by the adherents of *Sapieha*, to kindle a faction in their favour. This exclusion of the Deputies gave them such a shock, that, binding themselves closely together, they at last concluded a formal confederacy.

After the Deputies had retired, a great outcry was raised in the Diet against the *Sapieha* and against the Cardinal; but to the great surprize of the Court, that Prelate arrived six days after the opening. He set out from *Warsovia*, after having writ a letter to the King of *Sweden* on the 2d of *June*, to dissuade him from the siege of *Thorn*, as it was a town belonging to the Republick. The Court was much troubled at his arrival; for they had flattered themselves with his

his absence, by which means they might more easily have succeeded, either by persuasion or force, in their projects; which were to declare war against *Sweden*; to make an alliance with the Czar, and with *Denmark*; to condemn the *Sapieha*; and to annul the primatical dignity.

The Cardinal entered the town, as it were, in triumph, attended by his own retinue, and a numerous train of several Senators and Lords, who went out to meet him. He immediately sent one of his relations to the King to compliment his Majesty, and demand an audience; but was much surprized at the coldness with which his relation was received, and to hear, at the same time, that the audience was refused him. Which refusal was founded on an imagination that the Cardinal would not come to the Senate; he took, however, a resolution to go thither without having paid his respects to the King; which determined his Majesty to give him an audience three days afterwards. They had used many endeavours to bring him into the views of the court, but that Prelate always strongly opposed them, and would never take the least step, which might be looked on as an effect of weakness or cowardice. He had his public audience when the King was on the point of going to the Senate, whither he accompanied him, and took his place, without waiting till he was called.

The affair of the Cardinal coming on the carpet, some of the Deputies would have declar'd the dignity of Primate vacant, as well as that of Archbishop, being desirous to make him pass for a traitor to his country, and a partizan of *Sweden*. Tho' he was accused of enormous crimes, and loaded with injuries, he did not attempt to defend himself, but heard all with patience, as he saw the assembly

assembly prejudiced and enraged against him, flattering himself that he should be able, by that means, to appease the first emotions of their anger. However, to exculpate himself, he desired that he might conform with the rest, and take an oath to the King, and to the Republic; which he instantly did, and all the Senators, and Members of the lower Chamber, even those who had not assisted at the great Councils of *Thorn* and *Marienburg*, followed the example of the Primate, and took an oath of fealty.

The Party of King *Augustus*, surprized at the Cardinal's constancy, sought after new opportunities to raise a storm against him, as well as Mr. *Towianski*, Palatine of *Lencini*, and his son, who was the Cardinal's minion. But after his Eminence had given a full scope to the animosity of the Nuncios, he ventured to speak at another sitting, which he did with so much force and vivacity, that he entirely removed from the assembly all the suspicions which had been raised against him.

It was remarked, that the profound silence of the lower Chamber, and the attention which they gave to the Primate's discourse, caused great uneasiness in the King. He afterwards spoke twice himself, and dwelt much on the blindness of the Republic, her disquiet, and weakness in the support of the liberty of her country. This he did with such violence, that the tables were soon turned.

The Nuncios, emboldened by this discourse, recovered their vigour, and spoke with more freedom: they exaggerated the elogiums of the Cardinal so far, as to call him the Father of his country.

The

1703. The diet, however, came to a resolution, which we shall mention a little lower, and the affair of the *Sapieha* was concluded with more moderation. The alliances with the Czar and *Denmark* were carried in the negative, as was the incorporating the *Saxon* troops with those of the Crown.

During these transactions, the King of *Sweden* answered, on the 29th of *May*, the letter which the Cardinal had writ to him, to dissuade him from the siege of *Thorn*. His Majesty, a little afterwards, sent Count *Stenbock* to *Dantzick*, to hasten the transport of the artillery, which would be necessary for that siege, in case the garrison would not capitulate before they were attacked in form.

The Count, immediately on his arrival at *Dantzick*, sent Couriers to *Riga* and *Carelscroon* to press the transportation; but as the convoy did not arrive in the road of *Dantzick* till the end of *June*, Count *Stenbock* made in the mean while his propositions to the Magistrates, to pay a pretty considerable sum of money to the King, in the form of a contribution. The town appeared strangely alarmed with this demand, and would willingly have avoided the taking a step which must be very disadvantageous, and of great consequence to them for the future. But as they entered immediately into serious reflection on the past wars, where their obstinacy in not paying had drawn great inconveniencies on them; and as they heard besides, that a new fleet was on the point of appearing in their road from *Sweden*, they conformed to his Majesty's will, and agreed with the Count to pay him in all 100,000 crowns, desiring, nevertheless, to reserve certain articles

very

King Charles XII. of Sweden.

very favourable to their commerce, but which were entirely refused them.

The town of *Elbing* was summoned at the same time by the Count, to pay their contributions to the King, which the Magistrates had the boldness to refuse, though the citizens offered willingly to comply; and we shall soon see the severity with which that town was punished for their refusal.

The garrison of *Thorn*, in the mean while, began by little and little to diminish, by the distempers occasioned through their fatigues, and want of necessary refreshments; not to mention their magazine, which was infinitely exhausted. They were obliged to keep from the troops a part of their ordinary allowance. However, as they had a large provision of powder and ball, they were extremely prodigal on that head, and fired on our quarters without cessation.

It is astonishing that his Majesty, who with his usual intrepidity visited the posts every day, and approached so near the town, that the Gunners were (if I may so express myself) obliged to fire several times at his little body of attendants, during the whole siege received no wound, nor did any of his attendants; for the balls flew either over their heads, or between the legs of their horses, or else past by them.

But what is as surprizing, and what is rarely practised among polite nations was, that they spar'd the King's quarters no more than the others, tho' it is usual to have the same regard and respect for those tents, as for crowned heads. At their morning and evening fire they never failed to distinguish the head quarters, where every one was in the greatest danger of their lives; and one morning particularly a bullet flew directly towards
the

the King's tent, but as it was wet, had not sufficient force to pass through it (ᵏ).

To replace the regiments of *Ridderhielm* and *Nieroth*, the King brought up Major-general *Morner*, with his regiment of horse, from *Rheinschild*'s army, which lay at four leagues distance; and ordered them to encamp on the *Vistula*, below the town, where the regiment of foot guards was likewise posted soon afterwards. His Majesty sent orders also to the same army to bring up two companies of *Lithuanians*, one of which, after having been some time at the camp, was detached with Colonel *Meyerfeld*, to join *Ridderhielm* and *Nieroth*, and to assist in the levying contributions.

About this time the Crown army, which might amount in the whole to 4000 men, joined the *Saxon* and *Lithuanian* bodies, who were posted at *Pultowsk*.

As these last had formed a resolution to deliver the town of *Thorn*, they thought that the conjunction of all those troops would furnish them with means of executing their project; a very fine one, if they had had courage to support so noble and bold an undertaking, which ended in only sending out parties with great diligence to discover what *Ridderhielm* and *Nie-*

ᵏ There is a circumstance in my father's journal, in regard to this, which I think not proper to be omitted. 'One morning, *(says he)* as I was in bed in my tent, near the King's quarters, I raised myself in my bed to give some orders to my servants. I had scarce laid down again, when a ball passed by, and broke a case of pistols to pieces which I had placed at my bed's head; the pieces of which fell on the bedsted with a violent noise. If I had not soon laid down again, this ball would infallibly have taken off my head.'

roth

roth were doing in their neighbourhood. A curiosity which cost them dear. For one of their parties, consisting of about 1000 *Poles*, under the command of *Potocki*, had the misfortune, together with some *Saxons*, to fall in with a *Swedish* detachment, who made ten of them prisoners, and killed a great number. This shock took from them all desire of giving us any farther trouble; nor did they any longer dare to think of raising the siege of *Thorn*, though they had given the strongest assurances of it to *Robel* and *Canitz*, by a letter which they had found means to convey into the town.

The enemy had, however, their revenge in *Ingria*. After they had taken *Noteburg*, *Nyenschantz*, and *Jama*, and built the fort of *S. Petersbourg*, the Czar turned towards *Finland* with part of his army, to attack Major-general *Cronbiort*, who had not quite 4000 men, both foot and horse. That General performed, nevertheless, whatever could be expected from an experienced officer.

To stop the torrent of so numerous an army, *Cronbiort* took possession of the pass at *Systerbek*, nine leagues from *Wibourg*, where he was attacked by 25,000 *Russians*, who had marched through defiles, morasses and woods, which were believed impassable. The battle lasted from six in the morning till two in the afternoon, with great obstinacy on both sides.

The *Russians*, who returned always to the charge with fresh troops, at last won the day, and forced the Major-general to think of a retreat before it was cut off, which was performed with so much order and boldness, that the enemy could never break the least line of our men, nor take from them their baggage and artillery. *Cronbiort*

biort then posted himself half a league from the field of battle, where he always repulsed the enemy, who undertook to force his new post.

His admirable disposition astonished the *Russians*, who lost all appetite of returning to the charge; and Mr. *Cronbiort* thought proper to take an opportunity, in the night, of retreating three quarters of a league from *Wibourg*. He lost in his whole retreat but 200 men killed, with four officers, but we do not include those who fell in the battle.

The regiment of *Tisenhausen* suffered much in this action. We had 171 men wounded, besides Lieutenant-colonel *Glasenapp*, Aid-de-camp-general *Armfelt*, Lieutenant-colonel *Leyon*, who lost an arm, with thirteen other officers.

When *Cronbiort* had arrived safely in the neighbourhood of *Wiburg*, he placed a battalion of foot in the town, which were followed by some others, who were all set to work on the fortifications. Baron *Lindhielm*, Governor of that province, was charged with the direction of the works; for they had no doubt of being visited by the *Russians* with the first opportunity. However, these undertook no such matter; but after burning *Walkisari*, and some other little places, killing or carrying away all they could find, they returned to *Nyen*, where they employed themselves in recruiting those regiments which had suffered the most at the battle of *Systenbek*. They provided themselves likewise with a good number of floats and bridges, to convey them into *Esthonia*, where they intended to attack *Schlippenbach*, as we learned from their deserters, and at the same time to take advantage of the harvest.

With this view they reinforced their detachment posted between *Nyen* and *Andowa*, and drew

together

together a considerable force near *Pitschur*, to make an irruption into *Livonia*, on that side near *Dorpt*.

But to return to the diet of *Lublin*, which concluded with great satisfaction to King *Augustus*; the articles of the convocation which we mentioned above, purported,

1. That, to augment the Crown army to 30,000 men, and that of *Lithuania* to 12,000, the fourth penny should be paid on all liquors; that a poll-tax should be levied to pay the arrears due to the army; and, for an acquittance of the Elector of *Brandenbourg*'s pretensions on the town of *Elbing*, every mill in the kingdom should pay two crowns.

2. That they should give the King of *Sweden* six weeks, to declare either for war or peace.

3. That the *Sapiehas* should be declared rebels, if after six weeks, which they further allowed them, they did not surrender themselves to the King; that they might in that case hope to preserve some of their offices and goods, otherwise the whole should be confiscated.

4. That no more thoughts should be entertained of dethroning King *Augustus*.

5. That, if the King of *Sweden* would not accept a reasonable peace, but would continue the war, King *Augustus* might enter into an alliance with what powers he thought proper.

6. That, when the troubles are quieted, the King shall be permitted to visit his hereditary dominions, as often as he thinks convenient, without being obliged to consult the Republic on those occasions.

1703. The Cardinal was afterwards obliged, by a *Senatus Concilium*, to reply to the King of *Sweden*'s letter of the 29th of *May*, which was in anfwer to one from his Eminence of the 23d of that month: but the Primate would not undertake it, at leaft unlefs the Commiffaries of the Republic would write at the fame time, which they did on the 12th of *July*, acquainting his *Swedifh* Majefty that they had been confirmed in their commiffion, and expected that he would fend Deputies, to enter into a negotiation for peace, in behalf of the Republic.

They at firft declared, that as the Republic had by a new oath bound themfelves to the King her mafter; and that his Majefty had by a new diploma engaged inviolably to preferve all her laws, liberties, immunities and treaties of peace, they were charged, by virtue of the fundamental laws of the kingdom, and of this new diploma, to make the following propofitions in the name of the Republic.

1. The articles of *Oliva*, as well as all the other treaties concluded with the Kings and Kingdom of *Sweden*, fhould be religioufly obferved, renewed and confirm'd by a new mutual engagement on oath.

2. It fhall be fo ordered, that the auxiliary troops fhall not remain in the kingdom, and the great dutchy of *Lithuania*, any longer than the continuance of the war, and fhall return thither no more, on any pretence whatfoever.

3. Care fhall be taken that his *Polifh* Majefty, or his fucceffors, fhall not make any alliance with the neighbouring Princes, nor any foreign Potentate, without the confent of the Republic; and that any fuch alliance fhall be declared void on the part of *Poland*.

4. His

4. His *Polish* Majesty, and his successors, shall be hindered from bringing, either directly or indirectly, by themselves or others, their own troops, or those of sovereign Powers either by sea or land, into the Kingdom of *Sweden*, and the provinces under her dependence; and they shall make no war or incursion there, much less suffer any troops to pass thither through *Poland*, or her frontiers.

5. Nothing shall be neglected to prevent his *Polish* Majesty, or his successors, from furnishing any subsidy or troops to the declared enemies of *Sweden*.

6. Matters shall be so regulated, that for the future none of the *Polonese* shall undertake enterprizes of this nature, without the knowledge of the Republic; and that if any one shall dare to enter on such forbidden measures, he shall be declared a disturber, and punished as a criminal.

7. Lastly, That the foregoing propositions, and those which shall be interchanged by the Commissaries, may be faithfully observed, the Estates of the Kingdom of *Poland*, and of the Great Dutchy of *Lithuania*, and of the allied Provinces, engage, in case of any breach whatever, to unite against those who break it, and to send their troops to the assistance of the party offended, for the preservation of peace and the laws; for which they desire a reciprocal security may be given.

The Cardinal, before he quitted *Lublin*, writ at the same time with the Commissaries, a very respectful letter to the King of *Sweden* on this head, who answered on the 21st of *July*; and at the same time ordered Count *Piper* to write to the Commissaries of *Poland*, that his Majesty would

would willingly hearken to their propositions, but remained firm in his resolutions, absolutely to place no reliance on the promises of King *Augustus*, though seconded by all the guaranty and assurance which the Republic could give him. At last, though the Commissaries, and particularly Count *Morstein*, did their utmost to renew the affair, and though the foreign Ministers joined their endeavours also to bring it to an issue, they could gain no ground, and the negotiation was entirely broke up by the steadiness of the King, who demanded the dethroning his enemy, who had so often broke his word, and of whose promises he could make no account. After the diet was separated, the *Imperial*, *English* and *Dutch* Ministers, sent their Secretaries to *Thorn*, who went down the *Vistula*, to inform his Majesty of all that had passed in this assembly.

Notwithstanding all the fair promises of the *Poles* to assist King *Augustus*, we continued to push the siege of *Thorn*, with all possible vigour. The transports from *Sweden* were already arrived in the road of *Dantzick*; and, some days after, others came from *Riga* with the heavy artillery. As the recruits for the army were without officers, his Majesty dispatched a proper number, chose out of the *Drabans* and Foot-guards, with orders to conduct them to the camp forthwith.

King *Augustus* being arrived from *Lublin* at *Otfock* (a castle belonging to Mr. *Bielinski*, Grand-marshal of the Crown, and situated a league from *Warsaw*) ordered a bridge to be thrown across the *Vistula* at *Prague*, over which he filed off the *Lithuanian* Army, and the *Saxons* who came from *Pultowsk*, in order to be nearer *Thorn*. Their design was to attack our troops, which were encamped on that side, while the garrison

made

made a vigorous sally, and endeavoured to join them at the same time: by this expedient *Augustus* hoping to preserve his best infantry, which he deemed in extreme danger in case it failed.

In the interval that Prince ordered a detachment to march into *Upper Poland*, both to reduce the Nobles, who began to be regarded and were now to be treated as rebels, and likewise to observe more closely the movements of the army under General *Rheinschild*, which gave him great uneasiness.

Prince *Wisniowiski* had obtain'd the chief command of the troops sent on this service, which had given such umbrage to Prince *Lubomirski*, that he continued at *Warsaw* without any inclination to follow it. He pretended it was against the laws of the realm, to admit the *Lithuanians* without the consent of the Republic. But this gave the King so little pain, that he left him to cool at leisure, persuading himself he would be easily regained, which actually succeeded soon after.

On the other side, General *Brand* was on the watch for all opportunities to surprize the *Swedes*, who were encamped in the neighbourhood of *Strasburg* and *Neumarck*, and who had sent out detachments as far as *Lauterburg* to raise contributions: Intelligence of which being brought to that General, and that one of these parties still remained there, he marched immediately with all his forces, amounting to 6 or 7000 men, in quest of them. As all the inhabitants were fled, and Major *Charles Creutz* of the Horse-Guards, who was the commanding officer, could not be apprized of the enemy's approach, he was attacked by them so suddenly, that he had scarce

1703 time to put his little troop, of about 400 horse, in a posture of defence.

They however behaved with such gallantry, that Mr. *Brand*, having made his utmost efforts to break through them, and being always repulsed with loss, at last gave orders for all his Dragoons to alight, while the horse entered the town in another place, to attack them on all sides at once. *Creutz* then seeing himself surrounded, had now nothing to do, but force his way sword in hand; which he executed with all imaginable bravery, bearing down all before him, and plunging into a pretty rapid stream, which he swam across, and happily landed on the other side; losing in the action, and in the water, a Captain, a Lieutenant, and near 180 Troopers, of which some were made prisoners, and conducted to *Warsaw*, whence they were afterwards exchanged against the *Saxons* taken at *Thorn*. The enemy, extremely surprized at the prompt resolution and intrepidity of *Creutz* in passing the river, durst not pursue him, but let him return quietly to *Neumarck*, having received but a slight contusion in the action.

Immediately upon his arrival there, Major-General *Nieroth* put himself at the head of his regiment, and, taking *Creutz* with him, marched full speed towards *Lauterburg*, where *Brand* yet remained in suspence; but, fearing at last he should be attacked in his turn, retired as fast as possible, not caring to hazard a second engagement. Mr. *de Nieroth*, at his arrival, having caused the dead to be interred, and gathered together certain of the wounded, who had hid themselves in the wood, returned to *Neumarck*, whither the King a few days after sent a reinforcement

forcement of 500 men, to secure them more effectually from the insults of the enemy.

Upon another side, Prince *Wisniowiski* and Mr. *Steinau* approached with their army, within seven leagues of *Thorn*, to put in execution the project which they had form'd, to save, if possible, the fine garrison inclosed in that city. But, as they had learned his Majesty had thrown yet another bridge over the *Vistula*, to render the communication more easy with the troops encamped on the other side, they had not the courage to attack us. Their parties however approach'd frequently so near our advanced guards, that they were obliged to fire upon them. The *Saxons* in *Thorn* on their parts likewise made a sally; but, in passing over the boats, to see if the succours promised them were arrived, and also to conduct certain head of cattle into the city, were repulsed and compelled to give over their design.

Prince *Wisniowiski* seeing then the impossibility of saving that city, wheel'd all at once towards *Great Poland*, in order to dissipate the confederates, who increased in numbers every day; and had not only elected a Marshal, but even assembled publickly in the little city of *Skroda*, deliberating on the state of the Republic, protesting against all the pernicious decrees of the Diet of *Lublin*, and entreating the Cardinal to place himself at their head.

General *Rheinschild*, who had marched from *Konari* to *Ruski*, *June* the 3d, from thence to *Scarzino* the 15th, the 17th to *Colo*, and the 1st of *July* to the city of *Camia*; from whence he turned towards *Great Poland* to procure intelligence of the confederates; proceeding the 13th to *Jagorow*, and the 16th to *Zirkzow*, an estate

belonging

1703. belonging to the General of *Great Poland*, a partizan of King *Auguſtus*; where having reſted till the 13th of *Auguſt*, he marched on to the little town of *Pizdri*; and, being here inform'd of the march and approach of Prince *Wiſniowiſki*, he decamped the next morning, and marched ſtrait on to *Wrezna*, a ſmall town two leagues from *Skroda*, in order to protect the confederates: ſome days after which he detached Lieutenant-Colonel *Konigsheim* to obſerve the motions of the enemy.

Who, having had advice about five leagues from thence, that *Wiſniowiſki* was yet thirteen leagues off, and that a party of 500 *Valoches* had paſſed within half a league of him to *reconnoitre* the army of *Rheinſchild*, believed it his duty to attack them. Accordingly he marched after them, encounter'd and defeated them, taking a pair of kettle-drums, and certain priſoners; after which he poſted himſelf in the village of *Mielezun*, and intrenched himſelf in the beſt manner he could.

But as misfortune would have it, a famous *Lithuanian* leader called *Bandonir*, who, by the order of *Wiſniowiſki*, had lain concealed in an adjoining wood with twelve companies of *Valoches*, ſix troops of *Pancernes*, two companies of *Tartars*, 280 *German* Horſe, 400 Dragoons, and 600 *Saxons*, ruſhed out ſuddenly on Mr. *Konigsheim*, and attacked him ſo briſkly, that, finding himſelf ſurrounded on all ſides, and oppreſſed with numbers, he was obliged to ſurrender himſelf priſoner, together with Mr. *Funk* Captain of Dragoons, having firſt ſeen an hundred of his men killed. General *Rheinſchild*, who was ſoon apprized of this incident, flew thither with two regiments of Dragoons to ſuſtain his party, and

repulſe

repulse the enemy, but arrived too late, they being already retired to the little town of *Slupsie*, and, tho' he pursued them even thither, found it impossible to overtake them, they having thought proper to make the best of their way, to avoid a second combat. Some days after the General made another visit to the same place, in hopes they would venture to return; but, finding the town deserted, he marched on to *Mielezun*, and the 29th to *Meroslaw*, a league and a half from *Skroda*, to be nearer the confederates, who, in the interval, had sent Deputies to *Wisniowiski*, to beseech him not to treat them as enemies.

Rheinschild, being obliged to decamp for want of forage, marched the 2d of *September* to *Kurnitz*, the house of a Nobleman, near the town of *Buny*, two leagues from *Posnania*. In passing by the camp of the confederates, they sent to desire he would not remain in that Palatinate; which message was owing to their Chiefs, who, having fair estates in those parts, were fearful those troops would prove but bad neighbours: But as Mr. *Rheinschild* gave them to understand, it was absolutely necessary for their safety that he should continue there, the enemy waiting only till his back was turned to waste all before them with fire and sword, they readily consented, and were afterwards highly pleased to be under his protection.

The Count *de Stenbock* had left *Oliva*, where he had been some time with his recruits, which amounted to some thousands of horse and foot, and a little after arrived happily in the camp before *Thorn*. His Majesty immediately distributed the infantry among the different regiments, and detached the cavalry under the command of *Rahsford*,

1705. *Ransford*, Adjutant of the *Drabans*, beyond *Dribentz* towards *Ploczko*, to oblige the Nobility to pay the contributions imposed upon them.

Some days after, the artillery and ammunition arrived on the vessels used in going up the *Vistula*, but could not reach *Thorn* by three leagues, because the water was then so extremely shallow; which obliged the King to transport the whole in waggons the rest of the way, not without infinite difficulty and labour; his Majesty himself attending to give the necessary orders, and exposing his person all the while to the fire of the enemy's cannon, one of which they actually levelled at him, and with so good an aim, that the ball grazed him in its passage, and imminently endangered his life. In the mean while a new reinforcement of troops arrived in the road of *Putsik*, a place seven leagues from *Dantzick*, in the possession of the King, who had caused it to be fortified, that he might have the command of a sea-port to serve him on all emergencies.

As soon as the artillery was in a condition for service, the King proceeded to attack the city with greater vigour than ever; and, not content with holding it blocked up, ordered a battery to be erected in a garden near the *Culm*-gate of four mortars and eight pieces of cannon, and, upon an adjoining eminence, another of six.

His Majesty order'd the trenches to be opened the 9th of *September*, between the hours of nine and ten at night, in two different places; *viz.* on the side of the *Vistula*, where a Major was posted, and at the foot of a hillock called *Bekersberg*; and, placing himself at the head of 800 infantry, who covered the pioneers, defeated the advanced guard of the enemy, taking a
Lieutenant

Lieutenant and six soldiers prisoners, and having six of his own wounded.

The works were carried on all night in profound silence, but being perceived at day-break by the *Saxons*, they made a terrible and continual fire upon us, both from the ramparts and a tower, where the citizens had mounted some cannon: notwithstanding which the King was always foremost to encourage the pioneers with his presence and forward the works. It happened the same day, that while he lean'd with his elbow on a parapet of fascines, and talked to the Colonel upon duty, a bullet passed between his arm and the parapet without doing him any harm; he barely smiling at the incident, without betraying the least emotion beside. As he every day visited the trenches, for the most part on horseback, it drew upon him a hail of musquet-balls from the enemy, which made every body tremble round him; but he always preserved the same tranquillity even in the midst of the greatest dangers.

On the side of the *Vistula* the trenches were carried on with the like industry. But the *Saxons* believing they should meet with fainter opposition there than at *Bekersberg*, made a sally with 200 of their best Granadiers, falling upon the peasants, who were cleansing the trench along the *Vistula*, and obliging them to retire. But the Baron *Erich Sparr*, who commanded that day, coming up, soon put these adventurers to flight, after having killed ten of their men, wounded a great many more, and pursued the rest to the very glacis of the counterscarp, the garrison looking coolly on from the top of the ramparts, without taking a step to sustain or relieve their fellow-soldiers. We had four men killed

1703. killed in this rencounter, and near upon twenty wounded.

We were never troubled with frolicks of this kind on the fide of *Bekerſberg*, but the garriſon continued a dreadful fire from their cannons and mortars, diſcharging from the laſt ſuch a quantity of ſtones, that we were obliged to build certain little outworks for our better ſecurity.

We had now a third battery erected near the *Viſtula*, which was mounted with twelve pieces of cannon; a fourth on the other ſide of the river with ſix 12 pounders; and a fifth cloſe under the city upon the hill of *Bekerſberg*.

As ſoon as theſe were in a condition to play, the King ordered them to fire from all at once. This began between four and five hours after it was dark, and continued without intermiſſion till break of day; and with ſuch ſucceſs, that we had ſcarce fired two hours before we ſaw the flames break out in three different places. One cannoneer in particular fired ſo exactly on the Town-houſe with a red-hot ball, that the ſteeple blazed out immediately like a flambeau, and ſet fire to that whole fine building. All the merchandizes laid up there were conſumed, as was likewiſe the corner of the market-place, where King *Auguſtus* had lodged; a magazine and ſeveral other houſes ſhared in the ſame fate.

This terrible fire continued all the following day till night, becauſe of the great number of bombs which we diſcharged inceſſantly. The damage which the poor city ſuffered, by the ruin of its churches and other fine buildings, was irreparable; and the miſchief ſpread the farther, as the inhabitants durſt not ſtir out to extinguiſh the flames.

In

In this distress, as they had several times already in vain solicited the commanding officer for leave to send deputies to the camp, they resolved to expose themselves to no more refusals; but, crowding in great numbers to the steeple nearest the walls, they sounded a trumpet, to express the extremity to which they were reduced. But this step so exceedingly incensed Mr. *de Canitz*, that he put them all into prison, and treated them with great severity.

The same day the King caused certain mortars to be transported from the battery before the *Culm*-gate to that near the *Vistula*, which was commanded by Mr. *de Bunow*, Lieutenant-Colonel of the Artillery; because the magazines of powder, which the *Saxons* preserved in the cloisters of the *Dominicans*, and in their neighbourhood, were more remarkably exposed on that side; after which we began again to bombard the city with great violence, and fired it in several places; but the flames were almost as soon extinguished as they broke out, by the indefatigable endeavours of the Governor, who had now learned more experience, by having suffered so greatly from the first bombs that were thrown.

It was during this siege, that by order of General *Rheinschild* the Baron *de Mardfeld* took possession of the city of *Posnania*, by whom the fact was related in the following manner.

' After the arrival of General *Rheinschild* the
' 2d of *September* with his army at *Kurnik*, situ-
' ated about two leagues from *Posnania*, he de-
' tached the same evening Lieutenant-Colonel
' *Wrangel*, of the regiment *de Horn*, with 200
' horse, to escort Captain *Funk* of the regiment
' of Dragoon-Guards, who, in quality of Com-
' missary,

' miffary, was to make certain propofitions to
' the city of *Pofnania* ; becaufe no queftion was
' made of its being difpofed to fubmit on any
' reafonable terms that fhould be offered.

' The detachment being arrived, and Mr.
' *Funk* with two other perfons admitted and
' heard by the Magiftrates, they told him, *They*
' *would confider of it*, without any farther expla-
' nation. The Captain having waited feveral
' days without bringing them to reafon, or ob-
' taining any pofitive determination, fent advice
' to the General of all which had paffed, that
' he might take fuch farther meafures as he
' thought proper; who, feeing there was no
' longer any hope of obtaining any thing by fair
' means of the inhabitants, refolved on the 6th
' of *September*, towards noon, to difpatch thi-
' ther Colonel *Gabriel Lilliehoeck* and Lieutenant-
' Colonel *Waidenheim* with 200 *Smolanders* and
' 200 of the regiment *de Sudermanlande*, all in-
' fantry, and four field-pieces, with orders to
' be there towards evening, and endeavour to
' carry the place by furprize; adding by way of
' reinforcement 100 of the Dragoon-Guards,
' commanded by Captain *Ornftedt*.

' The next morning, when it was broad day-
' light, an officer of the party returned to the
' General, to acquaint him that there was more
' difficulty than he could forefee to execute his
' orders; upon which I was commanded to re-
' pair thither forthwith with certain horfe for an
' efcort, to deliberate on the affair, and act as
' occafion offered. I got there by noon, and
' found Meffieurs *de Lilliehoek*, *de Waidenheim*,
' *Wrangel*, and *Funk*, meditating how to execute
' the orders they had received. They told me
' they had ladders, together with boats and lit-
' tle

'tle prames, all ready to pass the *Warta*, which washed the walls of the town, but believed it necessary to wait the return of the night before the attack was made. Captain *Funk* likewise laid before me a plan of the city and its works, which I found sufficiently exact, as near as I could guess, by surrounding the place.

'While I was yet employed in making this tour, I received a letter from General *Rheinschild*, signifying, that the Magistrates had solicited some days respite to consider more maturely what was to be done: But having received intelligence that they had sent to *Wisniowiski* for succours at the same time, he had thought proper to allow them but one hour.

'When this term was expired, without waiting for the 200 men, which the General purposed to send to me towards night, I determined to make two attacks on the place; one under the command of Colonel *Lillieboek* with 200 men, on the *Gerber Schantz*, and the other with 200 more, commanded by Lieutenant Colonel *Waidenheim*, on the work of *Breslau*. Having regulated the order of the march, Lieutenant-Colonel *Wrangel*, at the head of 100 horse, posted himself before one of the gates, *Ornstedt* with a like number before a second, and a Captain, who had 100 more under his command, was ordered to observe all that passed round the whole city, to prevent all surprize from the enemy. I made this arrangement behind the *Bernardine*-cloisters, whence we could march under cover within forty paces of the fortifications, which were all filled with people with pikes and other arms, who seemed to threaten us with

'an

'an obstinate defence. I then gave order, in
'case of resistance, to spare none who were
'found in arms; but at the same time expressly
'forbid the firing on the wretched out-works
'of the city, or on a party of beggars, about
'60, which the citizens had for soldiers, nei-
'ther of which were worth powder and shot.

'About four o' clock in the afternoon I gave
'order for the assault; but, when I was arriv-
'ed at the town-ditch, I saw issuing out of
'the gate of *Breslau* a person with a flag of
'truce, who blew a trumpet, and cried out,
'*The city would surrender.* To which I an-
'swered, the Magistrates should then immedi-
'ately bring me the keys: But as they de-
'murred to this reply too long, I ordered the
'scaling-ladders to be fixed, and the ramparts
'to be mounted sword in hand. The conster-
'nation of the citizens was then so great, that,
'being likewise at variance among themselves,
'they knew not what they did; some inclining
'to fire, and others forbidding it; and one
'among the rest attempting to discharge a can-
'non, a second caught him round the middle,
'and threw him off the walls.

'While all this was transacting I was before
'the gates, and forced them open without delay.
'The horse being enter'd, drew up, together
'with the infantry, in the market-place; after
'which having posted sufficient guards on the
'gates, I ordered the Magistrates to attend me,
'who immediately obeyed; and, presenting me
'with the keys of the city, I reprimanded them
'severely for not having sent them at my first
'approach, and for their having behaved in so
'stubborn a manner. I then put them all un-
'der arrest in the town-house, and order'd the

'citizens

'citizens to surrender their arms, as likewise to
'pay instantly 1000 crowns to the soldiers to re-
'deem the city from plunder.

'After having given the necessary orders for
'the defence of the place in case of an attack,
'I sent back in the morning to the camp at
'*Kurnyk* the reinforcement of 200 infantry,
'which came in the night with Mr. *de Wrangel*,
'the 200 horse, and the four field-pieces; and
'some days after repaired thither myself.

ARWID AXEL MARDEFELDT.

In this manner, without losing a man, or striking a blow, we became masters of a city well furnished with cannon and other arms, and populous enough to have made a brave defence, if the burghers had been united among themselves.

Some days after the reduction of the place, a letter from King *Augustus* to the Magistrates was intercepted, in which he exhorted them to hold out as long as possible, promising them immediate succour if they behaved as valiantly as might be reasonably expected from them. But this encouragement came too late, and the city was obliged, for having so long delay'd opening her gates, to pay a considerable sum of money, and furnish large contributions to the army. This conquest was so much the more important, as it enabled us to cover the assembly of the confederates, and, at the same time, keep them both in respect and awe, in case they took any measures contrary to the interest of his *Swedish* Majesty; and as it afforded us beside a safe retreat both for our baggage and wounded men.

But care was taken to render it more defensible; and the works, that were most debilitated, were put in repair forthwith. Col. *Lilliebock* had the command of it; and General *Rheinschild*, to take away all suspicion from the Confederates, immediately imparted to them his success, which was received even better than there was room to hope; they not only declaring themselves satisfied, but intreating the General to continue a strong garrison there, in case he himself should be obliged to march at a greater distance from it.

He likewise concluded, very reasonably, that the King of *Sweden*'s manifesto, which he communicated to them at the same time, and by which he assured the Confederates of his protection, had contributed to render them so tractable; and so much the more, as his Majesty threatened to use with the utmost rigour all such who declared themselves in favour of the Diet of *Lublin*. This extremely raised their courage, and animated them to pursue their design with vigour; which they declared was principally to maintain religion, preserve their liberties, and the publick peace, without any prejudice to the duty they owed King *Augustus*. They likewise proposed to mediate a stable and solid peace between the Kings of *Sweden* and *Poland*; in which view they had already sent a deputation, as well to King *Augustus* to assure him of their fidelity, to the Cardinal, to the army of the crown, as to the King of *Sweden*, to acquaint them all with their genuine sentiments.

Tho' it was with regret King *Augustus* gave these Deputies audience, he submitted to it notwithstanding: But the concession had not force enough to soften the resentments of the *Poles*;

on the contrary, as tho' it was by contagion, many other Palatinates joined with *Great Poland*, till the Confederacy infenfibly became univerfal, and tended finally to declare the throne vacant.

At the fame time the Palatine of *Pofnania*, whom the Confederates had fent to Prince *Wifniowifki*, fo effectually perfuaded him that his principals had no other end in view but the publick good, and confequently very ill deferv'd to be treated as publick enemies, that, all at once, he took a refolution to return into *Lithuania* with his whole army. Accordingly the crown-troops immediately divided from the *Saxons*, taking their rout to *Lemberg*, and the *Saxons* theirs to *Cracow* by the way of *Pierekow*.

While the enemy's forces in *Poland* were thus difperfing, the *Czar* prepared to make an irruption into *Livonia* and *Efthonia*, and actually effected it in the beginning of *September*, when he departed from *Nyen* with confiderable forces and twenty-four pieces of cannon ; and in his way paffing over the river near *Narva* to *Wefenberg*, he reduced that place to afhes, and laid all its appendages in ruins.

Major-General *Schlippenbach* was pofted at *Sommerfhaufen* near *Wefenberg*, and immediately difpatched Lieutenant-Colonel *Freiman* at the head of a party to *reconnoitre* the enemy. *Frieman*, having rencontred their advanced guard while preparing a bridge, deftroyed it ; but, as *Schlippenbach* found himfelf too weak to hinder the repairing it, much lefs refift fuch formidable forces, he retired under the cannon of *Revel*, to throw himfelf into that city in cafe the enemy threatened him with an attack.

The *Ruffians*, not thinking themfelves obliged to run their heads againft ftone-walls, and aim-

1703. ing at nothing but to ravage the open country, marched with all their forces from *Wefenberg* to *Kolka*, from thence to *Wittenftein* and other places, where they committed great diforders, and laid all wafte with fire and fword.

Another body of thefe troops having enter'd into *Livonia*, on the fide of *Pinfchur*, behaved there in the fame dreadful manner, carrying away all the young people, and maffacring all the old. After having fpent the whole campaign in deftroying the diftricts of *Gerven* and *Wirlande*, which make full half of *Efthonia*, and reduced to afhes the fuburbs of *Dorpt*, with the towns of *Wolmar, Wenden, Walk, Kalkus, Felin, Oberpahlen*, and half-burnt *Ruygen*, with *Mentfen* and *Sagnitz*, they repaffed the frontier with threats to return very fpeedily to *Narva*, which they propofed to befiege in form, having held it in a manner blocked up ever fince the taking of *Jama*; from whence they made continual inroads, and hindered all provifions from being thrown in for the fupport of the garrifon.

It is true, the *Dutch* greatly contributed to thefe devaftations of the *Ruffians*, by having furnifhed them with all forts of arms and ammunition, Mr. *Schlippenbach* having himfelf feen no lefs than nine large fhips of that nation under fail near *Affariem*. Very lively complaints were made to the Minifter of the States at *Stockholm* of this proceeding; but he threw all the blame on private adventurers, whofe conduct was highly difapproved by the Republic.

The fiege of *Thorn* ftill continued, and the King (*Sept.* 27.) growing impatient of wafting fo much time in reducing it, refolved to make a third attack near the new ravelin of the *Saxons*, and the garden which led to the tile-kiln. Having

ing possess'd himself of the last during the night, he ordered a line to be drawn towards the tile-kiln, which, in the morning, so greatly surprized the *Saxons*, that they thought fit to capitulate, and accordingly beat a parley forthwith. But the King, who was then in the trench, would give no ear to it; but pushing on the work with vigour, caused a new battery to be raised, mounted with 48 pounders, which were soon in a condition to play.

The next morning a Drum from the besieged presented a letter from the commanding officer, but was answered, that his Majesty accepted no other terms but that of surrendering at discretion. But though the garrison were extremely weakened by sickness and scarcity of provisions, they thought those conditions so severe, that they resolved to defend themselves to the last extremity.

A new battery on the *Vistula* being now completed, the whole six at once began a most terrible fire upon the city, which was returned by the enemy with wonderful ardour. The same day his Majesty resolved to attack an island over-against the city, which the *Saxons* had fortified both from the *Vistula* and the opposite shore, ordering the infantry for this purpose to march down to the side of the river, and embark themselves near the bridge of boats.

The Governor, perceiving all these movements, as likewise that the trench was advanced within a stone's cast of the counterscarp, thought it high time to submit to the King's pleasure; for which end he desired a conference with certain officers of distinction. The King then countermanded his troops which were preparing for the assault, and sent Mr. *Duker*, his Aid-de-Camp-General, into

into the city to confer with the *Saxon* Generals, who at last agreed to surrender at discretion.

Mr. *Duker* returned with this news to the King, who complimented both the Generals and Officers of the enemy with their swords and baggage. In the morning his Majesty order'd Count *Gaspar Sperling* to take possession of the city-gates with one battalion of guards, and disarm the garrison at the same time. Towards noon the Generals *Robel* and *Canitz*, with the Counts *de Reuss* and *Goltz*, Colonels, and many other Officers, came out to pay their compliments to the King. His Majesty kept the Generals and Colonels to dine with him, and received Mr. *de Canitz* in particular in the most gracious manner. Count *Sperling* also magnificently regaled in the city all the Officers of the garrison, the King having ordered 50 dishes out of his own kitchen for that purpose. At the same time a great number of sheep and cattle were drove into the city for the relief of the poor soldiers and citizens, who were almost famished.

In this manner King *Augustus* lost his best infantry, who could make no farther resistance, as having scarce any bread remaining; the rest of their provisions being likewise consumed, the garrison were reduced to live upon rotten herrings, which spread so inveterate a scurvy among the troops, that no more than 1583 men were capable of service, the remaining 2499 being disabled by the disease, and in their beds. 100 of their dragoons out of 188 were in the same condition, as were 282 artillery-men out of 509.

Among the prisoners were 2 Generals, 2 Colonels, 6 Lieutenant-Colonels, 9 Majors, 46 Captains, and 113 Lieutenants and Ensigns, all which

which had the compliment of their swords on their parole.

A great quantity of ammunition was yet remaining in the city, but the cannons and mortars were near worn out by the continual fire which had been made from the 16th of *May*, when the place was first blocked up, to the 3d of *October*, when it surrendered; towards the evening of which day, the whole army being under arms, his Majesty order'd a double discharge to be made, both from the cannons of the ramparts and those of the batteries.

At the instances of the *Saxon* Generals, the King afterwards permitted Colonel *Goltz* to repair to King *Augustus* at *Warsaw*, to acquaint him with all the particulars of the siege.

'Tis easy to judge how ill that Prince must have relished such disagreeable news, and above all the loss of his best infantry, which he regretted extremely. Some days after he departed from *Ottfok*, where he had been during that whole interval, and took the road to *Leopold*, to assemble the Senators and hold a council at *Jawarow*.

In the mean time the King ordered the fortifications of *Thorn*, which the *Saxons* had newly raised, at a great expence and much labour, to be totally demolished, as likewise the towers, from whence the citizens had annoy'd our troops; no more than the wall being left, just to defend the inhabitants from the inroads of the *Cossaques* and other military thieves. The Magistrates and Burghers were likewise obliged to lay down their arms, and likewise pay a large contribution to the King*.

The

* During the siege of *Thorn*, it was confidently affirmed in the publick news, that a *Saxon* officer, named *Muhlheim*, having quitted the city, and repaired to the *Swedish* camp

The LIFE and HISTORY of

The happy fuccefs of his Majefty's arms made fo much the greater impreffion on the Confederates, as their Deputies, being in the camp, were eye-witneffes of the glory which the King had acquired. They departed foon after, on the hopes he had given them of fending a perfon with certain propofals regarding the meafures he expected them to purfue; and Mr. *de Wachflager* was accordingly appointed for that fervice.

A great number of Deputies from the neighbouring Palatinates, as of *Dobrzin*, *Cujavia*, *Plotzko*, and of *Polifh Pruffia*, came to compliment his Majefty, and entreat they might be admitted into the number of the Confederates. His Majefty received them all very gracioufly, tho' it was eafy to perceive, that nothing but fear, and a defire to be foon difcharged from the contributions exacted by our troops, had prevailed with them to act in this manner. Neverthelefs, they deceived themfelves in this particular, the King refufing to remit thofe levies, to keep them within the bounds of refpect and obedience.

It was about this time that his *Swedifh* Majefty publickly acknowledged the Elector of *Branden-*

camp, pretending to be a deferter, and offering his fervice to the King to difcover the weakeft places of the fortifications, the King had twice walked out, accompanied by him only, to be let into thefe difcoveries; and that the third time the counterfeit fugitive threw himfelf at his Majefty's feet, declaring, that he was employed by General *Rebel* to affaffinate him, producing, at the fame inftant, a poinard from underneath his clothes, prepared for that purpofe; and adding, he was ready to die, as believing himfelf unworthy of life, after having embarked in fo execrable a defign.

It may have been thought, that there was fome truth in the narration; but there is not the leaft authority for it in the journal of my father, who would not have fail'd, according to his ufual exactnefs, to have mention'd it, if it had had the leaft foundation.

burg

burg as King of *Pruſſia*, which gave immediate rise to a report, that an important alliance was formed between the two Monarchs; a circumstance by no means favourable to the Republic, in case she refused to enter chearfully into a general Confederacy.

The *Swediſh* troops in *Courland* had frequent skirmishes with those of *Oginſki*, which, tho' always worsted, appeared nevertheless desirous of new trials. They for some time harassed Colonel *Banneer*, who was then ordered, together with Lieutenant-Colonel *Glaſenap* and 300 horse, to pass the frontiers and attack them, which he did *October* the 30th near *Janiſka*, and gave them an entire defeat.

The same night Lieutenant-Colonel *Lorentzen* marched from *Seelburg* with a detachment of infantry and 25 granadiers, and, paſſing the *Dwna*, proceeded to *Slaboda*, where he carried off the advanced guard, composed of certain companies of *Valoches*; after which he ſurprized the rest, 50 of whom were put to the sword, and 20 taken priſoners, together with a great number of horſes, without the loſs of a single man on our side.

Some days after, Colonel *Peſs* ordered Captain *Frommerie*, with 60 foot, to depart from *Bauſke* to levy contributions. In his return he fell in with 500 *Polanders*, conducting 20 waggons laden with provisions from *Courland* towards *Birſen*, who attacked him immediately, but were so warmly received, and so many of them killed, that they thought proper to retire, abandoning their convoy, which the Captain happily conducted into *Bauſke*.

About the same time eight companies of Dragoons and *Polanders*, commanded by a Major named *Broms*, carried off a party of ours poſted

at

at *Polangen*; which induced Colonel *Skytt*, who commanded at *Libau*, to detach 300 foot and horse, under the conduct of Major *Patkul*, with 100 of the troops of *Sapieha*, to give them chace. Captain *Metz*, who conducted the van with 50 horse and the *Polanders* of *Sapieha*, having fell in with them at *Cretingen*, attacked them immediately, killed 40, took 19 prisoners, and all their horses and baggage. Major *Patkul* being come up, they pursued the enemy, who, having been likewise reinforced, met us half way, and attacked *Patkul* in a certain village, but were repulsed with the loss of 40 men.

In the morning, the *Swedes*, being on their return to *Libau*, the enemy followed; and, overtaking them in a level field, near a bridge which they had already passed over, and where they drew up in order of battle, began their attack forthwith, but were repulsed and put to flight, returning over the bridge in confusion, and leaving above 50 men dead upon the spot. *Patkul* then continued his rout, but was again harassed by the enemy, who charged his rear, and were once more defeated with the loss of ten or a dozen men; after which they gave over the pursuit, and *Patkul* arrived happily at *Libau*.

After the reduction of *Thorn*, the Count *de Steinbock* had been sent to *Dantzick*, to take the necessary measures for transporting into *Sweden* the *Saxon* prisoners, and all the trophies atchieved in *Poland*; for which service several men of war were already arrived from *Carelscroon* in the road of that city.

At the same time his Majesty ordered one regiment after another to file off into the quarters prepared for them on the side of *Dantzick*; he himself still continuing before *Thorn*, till the sick

Saxons

Saxons were embarked, together with the artillery, to go down the *Vistula*, under the command of Colonel *Rank*, who was to escort them by water with his regiment. The other prisoners, with the three Generals *Beust*, *Robel*, and *Canitz*, and all the officers, followed some time after, guarded by a large detachment of dragoons. Some few were exchanged against the *Swedes* who were taken at *Warsaw*. The Count *de St. Paul*, Colonel, who had been made prisoner in the affair at *Pultowsk*, and was permitted to repair to *Warsaw* on his parole, for the cure of his wounds, obtained his liberty in exchange for Lieutenant-Colonel *Konigsheim* and Captain *Funk*, who returned to the army.

When the city of *Thorn* had paid the sum agreed upon, the King (*Novemb.* 11th) set out at the head of his Drabans, and crossed the *Vistula* near *d'Althusen* and the town of *Culm*, after having distributed his army along the borders of the river. His Majesty chose for his lodging the cloister of *Topolno*, five leagues from *Thorn*; the Drabans took up their quarters in the nearest villages on the side of the river, and the regiments of Foot-Guards in the towns of *Culm* and *Schwetz*.

In the morning the King repaired to *Dirschow*, about four leagues from *Dantzick*, to have an interview with the Count *de Steinbock* on the subject of the winter-quarters; when it was resolved upon to dispose the troops as well in the neighbourhood of *Dantzick*, *Marienburg*, and *Elbing*, as in the Bishoprick of *Warnice*. After which his Majesty returned on horseback, accompanied by the Prince of *Wurtemburg* and certain Officers, having rode thirty-two leagues in two days.

1703. The *Czar* returned to *Moscow* at the end of the campaign, after having sufficiently provided for the security of the frontiers, especially on the side of *Narva*, thinking of nothing now but how to render his entry into his capital more splendid and like a conqueror; for this end four triumphal arches were erected, under which he passed in a sledge, *Novemb.* 22d, followed by a superb train of Generals and other grand Lords. The poor peasants of *Livonia* and *Ingria* being led as in triumph between the ranks of the regiment of guards *Preubrasinski*, to induce the people to believe that 'twas a glorious campaign, which entertained them with the sight of such a number of prisoners.

King *Augustus*, on his side, being set out for *Jawarow*, as before mentioned, assembled there all the Senators of his party, to whom he strongly represented, that, having been authorized by the Diet of *Lublin* to contract alliances with foreign Princes, he could not believe they would dispute with him the privilege of sending a solemn embassy to the *Czar*, for the good of the Republic, who, being a Prince of great power and their near neighbour, and one who interested himself in the welfare of the Republic, might, by that means, be induced to exert himself in procuring her a safe and advantageous peace with *Sweden*.

He concluded with proposing the Palatine of *Culm* to negotiate this affair, and declaring that he was already on the road to *Moscow*. But Prince *Lubomirski*, with twelve other Senators, protested so vehemently against this measure, alledging, with great reason, it would be the means not only to retard the peace, but set the whole kingdom in a flame, that the King was obliged to

withdraw

withdraw his motion, and recall immediately the Palatine of *Culm*, by a solemn declaration made in council at *Jawarow*, *Novemb.* 24. Upon which occasion he extremely flattered the nation on the liberty he left in their hands, and added, that he would never violate it in the like circumstance. He was, however, so offended at the opposition that he had met with, that, under the pretence of the incommodiousness of so small a place to lodge so numerous an assembly, and of the Court itself's being greatly straitened in conveniencies, he adjourned the council, and retreated nearer *Saxony*, but without giving over his design of sending his Embassador to the *Czar*, as will presently be made appear.

As many Gentlemen had refused to join themselves with the Confederates, under the pretence of being obliged to reside at home to raise their quota of the contributions imposed upon them; General *Rheinschild*, who had orders to humour them as much as possible, removed the 19th of *September* from *Kurnik* to *Krotschin*, from thence the 24th to the little town of *Bobigecoski*, the 25th to *Klaskow*, the first of *October* to *Zornick*, and on the 3d gave his troops a few days rest at *Leknow*, two leagues from *Gnesnen*, being then out of the Palatinate of *Posnania*, arriving the 22d at *Gorkidombski*, where he began to canton out his troops; and, having sent advices of his march to his Majesty, he proceeded the 2d of *November* to the Lordship of *Stzrelte*, and on the 24th to that of *Lubin*, where he was greatly surprized to see the King arrive the same day.

His Majesty departed from *Topolno*, accompanied only with his Drabans and his Aid-de-Camp General, all whose horses he so effectually jaded

in

in so long a march, that only one Page, *Klinkow-strom*, accompanied him into *Lubin*.

Mr. *Rheinschild* trembled, when he came to reflect on the danger to which the King his master had exposed himself, the country being filled both with the enemy's parties and robbers. To prevent therefore all accidents and misfortunes, when he saw his Majesty fixed to return the next morning, he detached certain troops for his guard, by which means his Majesty returned happily (*Nov.* 25.) to *Topolno*, after having travelled 34 leagues in two days; neither did he condescend even then to allow himself any repose, but set out the very next day for *Dirschow*, many regiments being already in full march to their winter quarters.

In *Great Poland* several riotous parties embodied themselves to raise certain military contributions called *Hybernes*; and *Smigelski*, Starost of *Gnesnen*, at the head of a great many Gentlemen, made continual inroads into the lands of the Confederates, who complained bitterly to General *Rheinschild* of these outrages, and demanded succours; upon which several detachments were dispatched immediately to give the enemy chace; and one of these, under the command of Lieutenant-Colonel *Zulig*, had the good fortune to surprize a large number, of whom the greatest part were made prisoners.

Soon after this the General set out himself from *Lubin*, to be the better able to take the Confederates under his protection; the army marching in two columns, first to *Ziernewo*, a Gentleman's seat, *Decemb.* 11. to *Skodra*, where the Confederates had their rendezvous; the 12th to the little city of *Zzin*, the 14th to *Ziondz*, the 15th to *Zarodzin*, the 17th to *Plesko*, the 19th to *Kalis*, and

and *Jan.* 1. 1704. to *Blasice*, and from thence to *Siradia*, where the General seiz'd upon the castle, that nothing might be omitted that could beget a confidence in the Confederates, and at the same time convince the Palatinate of *Posnania* how nearly he regarded their welfare.

He was scarce arrived at the last-mentioned place, before the province to which it belongs sent their Deputies to beseech him to lessen the contributions with which they were charged, in consequence of their acceding to the confederacy. Those of *Lencize* and the territory of *Vielune* demanded likewise the same favour; and part of their demand was complied with, to encourage them to unite and continue firm to the article of deposing King *Augustus*, which was on the point of taking place.

All being ready at *Dantzick* for transporting the *Saxon* prisoners, trophies, and artillery, the squadron, under the command of Baron *Claes Sparr*, Vice-Admiral, which was come from *Carelscroon* to escort them, set sail from the road of *Putzig* with so fair a wind, that they soon came in sight of the coast of *Sweden*: but the joy on that occasion was but short-lived; a dreadful tempest the next day (*Nov.* 28.) coming on, which dispersed the fleet, and every ship was glad to make away for the nearest port. However, after they had long contended with the winds and waves, Mr. *Sparr* made a shift to reassemble the greater part of them, and thought it most expedient to steer for *Dantzick*.

One of these vessels, with 500 *Saxons* on board, arrived at *Pilkaw*; but they all made their escape as soon as the Captain had set them ashore at the entreaties of his crew. There was but one ship wrecked, which was on the coast of
Courland,

Courland, and which was freighted with powder and ball. Many *Saxons*, who, by the situation of their country, are little used to sea-voyages, lost their lives upon the occasion, testifying great apprehensions of death, and atoning, after a rate, by their incessant prayers, for the horrible oaths they had uttered to the very moment of their embarkation.

A little while after the fleet set sail again, and arrived in *Sweden* without any farther loss. As to the *Saxon* Generals and Officers of distinction, they were permitted to repair thither by land, as they thought proper, provided they arrived at the time prefixed by his Majesty.

Count *Steinbock* having demanded of the Magistrates of *Elbing* free passage for the *Swedish* troops, who were upon their march to their winter-quarters in the Bishoprick of *Vermia*, and, likewise, that they should immediately throw a bridge over the river near that city for that purpose; they did not presume to refuse it openly, but nevertheless made no preparations to put it in execution, alledging in excuse a great many false pretences, and, among the rest, that the *Brandenburg* troops, quartered in their suburbs, had forbid their compliance with that demand. Count *Steinbock* immediately resolved to advise his Majesty of this incident; to which he was the more moved, as he easily perceived that the sole reason of this delay was the fear of being punished for having refused some months before to pay the contributions imposed upon them.

The King, provoked with all those delays, but more especially that they should call in foreign troops to their succour, dispatched thither Lieutenant-Colonel *Von Scheven* and Major *Morner* with a letter from Count *Steinbock* to the Magistrates giftrates in his Majefty's name, enjoining them to anfwer categorically, whether they were inftantly difpofed to receive a *Swedifh* garifon, or not; who, on their return to the Count, inform'd him, that they behaved as haughtily, as if pride and infolence had turned their brain. Of which the King being advifed, he gave fecret orders to Major-General *Stromberg* to furnifh his regiment of infantry with horfes, and conduct them forthwith to a place called *Rufchow*, fituated between *Marienbourg* and *Elbing*, whither the regiment of Horfe-guards, with that of Major-General *Morner*, horfe likewife, had orders to repair at the fame time. On the other hand Lieutenant-Colonel *Schewen*, at the head of an hundred men, was commanded, under covert of the night, and by marching a long way about, to feize upon two fluices a league and a half from *Elbing*, by the help of which that city might lay all the adjacencies under water.

When all thefe preparations were made, we began to march at 11 o'clock at night, having firft given notice to the *Pruffian* Commander at *Elbing* of his Majefty's defign to pafs through that city.

The King was accompanied by the Prince of *Wirtemberg*, General *Morner*, Count *Steinbock*, and Colonel *Lagerfkrona*. As to Major-General *Stromberg*, he had pufhed on before with fome horfe to take poffeffion of certain prames, by the help of which he propofed to pafs the river in the dark, and poft himfelf on the other fide. But, when he came to the place, all thefe prames were already on the other fide; upon which he called to the *Pruffian* guards to fend them over; and being anfwered, that they durft not without express orders from their Officers; he sent a Captain of Horse, with some few Troopers, to cross the river in a little shallop with all possible silence, who, after some warm language on both sides, returned with the prames at the instant that the King arrived with the Horse-Guards. His Majesty, the Prince of *Wirtemberg*, the Generals, and about thirty horse, passed over immediately, and advanced towards the city to examine the avenues, as far as the ditch, without being suspected: but the guard at one of the gates at last taking the alarm, demanded the word; and receiving no answer, fired several shot, by which one horse was killed.

The King, to avoid a discovery, then retired full speed to the suburbs, where he lay as close as possible; but soon after sent Colonel *Lagerskrona* with a trumpet to the Magistrates, to demand once more whether they persisted in their refusal to satisfy his Majesty, by admitting a *Swedish* garrison. In this interval the King, who had passed over all his cavalry, posted them in all the avenues round the city; and, about 9 o'clock in the morning, Mr. *Lagerskrona* returned, and signified to his Majesty, that the city desired three hours time to deliberate on the proposal, when they would send Deputies with the resolution they had taken. The King took advantage of this opportunity to advance his troops as near the walls as possible, which were so concealed behind the houses, gardens, and hedges, that the city perceived nothing of the matter. Which done, the term demanded expired, and no Deputies appearing, his Majesty, growing impatient, sent Count *Steinbock* into the city, with express orders to stay but one quarter of an hour, and to demand absolutely and in few words their final resolution.

tion. The Count found the Senate still assembled, and, having made a lively representation of the extreme peril which their obstinacy would expose them to, if they exasperated his Majesty any farther, and that in such case the utter ruin of the city would be unavoidable, he induced them at last, partly by arguments, and partly by menaces, to open their gates, and submit themselves to the King's clemency; with which resolution the Count return'd to his Majesty, whom he found surrounding the city, and examining the fortifications.

As soon as the gates were opened, the King made his entrance, and immediately visited the ramparts, &c. giving orders for the three regiments to march in at the same time. His Majesty then made choice of his own quarters, and, by mere chance, pitched upon a house where his illustrious grandfather, *Charles Gustavus*, of glorious memory, had formerly lodged with his spouse *Hedwige-Eleonora*, born Princess of *Holstein-Gottorp*.

After the King had given what farther orders he thought proper, the Magistrates, terrify'd for the mistake they had committed, in exposing themselves so rashly to the resentment of so formidable a conqueror, besought the honour of throwing themselves at his Majesty's feet, together with their fellow-citizens, to implore his forgiveness. To this they received an answer in writing, which exemplified all the provocations they had given, and thence insinuated how unworthy they had rendered themselves of his Majesty's clemency: In conclusion it condemned them to pay 200,000 crowns contribution-money, beside the 50,000 imposed at first, and 10,000 more for not having sent, last summer,

1704. summer, the hundred waggons which had been demanded of them, for transporting to the camp before *Thorn* the ammunition sent from *Sweden*.

This writing spread a general consternation through the inhabitants of *Elbing*; but, as they knew their collusion with respect to the *Brandenburg* troops was discovered to the King, they durst not alledge the least thing in their own excuse, and, at the end of two days, offered to pay the whole money required of them; after which they were admitted to kiss his Majesty's hand.

When we were thus masters of the city, we visited the arsenals, where we found 180 pieces of cannon, great and small, (what belonged to the Republic and the *Saxons* included) abundance of ammunition, and 160 quintals of powder; all which was put under a strong guard of *Swedes*. We then disarmed 500 soldiers in the city pay, and made 400 *Poles*, who were part of the troops of General *Taube*, prisoners of war, together with the military commander of the city. The next step we took was to demand of the *Prussians* in the suburbs to surrender their quarters to the *Swedes*, who wanted room in the city, and were beside to be reinforced by a regiment of foot, then in full march to the place; which arriving a few days after, the King ordered two regiments of cavalry to march to their winter-quarters in the Bishoprick of *Warmia*.

Count *Schlippenback*, Major-General of *Prussia*, repaired about this time to *Elbing*, and had an immediate audience of the King; after which, and certain conferences had passed between him and Count *Steinbock*, he order'd his master's troops to retire, excepting only a few men, who, for the sake of certain pretensions of his *Prussian* Majesty

Majesty on the territory of *Elbing*, were permitted to remain.

The Court, the *Drabans*, the regiment of Foot-Guards, and that of *Dahl-Carlia*, having quitted their quarters at the same time, which were in the neighbourhood of *Topolno*, marched through *Neuberg*, *Meve*, and *Marienbourg*, towards *Elbing*. Some troops were left at *Graudentz* to levy contributions. Colonel *Axel Sparr* continued at *Strasburg*, and Lieutenant-Colonel *Claes Bond* joined him with certain cavalry, to lay all the country above *Dribentz* under contribution.

As to the King of *Poland*, ill-satisfied with what had passed in council at *Jawarow*, Decemb. 10. he set out for *Cracow*, where he kept his *Christmas*, and afterwards repaired to *Saxony* to convene the estates of that country, and demand of them a free gift and succours.

The ill state of his affairs, however, did not hinder him from passing his time agreeably at *Leipsick*, where he did not seem to regard much what happened in *Poland*; having only order'd 5000 of his troops to assemble themselves in the best manner they could in the neighbourhood of *Cracow*, there to wait his return.

The King of *Sweden*, on his side, having waited only at *Elbing* the arrival of his Court and the *Drabans*, set out the next morning (*Dec.* 15.) for the village of *Neukirchen* (3 leagues,) proceeding thence to the village of *Braunsberg* (2 leagues,) where the *Prussian* troops then were, but decamped at our arrival. From *Braunsberg* we marched on through *Toldorff* (2 leagues) and *Lichtenau* (2½ leagues) to *Hielsberg*, the residence of the Bishop of *Warmia*; where the King took up his quarters,

1703. quarters, *Decemb.* 22. and continued all the winter.

The troops attending his Majesty were lodged in the houses of the gentry and peasants, where they were quite at ease, and fared well. The rest of the army extended from *Warmia* as far as the country of the *Cassubes*, and from thence along the *Vistula* as far as *Thorn*[b].

The morning after his arrival at *Heilsberg*, his Majesty, who never lost sight of his design to dethrone King *Augustus*, proposed to the Confederates, who were more and more exasperated every day, Prince *James Sobieski* to be head of the Republic, by a publick declaration, dated *Decemb.* 23.

The Cardinal had already published his *Universalia* to convene all the Nobility of the kingdom at *Warsaw*, *Jan.* 14. But as he found there only a few Deputies, he deferred the opening of the Diet to the 30th; when the Deputies of the Confederates being there assembled from all parts, and seeming disposed to deliberate seriously on the means to procure a solid peace, and give all imaginable satisfaction to the King of *Sweden*; he, who saw well enough their inclinations, but, to all appearance, did not believe they had taken the necessary measures to dethrone King *Augustus*, or for some other reasons, so well concealed his sentiments, that the assembly did not intend at first to declare the throne vacant, tho' some persons proposed it.

This Prelate, to keep up the strictest decorum, did yet more; and even sent King *Augustus* ad-

---

[b] All our troops in *Poland* and *Prussia*, at the end of this campaign, amounted to 17,700 foot, 9,500 horse, and 4,000 dragoons, without reckoning the four new regiments which the King had raised.

King Charles XII. *of* Sweden.

vice of all that paſſed. The intention of the Diet, as has been ſaid, was only to eſtabliſh a firm peace with the King of *Sweden*; and, as the Cardinal had intreated his Majeſty to ſend thither his Commiſſaries to begin the treaty, Baron *Arwid Horn*, Major-General, had a commiſſion for that purpoſe, together with the Reſident *Wachſlager*, who arrived at *Warſaw* firſt, and had immediate audience of the Cardinal.

The Congreſs was opened ſome days after with a proceſſion, at which the Cardinal aſſiſted at the head of the Deputies, with a taper in his hand. To this ceremony ſucceeded a ſolemn maſs and ſermon, at the concluſion of which his Eminence repaired to the place of holding the aſſembly, where he expreſſed himſelf to this purpoſe:

' That tho' the councils of *Thorn*, *Marien-*
' *bourg*, and *Jawarow*, as well as the Diet of
' *Lublin*, were not able to effect the peace ſo
' much deſired; but, on the contrary, had pro-
' duced nothing but afflictions and diſappoint-
' ments, he had nevertheleſs made it his ſtudy to
' remove the obſtructions; that, for this end, he
' preſented himſelf, as one bearing his croſs, and
' called upon to contend for that liberty, which
' was the ſole ſupport of the Republick: that
' he thank'd the illuſtrious Confederates of *Great*
' *Poland* for having united themſelves to him,
' as the children of Peace, and exhorted them
' to perſevere: That, tho' his Majeſty was re-
' tired, he would not however abandon the throne,
' deſiring to repreſent, if not Majeſty, at leaſt
' the idea of Majeſty, as having always had the
' good of his country at heart, even to the pre-
' judice both of his health and intereſt.

The LIFE and HISTORY of

After he had finished, the Marshal of *Great Poland* complained, that that part of the Republic had been treated as if in rebellion, both by the contempt thrown upon it by the Diet of *Lublin*, and the excesses committed there by the *Saxons*; and that, for these reasons, the Confederates had thought proper to put themselves under the protection of his Eminence.

On *Decemb.* 31, in the morning, they proceeded to the election of a Marshal of the Confederacy; and the choice fell upon Mr. *Bronitz*, Starost of *Pisdriski*, and Marshal of *Great Poland*, the same who had before declaimed with such vivacity and courage; who immediately took the oath, and received his staff of office. Some days after they enter'd into conference with Major-General *Horn*, who was now arrived at *Warsaw*, and had produced his credentials in quality of Commissary, authorizing him to negotiate a peace with *Poland*, and receive proposals for that purpose.

During these transactions, the King levied new contributions, as well in the Bishoprick of *Warmia*, as in the *Werders* of *Dantzick* and *Marienbourg*, which were to defray the expences of a new regiment of Foot and four of Dragoons. Count *Steinbock* raised one of these regiments, Colonel *Meyerfelt* the second, and the Aid-de-Camp-Generals, Messieurs the Barons *Taube* and *Duker*, in complement to their distinguished merit, the other two. Lieutenant-Colonel *Ekeblad* had the regiment of Foot, which consisted of 1200 men.

At the same time a promotion was made of Colonels and General-Officers. Baron *de Spens*, Lieutenant-General, and Colonel of the Horse-Guards, was made General of the Horse, and
Inspector

Inspector of the Fortresses and Reviews in the realm of *Sweden*. Baron *Frolich*, Lieutenant-General, was created General of Foot, and Governor of *Riga*. Baron *Charles Morner*, Major-General, was made Lieutenant-General, and Inspector of the Reviews and Fortresses of *Sweden*. *Alexander Stromberg*, Major-General, was promoted to be a Lieutenant-General, and Governor of the Province of *Geole* in *Sweden*. Major-General *Ridderhielm* was appointed Lieutenant-General and Governor of *Wismar*, in the room of the late General *Liewen*, killed at the siege of *Thorn*. The Majors-General *Nieroth* and *Horn* were made Lieutenants-General; the last being continued notwithstanding in his post of Captain-Lieutenant of the *Drabans*.

Baron *Charles Creutz* was made Colonel of the Horse-Guards in the room of General *Spens*. Lieutenant-Colonel *Burenscholdt* had the regiment of *Ostrogothia*, cavalry, before commanded by General *Morner*. Baron *Gustavus Horn*, Quartermaster of the *Drabans*, succeeded Mr. *Ridderhielm* in the regiment of *Nordor-Scania*, cavalry; and Lieutenant-Colonel *Charles Ornstedt* to that of *Suder-Scania*, after General *Stromberg*.

Some little time after this, by a new promotion, the Colonels *Lagerskrona*, *Hummerhielm*, and *Meyerfelt*, were declared Major-Generals. As to Mr. *Hummerhielm* he had been detained prisoner all this while in the hands of *Wisniowiski*, after the affair of *Dorfuiki*, nor was exchanged till *March*, against Mr. *de Goltz*, a *Saxon* Colonel.

King *Augustus*, after having dispatched the Palatine of *Culm*, *Jan*. 6. as his Embassador to the *Czar*, in spite of all the remonstrances of numbers of Senators and Generals of the Crown

1703. to the contrary, had still continued in his hereditary dominions, as hath been already said, to assist at the opening of the assembly of the States: which, at length, taking place, he demanded of them, among other aids, 500,000 crowns and 16,000 new levies, all which was cheerfully granted. Having then received by several couriers a melancholy account of the general Confederacy of the Nobles at *Warsaw*, he repaired forthwith to *Cracow*, where he had the shadow of an army, both to cover that place, and expect the issue of a crisis which held all *Europe* in suspense, tho' not believed to be so near a decision: Nor had he been there long before it reached him in the most forbidding shape, signifying, that the Confederacy, with the countenance and support of the Cardinal, were on the point of declaring the throne vacant: That the Marshal had proposed to reduce it into an act; that the *Swedish* Commissaries absolutely refused to treat before the article of the deposal of *Augustus* was confirmed; and that at last, *Feb.* 6. after some slight debates, the following resolution had been taken.

'Since the most serene King *Augustus*, Duke
' of *Saxony*, has neither observed our laws, nor
' regarded our rights, and that, by the tenor of
' the *Pacta Conventa*, we are absolved from our
' allegiance, we now renounce it, and take the
' exercise of justice into our own hands. We
' likewise discharge his Senators and Mini-
' sters, and will no longer adhere to him. We
' declare all those to be enemies to their coun-
' try who assist in his councils; and we intreat
' the most eminent Primate to publish the inter-
' regnum, to officiate in the distribution of jus-
' tice

' tice and the care of the finances, and to pre-
' pare the conditions of a new election.

Some days after, this declaration was confirmed by the subsequent resolutions.

' 1. That two forms of an oath should be
' agreed upon, one for the Senators and Officers,
' and the other for the Nobles, which all, who
' joined the Confederacy, should be obliged to
' take.
' 2. That the said oath should be taken before
' the Marshal and Deputies of each Palatinate,
' of which they should give a certificate.
' 3. That, when they had provided for their
' safety at home, they should proceed to guard
' against what might happen from abroad ; and
' that the Marshal should convene the Commis-
' saries of the Republick to assist at the treaty,
' the project of which shall be framed by men
' of experience and capacity, and afterwards re-
' ferred to the Marshal.
' 4. That, during the inter-regnum, his Emi-
' nence shall convene the *Russien Pospolite*.
' 5. That, as the Dietines of *Little Poland* ap-
' proached, the instrument of the general Confe-
' deracy should be signed, and deliver'd into the
' hands of the Cardinal Primate, the Marshal,
' and the Deputies, to be sent to each of the
' said Dietines respectively.

Agreeable to these resolutions, the oath was forthwith taken by the Senators and Deputies, and instant advice of all was given to his Majesty by the Starost *Wiouski*, to whom it was sent at *Heilsberg*. King *Augustus*, now seeing affairs take so malicious a turn, preconceiving beside his enemies would not stop here, but proceed to the choice of a new King, resolved, with the Council of those Senators who still attended him, to consider the assembly at *Warsaw* as illegal, and consequently both to treat them as rebels, and declare all their resolutions null and void.

The *Czar*, at the same time, writ to the Cardinal, the Senators, and the Orders of the Republic in the most pressing terms, and even menaced them with the utmost rigour, if they persisted in their design of dethroning King *Augustus*.

As *Augustus* suspected that Prince *James Sobieski*, son of the late King of *Poland*, would cabal for the crown, and likewise knew he was both greatly favour'd by the Nobles, and esteemed by the King of *Sweden*, he thought it expedient to find out ways and means to arrest him.

Prince *James* received notice in time; but, whether he did not believe it, or despised the danger, as not imagining they would dare to seize upon the Emperor's brother-in-law in *Silesia*, the dominions of the Emperor, he continued quite at ease as before, and took no one measure to avoid the snare: so that one day, being in the road from *Breslaw* to his castle at *Wolaw*, 30 *Saxon* horse, with certain officers under the command of Mr. *Wrangel*, who had lain perdue, arrested him, and, without loss of time, conducted him to *Leipsick*, together with his youngest brother Prince *Constantine*, who would not leave him. They were both lodged in the castle, and were treated with all the honours due to their rank.

King

King Augustus did not fail to send the news to the Emperor, and ordered a memorial, at the same time, to be laid before the Diet at Ratisbon, containing the reasons which induced him to proceed to this extremity: what effect it produced in Poland we shall see presently.

The King of Sweden now saw himself solicited on all hands not to drive his enemy to extremities. The Queen of England, in particular, writ to him in the most obliging [c] terms, to persuade him to a reconciliation; Count Zinzendorf likewise presented him a memorial on the same subject some time after. But neither had any effect; his Majesty sending orders notwithstanding to General Rheinschild to march towards Cracow in order to surprize Augustus, who, after having persuaded the Palatines of Siradia and Lencizi to accede to the Confederacy, advanced with his

[c] All sorts of expedients were tried to bring about a peace; and, as it was well known, his Majesty emulated the great Gustavus-Adolphus, the following Latin verses, a language which he perfectly understood, were addressed to him from Germany, to induce him to deliver the Empire, as Gustavus had done before him.

Ad invictissimum Suecorum Regem.

CAROLE, vicisti! Sat' est, moderare triumphos;
  Sarmata ab invicto fædera Rege petit.
Da veniam victis; habeat jam Vistula pacem;
  Gloria servato major ab hoste venit.
Huc tua fas & honor semper victricia duxit
  Agmina: nunc alio te bona causa vocat.
Respice triste jugum, quod terris fata minantur!
  Publica felici pendet ab ense salus.
Maxima gessisti, sed adhuc majora supersunt,
  Si quæris Proavis digna trophæa tuis.
Europæ succurre malis, & frange catenas,
  CAROLE; Gustavi sic imitator eris.

troops,

1703. troops, *Jan.* 11. from the city of *Siradia* to *Zlozow*, the 13th to the little city of *Wielun*, the 21st to *Irzebutzow*, a Gentleman's seat near the city of *Jalupu*, and from thence to *Czenstakowa*, a very rich and potent monastery, where *Rheinschild* posted Colonel *Horn* with his regiment; marching with the rest of the army from the other side of *Czenstakowa* to *Redziny*, where he learn'd King *Augustus* was still at *Cracow*, and that his troops were encamped round the city. In order to surprize them therefore he push'd on to the Lordship of *Krusnia*, and, the next morning to *Radomski*, where two companies of the Starost *Bobrowski*, belonging to *Sapieha*, and commanded by *Grusinski*, joined the army.

The *Valoches* here likewise made certain *Saxons* prisoners, who confirmed the intelligence from *Cracow*, which induced *Rheinschild* to hasten thither with the greater speed. Accordingly, *Feb.* 22. he decamped from *Radomski*, and marched to *Zitna*, thence to *Koniespoli*, the 24th to *Siekuzewo*, and the 26th to *Wolbron*, where our van surprized a *Saxon* Ensign with certain soldiers, whom General *Venediger* had detached to observe our motions. But whatever diligence *Rheinschild* used, he could not hinder the enemy from being informed of his approach; and, being arrived the 27th at *Jangorad*, he learned King *Augustus* was already retired from *Cracow*, having first broke down the bridge of communication. The General however marched on a little farther, but finding it to no purpose, he returned to *Jangorod*, from whence he detached in the morning Lieutenant-Colonel *Funk* with 300 horse towards *Cracow* for a supply of provisions for the army. *March* the 1st, he advanced himself to *Zierkovice*, within 2 leagues, where he learn'd that

that King *Augustus* had taken the rout of *Sendomir* to throw a bridge over the *Vistula*, as well to keep the communication free with certain Nobles, who had assembled by his orders at *Osiez*, as to recall one of his parties which was on the other side of the river.

To disperse these Nobles, General *Rheinschild* decamped, having first received the provisions he wanted by Mr. *Funk* from *Cracow*; and, drawing towards *Sendomir*, he repair'd *Mar.* 5. to *Skalmiers*, where the assembly of the Nobles at *Osiez* was confirmed; upon which (the 7th) he hastened his march towards *Slota*, and from thence (the 10th) to *Piestritz*, the 12th to *Schieditz*, and the 14th to *Klimentow*, where he had advice, that, after the bridge near *Sendomir* was broke down, King *Augustus*, not caring to wait the arrival of the *Swedes*, had posted on to *Zavigost*. *Rheinschild* then instantly detached a Captain with forty horse to observe the enemy, who took a *Saxon* Corporal and four soldiers prisoners, by whom he was informed, that King *Augustus* was marching on towards *Pietrovin*, to throw a bridge at that place over the *Vistula*.

In this interval Prince *Alexander Sobieski* had writ from *Breslau* to the Cardinal, to complain of the King of *Poland*'s seizing his two brothers; at the same time aggravating the action, as being committed in the dominions of the Empire, and imploring the protection of the Republic both for them and himself.

This incident did not a little contribute to irritate the resentment and inflame the animosities of the assembly at *Warsaw*, where the letter was several times read, and the arrest canvassed.

They

1704.

They regarded this step of King *Augustus* as an outrage; and the Cardinal writing a very poignant letter to the Pope on the designs of King *Augustus* on the liberties of the Republic, concluded with the seizure of the Princes; ' Children (said he) of a great King, who had ' delivered *Vienna* and guarded *Italy* from the ' *Turk*; who was the idol of his country, the ' admiration of strangers, and the terror of the ' barbarians.

Prince *Alexander*, on his side, not believing himself safe at *Breslau*, and, hearing on all hands the sentiments of the King of *Sweden* in his favour, thought it necessary to throw himself into the arms of a Prince, from whose friendship every thing was to be expected, as he had once already made manifest [d]. But, at his intreaty, to

---

[d] To demonstrate that the friends of the King of *Sweden* had every thing to expect from the gratitude and acknowledgment of his Majesty, a certain wit made the following verses on the death of a favourite dog of the King's, called *Pompey*, whose corps was sent into *Sweden* to be buried. *A very singular note!*

Pompeius *egregius canis, invictissimo* Suecorum *Regi merito charus, in* Polonia *mortuus, inde in* Sueciam, *ne extra patriam tumularetur, transmissus.*

> *Hic est, qui dominum per tela secutus & ignes,*
>   *Dignus* Hyperborei *Regis amore fuit.*
> *Rex amat extinctum, patriamque remittit ad Arcton,*
>   *Sic hosti has etiam sustulit exuvias.*
> Pompei *cineres, & clari nominis umbra,*
>   *Debita* Parhasio *sunt monumenta polo.*
> *Quid modo non præstet fidis Rex gratus amicis,*
>   *Si neque dilecti negliget ossa canis?*

avoid

avoid running any risk on the road, a detachment of 100 horse and 150 foot, commanded by Lieutenant-Colonel *Weidenbeim*, was sent from the garrison of *Posten* to be his guard; who, after having left the foot at *Ranitz*, on the frontiers of *Silesia*, marched on to *Breslau*, and thence conducted the Prince to *Posnania*, without incurring any accident by the way.

Smigelski was extremely desirous of making an attempt, but was too timorous to undertake it, and the Prince with a second escort arrived happily at *Warsaw*.

If the seizure of the Princes *Sobieski* caused such violent agitations among the Confederates, the treaty, lately concluded with the *Czar* by the Palatine of *Culm*, exasperated them yet much more. It contained in substance, ' That there
' should be an alliance offensive and defensive
' between the *Czar*, King *Augustus*, and the
' Republic of *Poland*: That the first should furnish the Republic with 12,000 men at his own
' expence, together with two millions of florins
' *per annum*; and that the cities of *Poland*, of
' which he was master, should be ceded to *Poland*.'

Unquestionable intelligence however was received, that the treaty contained secret articles, contrary to the last stipulation, the *Czar* having reserved to himself the sea-ports; all which augmented their jealousies and resentments to such a height, that they no longer spared King *Augustus*, but proceded at last to a new election.

In *Lithuania* Count *Lowenhaupt* dispersed every where a Manifesto, dated at *Mittau*, Mar. 1.

1704. which was addressed to the Nobles of that province, and invited them to join the general Confederacy at *Warsaw*. *Lowenhaupt* then repaired to *Samogitia*, having first received a reinforcement of 400 foot from the garrison of *Riga*, commanded by Colonel *Stakelberg*. The Count led with him all his troops, which amounted to about 3000, horse and foot; his design being both to supply himself with provisions, and likewise reduce the inhabitants to reason.

To this purpose he marched through *Samogitia* towards *Lithuania* and the city of *Chelm*; and, that he might have nothing to fear from the garrison of *Birsen* and the parties of *Oginski* behind him, he left Colonel *Stakelberg* and Major *Appelman* at *Linkau*, which is three leagues from *Bauske*, and six from *Birsen*, with some hundreds of infantry and a thousand horse; who surprized the Regimentary *Odakowski** and 600 *Poles* not far from *Birsen*, and totally routed them. In the mean while *Lowenhaupt*, having continued his march from *Chelm* towards the city of *Keydan*, so managed it, that all the Nobles of those parts appeared disposed to declare for the Confederacy; designing to proceed farther still, if Mr. *Stakelberg* had not given him hope, on the credit of certain deserters from the garrison of *Birsen*, that he might render himself master of that city only by appearing before it. He resolved therefore to try what might be done, and returned with all his troops towards that city, but found the garrison in so good a state, and so disposed to de-

---

* This Regimentary afterwards submitted himself to the protection of the King, *April* 29.

fend

fend themselves to the last extremity, that he gave over the enterprize. It was however attended with this advantage, that he discovered by it what were the designs of the enemy: For he was scarce approached, but the *Russians*, posted on the frontier, began to make such motions, as obliged him to return into *Courland*, to observe their measures, and suit his own accordingly.

The King, who had never yet quitted *Heilsberg*, about this time took a resolution to visit the quarters of the army. Setting out therefore the 12th of *March*, accompanied by the Prince of *Wurtemberg*, and his ordinary train, he repaired first to *Dantzick*, where the guard in the suburbs refused him admittance, as not knowing he was the King; upon which his Majesty put spurs to his horse, and rid over the centinel, passing through the suburbs without interruption, and continuing on his way to *Putzig*, where Colonel *Clerk* and his regiment were in garrison, and where he arrived very late.

The guard admitting no body after it was dark, before they had given notice to the commander; and the King growing impatient, found, after a little search, a place in the palisades, where he could pass through; and, taking the Prince of *Wurtemberg* with him, scaled the ramparts, and went strait on to the quarters of Mr. *Clerk*, whom he found in bed, and greatly surprized to see his Majesty, without having been advertised of his arrival. The King made but a short stay, only visiting the fortifications, and giving orders for the transportation he designed; after which he returned directly to *Heilsberg*, where he found Count *Stanislaus Lescinski*, Palatine of *Posnania*, who was arrived from *Warsaw* with several propositions from the Confederates.

Stanislaus was a young Lord, between 20 and 30 years of age, perfectly handsome, well made, and polite. He was the son of the General of *Great Poland*, who was afterwards made Treasurer of the Crown. The famous Count *Raphael Lescinski*, his great grandfather by the mother, was the grand General *Jablienowski*, so loved and honoured by the Republic. The young Count *Lescinski* was made Senator of the realm and Waywode of *Posnania* at the age of twenty-one, as well in compliment to his personal merit, as his high birth.

He had audience of the King the next morning after his return, being commissioned to entreat his Majesty to honour the Confederacy with his constant protection, and to declare himself in favour of the person whom the Nobles should proceed to elect; as likewise to represent the necessity of gaining over the crown-army, which was to be done by distributing among them certain sums of money.

The King replied to the Count, ' That he
' would confirm the instrument of security which
' he had given out the year before, without
' pretending to dismember the provinces or
' lands of the Republic.' That, when the inter-
' regnum should be declared, and they should
' elect a new King, he would withdraw his
' troops, and lend the Republic 500,000 crowns
' for the payment of their army. That, when
' *Poland* had joined her forces to those of *Swe-*
' *den*, his Majesty would leave to the Confede-
' rates all the conquests they should make; and
' lastly, that he would release all the prisoners
' that were yet in the hands of the *Swedes*.

The

The 500,000 crowns were however never paid to the army; for Prince *Lubomirſki*, Great General, who was now among the Confederates, and had repaired to *Warſaw* with ſuch views, as we ſhall ſpeedily unfold, having changed ſides again after the election, and declared anew in favour of King *Auguſtus*, his *Swediſh* Majeſty look'd upon himſelf as under no tye, to perſons whoſe love or hatred were equally inſignificant, and from whom he had nothing to hope or fear.

This occaſion furniſhed Count *Staniſlaus* with ſuch means to inſinuate himſelf into the affections of the King, that it paved his way to the throne, his Majeſty being poſitive for him only, after Prince *Alexander Sobieſki* had refuſed it.

General *Rheinſchild*, having now quitted *Klimentow*, *March* 17th advanced to *Loſtow*, and the 19th to *Boſſoſum*. In paſſing by the city of *Opatow*, a great number of baggage-boys and ſutlers, being left at ſome diſtance behind, were fallen upon by a party of *Saxons* and *Valoches*, who put the greateſt part to the ſword, and made priſoners of the reſt. The 21ſt we continued our march to *Tarlow*, where the General learned that King *Auguſtus* was at *Pietrowin*, that his bridge over the *Viſtula* was completed, and that a great part of his troops were already paſſed over to our ſide, with intention, as it was ſaid, to attack us.

Upon this intelligence the army was ranged in order of battle; and, after having left the baggage near a paſs with ſome troops for a guard, we marched to the village of *Solecs*, which is ſituated oppoſite to *Pietrowin*. When we were yet a league off, the General, accompanied with ſeveral officers on horſeback, advanced to *reconnoitre* the enemy with the *Valoches*, who having diſcovered

discovered certain persons on the side of the *Vistula*, galloped thither full speed, and returned with a Page of King *Augustus*'s, a Lieutenant of *Janissaries*, and a *Saxon* Ensign, who had followed that Prince and Marshal *Danhoff* a hunting on this side the river; which last had been taken prisoner, if he had not been exceedingly well mounted; and King *Augustus* himself had run a very great risque, if he had not passed the bridge among the foremost. The General then ordered the army to march, and, as there were abundance of bushes along the brink of the *Vistula*, behind which he could easily conceal his infantry, he led the way himself, and the cavalry followed him to the bridge-foot, where the enemy had thrown up certain works, and had posted 300 foot to defend them.

Rhenschild immediately ordered the attack to be made sword in hand, and, after a very slight resistance, obliged them to retire with great confusion to their barks and prames, which they had collected together, after having first turned adrift above a third of the bridge, to hinder us from passing over. On the other side of the river they had planted 13 cannon, with which they fired incessantly, but with such poor success, that we had but 9 either killed or wounded.

After having lodged the infantry in the redoubt, and left Colonel *Hamilton* with 500 horse to cover them, the General marched in the same order towards the nearest villages, where the regiments were distributed; but there being a scarcity of forage, we removed a league farther off, to an estate of *Danhoff*'s, called *Lipkow*.

The 27th at night King *Augustus* ordered the rest of the bridge to be broke down, which the stream lodged on the enemy's side: He likewise ordered

ordered his prames to depart at the same time, the greatest part of which were laden for *Casimir*; which gave our General some reason to fear the design of that Prince was to break up the Confederacy; more especially, as it was reported he had received a reinforcement.

To prevent which misfortune, he decamped from *Lipkow*, drew towards *Warka*, and marched on to *Kazzanow*; from whence he repaired the 2d of *April* to *Godow*, thence to *Jedlinka* and *Gustow*, and arrived the 8th at *Warka*, where he distributed his regiments along the other side of the river of *Pilsa*, which passes near that city, and discharges itself a little below into the *Vistula*.

He threw at the same time some infantry of the regiment of *Sudermanland* into the city of *Novamiasto*, which was at the other extremity of our quarters on the same river, for our security on that side; and on the 22d of *April* advanced half a league with his whole army: But, being informed, that King *Augustus* was returned to *Sendemir*, where he had thrown over a bridge, and posted a strong garrison in the city to intrench himself there, and resolving not to lose sight of him, he passed the *Pilsa* at *Novamiasto*, arriving *May* 4th at *Przitalowise*, and the next morning at *Sporzina*, near the city of *Srinno*.

The Palatine of *Posnania*, at his return to *Warsaw*, did not fail to inform the Cardinal and the Confederates of the good intentions of his *Swedish* Majesty with respect to the Republic, and the resolution he had taken to pay the crown-army, in case they joined their forces to his; which Prince *Lubomirski* the Grand General agreed to do, and was already arrived at *Warsaw*, where so favourable a declaration from the

1704. King of *Sweden* spread an univerfal joy. In the beginning of *May* they proceded to declare the throne vacant, and to invite the Dietines to repair to *Warfaw* by the 19th of *June*, in order to elect a new King; and, at the fame time, notified the refolution they had taken on that head to his *Swedish* Majefty; who, as foon as the interregnum was publifhed, gave orders to his Commiffaries to enter into treaty with the Republic. On which occafion they were conducted with great pomp to the place of affembly, where General *Horn* read a paper, which contained in fubftance, ' That the intentions of the King his ' mafter, tending only to maintain the treaty of ' *Oliva*, to confirm the alliance, and re-eftablifh ' peace, his Majefty had fent him as his Em' baffador: That he was ready to begin the ' conferences whenever they pleafed; and that ' he defired them to name the Commiffaries ' with whom he was to open his negotiation.' Some days after he prefented to thofe Commiffaries the inftrument which the King had promifed them; and the Cardinal, on his fide, fent forth circular letters to all the cities of *Poland* to invite them into the Confederacy.

Tho' feveral pretenders appeared for the throne, the greateft part of the Confederates declared for Prince *Alexander Sobiefki*, a Nobleman of great merit, and as greatly efteemed. But as his brothers were prifoners, whom he tenderly loved, and as he thought their fafety would be endangered if he accepted the crown, he gallantly refufed it, and intreated the Confederates to think of him no more.

Many have believed, however, that the Queen his mother and the Imperial Court had greatly contributed to this refolution of his, by reprefenting senting it as a crown of thorns, and what would ruin him to support it. But, whatever was the motive of his refusal, he persisted in it with firmness and grandeur; and, at the same time, that his conduct might not irritate the King of *Sweden*, he repaired to *Heilsberg*, April 29. to explain the reasons on which it was founded; thanking his Majesty at the same time for the honour of his friendship and protection, which he had extended both to him and his whole house. He staid some days at *Heilsberg*, where he was lodged in the castle near the King; and, *May* 5. returned to *Warsaw*, greatly satisfied with the gracious reception which his Majesty had even been assiduous to give him, but immoveable to the most lively remonstrances that were made to induce him to mount the throne [f].

When it appeared there was no longer any hope of him, several foreign Princes were put in nomination; among whom were the Elector of *Bavaria*, the Prince of *Conti*, Prince *Ragotski*, Prince *Odeskalchi*, and some others. But the Confederates refused them all, tho' nominated by the Cardinal, and demanded for their King a *Piaste*, born in their own country; and, as the King of *Sweden* likewise inclined the same way, there was no more mention made of bestowing the crown on a foreigner.

On an examination then of what *Poles* were qualified to be candidates, much talk at first occurred of the Princes *Lubomirski* and *Radzivil*, the Palatine of *Posnania*, and, above all, Mr. *Opalinski*, a Lord, not only extremely rich and

[f] The day of the departure of Prince *Alexander* from *Heilsberg*, Hard, the Master of the Horse, had the misfortune to be killed.

in great esteem, but who had likewise been upon the list before; nevertheless, as he was exceedingly covetous, he was soon set aside, and withal died soon after.

The majority then agreed upon Count *Lescinski*, Palatine of *Posnania*, both as he was a *Piaste*, and agreeable to his Majesty, whose esteem he had entirely gained; and also, as that choice seemed to be the most plausible expedient to re-establish forthwith the peace and tranquillity of the realm.

Our Commissaries having orders to exert themselves to the utmost in the young Count's favour, the Cardinal at first testified no sort of displeasure to him, nay, even promised not to oppose his election. But the event will soon manifest the contrary, and that he had quite other views. He dissembled nevertheless till the marriage was celebrated between the young *Towianski*, son of the Waywode of *Lencici*, with the daughter of Prince *Lubomirski*, when it was imagined this alliance would have contributed greatly to bring the Cardinal over to the side of the Palatine of *Posnania*; inasmuch as he was esteemed entirely in the interest of the last, and became nearly allied by this match to *Lubomirski*; *Towianski* being his kinsman.

Our Embassadors, whose business was to stickle strongly for the Palatine, were highly pleased to see their affairs in so good a train; not being able to think the Cardinal, after such positive assurances, had any thought of electing the Grand General; for whom nevertheless he laboured, under hand, with all possible ardour, as we shall see by and by.

All being ready in *Sweden* for a fresh transport of recruits for the army, those troops arrived in parties

parties in the road of *Dantzick*. Four new regiments of Dragoons were likewise raised, those of *Stenbock*, *Meyerfelt*, *Taube*, and *Ducker*, who were all in *Prussia*, and ready to march at the word of command.

The King had not reason to be over and above content with the city of *Dantzick*, and that misunderstanding might have been attended with dangerous consequences, if the Magistrates had not thought it expedient to conform forthwith to his Majesty's pleasure. Count *Stenbock* had sent to dispose them to accede to the Confederacy of *Warsaw*; and they, looking upon it as a very critical step, had several times evaded a positive answer.

The King, piqued with these delays, ordered some regiments to march thither, whom he conducted himself; and, *May* 20th, sent a letter to the Magistrates by General *Stenbock*, wherein he prefixed a time for the city to declare itself, and imposed a fine of 1000 crowns, to be paid within an hour after, in case they suffered it to elapse.

As it was dangerous to persist in their obstinacy, or fall into disgrace with a Prince so potent and successful, they accepted the conditions proposed by Count *Stenbock*; and gave it in writing, 'That they not only renounced their
' oath made to King *Augustus*, but likewise so-
' lemnly espoused the Confederacy of *Warsaw*;
' declaring, at the same time, King *Augustus* and
' his whole party enemies to their country:
' That, as his *Swedish* Majesty had graciously ac-
' corded his high protection to their commerce,
' they engaged, on their side, not to assist in any
' manner, directly or indirectly, the enemies of
' *Sweden*, and, on all occasions, to testify their
' zeal for his Majesty's service.

The

The *Dantzickers* likewife paid, upon this occafion, an old debt contracted in 1500, during the reign of *Charles Canutfon*, who, being compelled by *Chriftiern* King of *Denmark* to retire to *Dantzick*, refided there fome years, and at his return to *Sweden*, left behind him twenty odd thoufand crowns, for which they gave a bond, fince found in the archives of the kingdom. As the families of *Gyllenftierna*, *Stenbock*, and fome others, who had allied themfelves with the defcendants of King *Canutfon*, were interefted in this money, the *Dantzickers* were held accountable for it, and obliged to pay it. After which, his Majefty being fatisfied with the conduct of that city, returned to *Heilfberg*, where he made all the neceffary preparations to decamp forthwith, and open the campaign.

We left General *Rheinfchild* at *Sporzina*, near the city of *Srinno*, upon the road to *Sendomir*, where King *Auguftus* was encamped on the other fide the *Viftula*. That General there received intelligence that 18 companies of the crown-army, commanded by *Baranof*, and which had been detached to harafs him in his march, had furprized the Quarter-mafter of the regiment of *Craffau*, named *Korff*, with 30 troopers, and put them all to the fword (except *Korff* himfelf, who was taken prifoner) after a long and obftinate defence, which lafted till their ammunition failed.

The army, having decamped from *Sporzina*, marched to *Ziedlovice*, and from thence in the morning to *Illfe*, proceeding afterwards to *Grabovice*, which is but fix leagues from *Sendomir*, and arrived *June* 3d at *Bodzekof*, having paffed near *Oftrovice* in its way.

It

It was here we learned that the *Saxons* had repassed the *Vistula*; that they had left none but their infantry in the city of *Sendomir*; and that they had even pulled down that part of the bridge which was near the city. Upon which the General detached, some days after, two parties of 300 horse each, the first of which was commanded by Lieutenant-Colonel *Wolffrath*, with orders to take different roads, and both levy contributions and search for provisions; the Nobles of all these parts having abandoned their estates and retired elsewhere.

The same day (*June* 7.) the *Poles*, to the number of 4000 horse, together with 600 *Saxon* troopers, were dispatched by King *Augustus* to make an attempt upon our camp; which accordingly they did at ten o'clock at night, attacking the advanced guard, and killing a Captain-Lieutenant of the *Pomeranian* horse, commanded by General *Mellin*; but, finding more resistance than they expected, retired full speed in quest of our detachments, to whom Mr. *Rheinschild* had sent, to warn them to be upon their guard: But, as Mr. *Wolffrath* did not receive the advice, he was surprized at four o'clock in the morning, when returning in full march to the camp.

The enemy fell in first with Captain *Lowisen*, in the van, and began the attack at the same instant; but *Wolffrath* coming up almost as soon to his assistance, the *Poles*, who, till then, had hid the *Saxons* behind them, opened themselves to the right and left, and, while the last advanced to the front, surrounded the *Swedes* on all sides, and obliged them to make head every where at once.

Wolffrath,

Wolffrath, at first, made his principal push against the *Saxons*, charging them no less than five times, and having, in the beginning, the good fortune to repulse them; but, as the *Poles* fell every time upon his flank and rear, and cut to pieces abundance of his men, he saw no other way to escape, but to fight his way through sword in hand: Turning then all at once upon the *Poles*, he broke, routed them, and, rushing through the midst, at last made a shift to reach the camp, with a Captain of horse, a Cornet, and 140 Troopers, the greatest part of whom, as well as himself, being wounded.

Mr. *Rheinschild*, fearing the same misfortune would befal the other detachment, ordered out immediately 300 horse and 200 foot to sustain Lieutenant-Colonel *Rentes* in case of need. But he had regulated his march so well, according to the notice he had received, that the enemy could never find an opportunity to attack him.

These little advantages obtained over the *Swedes* mightily puffed up the Confederates, who were assembled at *Sendsmir*, in favour of King *Augustus*; and so much the more, as Mr. *Rheinschild* was not strong enough to molest them. These were the Nobles of *Poland*, who, under the direction of Marshal *Danhoff*, declared all those to be rebels and traitors to their country, who had signed the Confederacy of *Warsaw*, allowing them a month's time to return to their duty, and declaring whoever should be proclaimed King an usurper.

'Tis easy to imagine they did not spare the Cardinal any more than the rest; on the contrary, they sent to the Pope's Nuncio to entreat him to induce his Holiness to degrade both him and the Bishop of *Posnania*, and to sequester their ecclesiastic

King CHARLES XII. *of* SWEDEN.

ecclefiaftic revenues for the payment of the crown-army.

King *Auguftus*, accompanied by fixteen Senators, being repaired to the affembly, made a long harangue, in which he declared himfelf ready to take the new oath they demanded of him, profeffed an abhorrence of all abfolute power, and promifed to maintain the laws and liberties of the realm. This was executed *May* 23d, and was received with loud acclamations both from the Nobles and people. The Senators and the Nobles then fwore to and figned the Confederacy, by which they all engaged to attend his perfon, and then adjourned to *July* 1, having firft fung *Te Deum* in the church of *Sendomir*, under the difcharge of the artillery.

The *Czar* likewife, on his fide, contributed greatly to keep them in fpirit by the fuccefs of his arms in *Ingria* and *Livonia*, which gave them reafon to hope every thing.

Lieutenant-Colonel *Maidel*, who commanded our troops in *Finland*, had frequent bickerings, during the winter, with the *Ruffians*, which the *Czar* had quarter'd in *Ingria* at the end of the laft campaign; tho' our forces, who were pofted in the city of *Wiberg* and the adjacencies, were for fome time in perfect tranquillity: But this continued only till the fea was frozen over, when (*Jan.* 14.) a party of about 2000 *Ruffians* paffed over an arm of the fea between *Ingria* and *Finland*, and fell upon an advanced poft, guarded by 60 horfe, which they feveral times attacked with all imaginable fury, but were always bravely repulfed, till they had quite furrounded our troops; and, even then, the officer who commanded them broke his way through the midft of them fword in hand, and happily reached

reached *Wiberg*, 8 men only being killed, and 20 wounded and taken prisoners. The enemy bought this little advantage very dear, and retired without attempting any thing farther.

Some days after, Mr. *Maidel* detached a party over the ice, who, in spite of the deep snows, penetrated into *Russia*, surprized two posts, killed abundance of the enemy, and returned safely with a great number of prisoners.

A little time again after this, in the month of *February*, 1000 *Russian* horse and some foot likewise took their turn to cross the sea, and, tho' vigorously resisted, obliged our advanced guard to retire: who, being reinforced with 100 horse from *Wiberg*, returned to the charge, and obliged the enemy to repass the ice with all possible expedition.

The *Czar* now proposed to enter with considerable forces into *Livonia*, and lay siege to *Narva* and *Dorpt*; and especially as Mr. *Schlippenbach*, being too weak to keep the field, was obliged to withdraw under the cannon of *Reval*. Accordingly he ordered all the regiments in the neighbourhood of *Petersburg* to defile towards *Narva*: He even enlisted the fifth man of all the vassals of his *Boyars*, and sent out parties continually on all sides to *reconnoitre* our troops; one of which was attacked by a little detachment of *Swedes*, less in number, but much more brave, who pressed them so vigorously, that, after losing 20 prisoners, they were obliged to take shelter in certain houses, which, being immediately set on fire, they perished in the flames.

From the beginning of *April* the enemy had held *Narva* blocked up on that side next the sea; whence it was not without extreme difficulty that Major-General *Horn* threw into the city

city one regiment of foot to reinforce the garrison: But, to prevent our doing the like again, they raised certain batteries upon the river, which, thenceforward, cut off all communication.

About the same time our Vice-Admiral *Prou* arrived with his squadron on the coasts of *Wiborg*, and took on board 1200 men, which General *Maidel* designed for *Narva*, together with a vast quantity of provisions: But, as the *Russians* were masters of the entrance of the river, which they had beset with batteries on both sides, they found it impossible to reach the city; upon which they steer'd towards *Reval*, where they disembarked the troops, to join those under the command of *Schlippenbach*.

In *June*, when there was forage for the horse, Mr. *Maidel* took the field in *Finland*, with about 4000 foot and cavalry; and, at the same time, the *Russians* marched towards *Wiborg* with numerous forces, as if they designed to undertake the siege. But this was apparently no more than a feint; for, all at once, they wheeled about, and, having fill'd their whole frontier with troops, sat down before *Narva*, which was now totally blocked up both by sea and land.

In the absence of the *Czar*, General *Schonbek* had, at first, the direction of the siege, but it was, afterwards, committed to Field-Marshal *Ogilvi*, who had been formerly in the service of the Emperor.

As to Field-Marshal *Scheremetof*, the *Czar* had detached him towards *Dorpt* with another army to render himself master of that place; where Colonel *Charles Skytte* had done his utmost to strengthen the fortifications, and prepare for a vigorous resistance.

As this last siege could hardly ever succeed, while the *Swedes* were masters of the lake *Peipus*,

Vol. I.   X   where

where they had 14 or 15 good veſſels, the *Czar* had prepared, in the ſpring, a number of armed barks to back his deſign, and attack thoſe of ours, which, during the winter, had been laid up in the river under the cannon of *Dorpt*; but, as ſoon as the ſeaſon permitted, the Commander *Loſcher* fell down the river to cruize upon the lake, as uſual; which the *Ruſſians* being apprized of, they advanced with their *flotilla* to the iſle of *Porkazari*, which is in the mouth of the *Embach*; from whence they advanced yet farther up the ſtream, and, where it was narroweſt, lined both the ſhores with infantry, through which *Loſcher* muſt neceſſarily paſs: who accordingly puſhed on, without regarding the preparations made for his reception, tho' his veſſels could afford no aſſiſtance to each other, nor make any uſe of their artillery againſt the enemy, who were poſted on very high ground on both ſides, and from whence they killed every man who made his appearance on the deck. It became thus a very eaſy taſk to ſeize them all one after another in a very little time: when therefore the Commander was convinced of his raſhneſs, he blew up himſelf, together with his veſſel, which was called the *Charles*, that he might not be a witneſs of the fatal conſequences [g]. Not above 200 men of all that were on board this fleet eſcaped, and even the greateſt part of them were dangerouſly wounded.

The *Ruſſians* obtained this victory *May* 4, and by it became maſters both of the lake *Peipus* and the river *Embach*, by which they tranſported 8 or 9000 men within three leagues of *Dorpt*.

[g] The King being informed of this incident, turned to thoſe in the preſence, and ſaid, Loscher *died like a ſea-man, but not like a Chriſtian.*

About the beginning of *June* they made their approaches to that place, blocking it up on all sides, and even ordering their vessels up the river to distress it from thence.

The Governor immediately set fire to the suburbs; and the enemy, on the other hand, threw a great number of bombs and red hot bullets into the city, to favour the opening of the trenches, which was done in three places at one time. We shall see, by and by, an ample detail of this siege, sent to his Majesty by the Governor Colonel *Skytte*. The *Czar* repaired thither in person; and, that nothing might be neglected at *Narva*, he pass'd and repass'd continually, in order to hasten both sieges at once.

Major-General *Horn* was extremely solicitous to convey a letter to Mr. *Schlippenbach*, to let him know how greatly he stood in need of relief; the siege of that city (*Narva*) being open'd *May* 24th in form; the bearer of it fell into the hands of the enemy, which gave the *Czar* an opportunity to try a stratagem, which in part succeeded. As the besieged were confident of immediate succours, he undertook to ensnare them into an opinion that they were really come, in order to draw the garrison from behind their walls.

Accordingly, one dark night, he detached some thousands of men out of his camp, whom he habited in blew like the *Swedes*, and ordered them to appear the next day about two o'clock in the afternoon, at a certain distance from the city, from whence they made certain vollies by way of signal, as directed in the letter. In answer to which, Mr. *Horn*, not doubting but that they were the reinforcement he expected, discharged two pieces of cannon; upon which they advanced towards the city, and feigned an engagement with the advanced guards of the besiegers; who, seeming to be greatly alarmed, struck their tents, and withdrew the advanced guard, which they had posted on that side next the city. In short, they did all that was necessary to convince the besieged that they were preparing for an action. The two armies then advanced towards each other, first discharging their cannon and then their small-arms; and, after continuing a brisk fire for some time, the *Russians* seem'd to give way, and tend towards the bridge, which was over the river, for their preservation.

Mr. *Horn*, being then convinced of the arrival of the *Swedes*, detached, in the heat of the combat, Colonel *Morat* with 150 horse, and Colonel *Loode* with 800 foot, to sustain the troops which he thought were come to his assistance, and concluded to be already victorious. Certain citizens, who believed they were rather going to reap the fruits of a conquest, than a battle, likewise followed the detachment, which soon fell into an ambuscade, that lay in wait to receive them.

The cavalry, being foremost, saved the infantry, and were all cut to pieces, or taken prisoners; in the number of which were a Lieutenant-Colonel, two Captains, and some other Officers. But Colonel *Loode*, who commanded the infantry, having discovered the snare betimes, retired with all speed to the city with his 800 men, without losing one by the way; where he gave the Governor to understand what had happened, and that he had no succours to expect.

This disappointment, however, did not abate his courage; he resolved to defend himself to the last extremity, often making vigorous sallies to incommode

incommode the besiegers, and burning, at times, all the houses in the suburbs, as well as all the trees and bushes that could afford them any cover.

This affair having thus answered the expectations of the *Czar*; and that Prince being inform'd, on the other side, that Major-General *Schlippenbach* was posted between *Reval* and *Narva*, in a place called *Lesna* in *Weyerland*, with three regiments of Horse and Dragoons, which amounted in all but to 1400, he commanded Colonel *Renne* with 8000 to dislodge them from that post. The *Swedes* at first retired; but the *Russian* Commander having overtaken them (*June* 16th) between *Wittena* and *Tillejogi*, they were obliged to face about, and come to an engagement.

Schlippenbach defended himself with abundance of bravery; but, as the *Russians* were greatly superior in number, and he perceived they began to surround him, in order to cut off his retreat, he thought it necessary to prevent them, and retire without loss of time: But, whatever efforts he made, he could not avoid being totally defeated; not above 200 horse making their escape, and the rest being all dispersed, killed, or taken prisoners, among which last was Colonel *Fritz-Wachtmeister*. *Renne* returned strait to *Narva*, the journal of which siege we shall see hereafter.

The King of *Sweden*, having now formed the plan of the campaign, prepared to open it forthwith. His troops quitted their winter-quarters, which they had held in the Bishoprick of *Warmia* and *Polish Prussia*; and, for the better regulation of his march, his Majesty took his rout from *Heilsberg*, thro' the city of *Melsach*, where the regiment of Guards was posted, in order to make

make *Elbing* and the other quarters in his way. The Princes of *Saxe-Gotha* and *Wirtemberg* accompanied him, and, finding all the regiments in good condition, he ordered the whole army to decamp forthwith.

Count *Piper*, together with the Court and the *Drabans*, commanded by Count *Charles Wrangel*, Colonel, during the absence of Lieutenant-General *Arwid Horn* received orders to proceed strait on to *Poland*, through the territories of *Brandenbourg*. These troops marched the first day (*June* 12th, 4 leagues,) as far as *Ottendorf*, the 13th through the city of *Wirtemberg* to *Schavaden* (3 leagues,) the 14th to *Butrin*, a village on the frontiers of *Brandenbourg* (3 leagues,) the 15th, traversing the said frontier, through the city of *Janowa*, towards the village of *Schembroffski* (5½ leagues,) where they rested one day, the 16th; proceeding the 17th to *Krzyvanowa* (2 leagues,) and from thence the 18th to *Prasnicz*, (2 more.)

The regiment of Foot-Guards and that of Horse took the same road, but the other troops different ones, which hindered them from joining all on the same side of the *Vistula*.

The King repaired to the head-quarters at *Prasnicz*, after having ordered the march of the whole army, and rid above an hundred leagues in a few days. From hence his Majesty (*June* the 20th) advanced to *Cziecanowa* (3 leagues,) the 21st to *Novamiasto* (3 leagues,) whence he led the way the 22d to *Zalkrotzin*, a village upon the *Vistula*, in order to chuse a commodious place for passing over his troops. The same day the Court and the *Drabans* marched (4 leagues) to the village of *Muttelin*, where the *Bug* discharges itself into the *Vistula*. At this place the King

King halted for some days, and, after all the baggage had passed over in prames, his Majesty (*June* 25.) followed with the *Drabans*, and marched (2 leagues) to *Tratzowa*, four leagues from *Warsaw*.

When General *Horn* had received advice of the King's approach, he set out to meet him, and communicate the present posture of affairs, with whom his Majesty repaired to *Warsaw*, where he gave audience to the Cardinal-Primate, to Prince *Lubomirski*, Grand General, and many other Senators: with the Primate, in particular, he had a long conference on the person he recommended to be elected King.

All things were already ripe for that august ceremony. The Deputies of the Provinces and Palatinates of the Confederacy arrived at *Warsaw* the last month. The assembly was open'd *June* the 9th with a solemn mass and a sermon, after which they repaired to the field of election, where were present the Cardinal-Primate, the Grand General *Lubomirski*, the Grand Treasurer *Sapieha*, the Palatines of *Posnania*, *Siradia*, and *Lancicia*, together with his son; the Crown-Cup-Bearer, and the Grand Marshal of the Confederacy, with the Deputies.

The Starost *Bronitz*, Marshal of the Confederacy, had been unanimously declared Marshal of the Diet of Election, and the session, after some debates, put off to the 16th, when several foreign Princes, already mention'd, were proposed, but all as soon rejected; the Confederates being resolved to give no ear to any but a *Piaste*; and the greatest part of them declaring in behalf of the young Palatine of *Posnania*, whose election our Commissaries had orders to support to the utmost.

The Cardinal had feigned, till then, that he would not oppose him, waiting the conclusion of the marriage of young *Towianski* with the daughter of Prince *Lubomirski*, and which the Palatine of *Posnania* labour'd to accomplish, in hope, by that means, to win *Lubomirski* over to his party, as believing himself already secure of the Cardinal.

But, notwithstanding all this, as soon as these nuptials were solemnized at *Warsaw*, his Eminence pulled off the mask, and declared openly he had never any intentions of contributing any way to the elevation of the Palatine to the throne; Tho' he had before proposed him to Mr. *Horn*, who was so shocked at this double-dealing of the Cardinal's, that he expressed himself upon the occasion, at a conference held some days after, in the most pointed terms, which put an end to all farther harmony between them.

This, however, did not hinder the Cardinal from labouring openly for Prince *Lubomirski*; nor could the instances of Prince *Sobieski*, who interested himself vigorously for the Palatine, nor the considerable offers made by the last to Madam *Towianski*, cousin and intimate friend to that Prelate, nor, in short, all the endeavours of others engage him to alter his sentiments.

As, moreover, the Marshal of the Diet greatly inclined to side with *Lubomirski* and the Cardinal, he knew so well how to manage matters with the adherents of that party, that they started continual difficulties, and spun out several sessions, without coming to any conclusion at all.

It was at this juncture the King of *Sweden* arrived, and demanded instantly their proceeding to the choice of a new King, recommending, at the

the same time, the Palatine of *Posnania* to be exalted to the throne. Some days after which (*June* 29th) his Majesty having drawn the army to *Blonia*, nearer *Warsaw*, that neighbourhood, and his peremptory declaration for the Palatine, struck a terror into the contrary party.

The Cardinal then applied himself, by all imaginable means, to defer the election till the arrival of Prince *Lubomirski*, brother of the Great General, and Chamberlain to the Crown, who was on the road with some thousands of *Poles*; in hope that, if he was present at the election, he might be able to carry his point by a plurality of voices.

On the other hand, the Palatine's party, perceiving the intention of the Cardinal, made such lively and effectual remonstrances, that the 2d of *July* was fixed for the election, without admitting the least mention of any farther delay. In the interval, however, the Cardinal and Grand General were importuned incessantly to give up their pretensions, and repair to the field of election, but without effect; they pretended indisposition, to excuse themselves, and demanded continually to have the nomination postponed to the 4th, because, by that time, they expected the arrival of the Chamberlain.

On *Saturday*, the day appointed for the election, the Bishop of *Posnania*, the Constables of *Bresz*, *Cujava*, *Radzious*, *Czersk*, and *Inowlodaw*, with all the Nobility, repair'd to *Kolo*, the field appointed for that ceremony, about 3 o'clock in the afternoon. After which, the first step that was taken was to send Deputies yet once more to the Cardinal, the Grand General, the Palatines of *Posnania*, *Siradia*, *Lancicia*, and *Podlachia*, with an invitation to join them. But the Cardinal

1704. Cardinal continued stedfast to his first proposal of deferring the election to the day following; Prince *Lubomirski*, who was with the Cardinal, did the same, and both promised, on that condition, to be present at the assembly.

The Palatine of *Lancicia* and the Constable of *Plosko* declared to the like purpose. Those of *Siradia* and *Podlachia* excused themselves on account of their infirmities, and added, they would approve of all that should be done. The Palatine of *Posnania* alone repaired to the assembly, followed by the Gentlemen of his party.

After the Deputies had made their report, the Marshal of the Election, in support of the party of *Lubomirski*, did not fail to represent how much precipitation was to be feared in a choice of such importance; that there was yet much remaining of the term prefixed for that ceremony; that it was not usual to proceed to the election till towards the close of that term; that, by waiting a little longer, the Deputies of the Palatinates of the realm might yet arrive, and, by their presence, render the election more legitimate; and finally that, to render it in all respects authentic, it would be unpardonable, for a few days, more or less, to overlook the representations of the Primate and the principal Lords of the realm.

On the contrary, those, who sided with the Palatine of *Posnania*, easily perceiving the drift of their antagonists, refuted, in the amplest manner, the reasons which had been alledged; and made it appear with great force, that, in the present situation of the Republic, they had not a moment to hesitate; that all delay was to be extremely feared; that customs, perhaps very dubious in their natures, were not to be deemed laws;

laws; especially in *Poland*, where the Republic had power over the laws themselves, and could change them at pleasure; that they did not conceive what end these demurs could answer, unless to set the whole realm in a flame; that, as to his Eminence and Prince *Lubomirski*, they had nothing to reproach themselves with, having used all honest and fair means to reduce them to reason; and lastly, that they knew not what to make of their conduct, which appeared so much the more extraordinary to the Confederates, as it was visibly contrary to their good intentions.

Upon this the debate grew more and more vehement, and lasted even to sun-set. As the *Swedish* Commissaries had great reason to fear they would again postpone the election till another time, they made their utmost efforts to win over their opponents, as well by the arguments they urged, as by their entreaties and exhortations.

They were well supported by the Bishop of *Posnania*, who besought the assembly to have no regard to the absent, nor to the sentiments of the Senators, who were for electing Prince *James Sobieski*, because his confinement put it out of his power to accept of the crown. Upon which certain persons threw up their bonnets into the air, and cried out, *Vivat* STANISLAUS *Rex!* But almost at the same instant certain others, who were the Deputies from *Podlachia*, put in their protests to that election, by as loudly interposing a *Niepofvelem*.

Mr. *Jeralski*, in particular, one of these opponents, took occasion to say he would never consent to that election, at least till the treaty was signed and concluded with *Sweden*; to which he added many other reasons to justify his dissent:

But

1704. But all this serv'd only to excite great clamours against him, and to renew the acclamations in favour of the Palatine of *Posnania*. At last the Bishop of that place, having first signified, that those who would not give their voices had nothing to do but to withdraw, proclaimed *Stanislaus* King of *Poland* according to the following form: *In nomine Domini nomino Regem Poloniæ & Magnum Ducem Lithuaniæ,* STANISLAUM LESCINSKI, *& precor,* &c.

The new King, at the same instant mounting on horseback, during the incessant discharge of muskets and pistols, and while their bonnets flew into the air, was conducted about 9 o' clock at night towards the Cathedral, where the Bishop of *Posnania* confirmed him before the altar, as was customary, by repeating the *Vivat* three times; after which the *Te Deum* was sung, and a prodigious multitude of people shouted forth their acclamations, as common upon such occasions.

'Tis easy to judge how deafening these were to the ears of the Cardinal and *Lubomirski*; who, seeing it would be fruitless now to oppose the election any longer, came immediately to acknowledge the new King. A little after which the Chamberlain *Lubomirski* arrived at *Praag* with 60 *Polish* companies. He had already sent, when some leagues off, an express to Lieutenant-Colonel *Claes Bonde,* who was posted in that place with an hundred horse, to demand an escort of some hundreds of men to guard him safe to *Warsaw,* a *Saxon* party being continually at his heels. *Bonde* immediately repaired to him with the few he had, and conducted him in security to his journey's end; where he had the mortification to be informed the election was

over,

over, and that he had nothing to do but make his submission, according to the example of others; which he did immediately, and paid his compliments to the new King; as the Ladies, on the other hand, did to the new Queen.

The King of *Sweden*, who had not stirred out of *Blonia*, was, that night, about 11 o'clock, agreably surprized, by his Page *Klinkowstrom*, with the news of the election of King *Stanislaus*, who did not fail to notify it in form to his *Swedish* Majesty the next morning, and instantly received in return a letter of felicitation, equally polite and affectionate: After which both the Kings mounted on horseback to meet each other half way, where, having embraced with all the tokens of the most perfect friendship, they entered into close conference for several hours, none but Count *Piper* being present, to deliberate on the most effectual means to re-establish the peace of *Poland*, and for ever remove their common enemy, King *Augustus*.

The Confederates had importunately demanded, a long time before, and during the election, that the King of *Sweden* should enter into alliance with them; and his Majesty had not only promised it, but had already entered into a negotiation with them, with assurance that, when the election should be made, he would put the last hand to it. As, therefore, he was always tender of his word, he did not fail to nominate three Ambassadors immediately to treat with the new King and the Republic; which were Lieutenant-General *Arwid Horn*, as first in the Embassy, the Secretary of State *Wachslager*, who had been long Resident in the Court of *Poland*, and Mr. *de Palmberg*, Vice-President of the Tribunal of *Dorpt*.

The

The necessary instructions were likewise dispatched as fast as possible, for their conduct to the new King, and for concluding a firm alliance with *Poland*.

It will not perhaps be disagreeable to insert here the following piece, writ by Mr. *Wachslager* some days after the election.

An extract from a French *letter from Mr.* Wachslager, *Secretary of State, to Mr.* d'Adlerfelt, *who was then at* Blonia, *and who had put several questions to him on the situation of affairs at the election.*

'WHEN it was thought proper to put a
' period to the *inter-regnum*, and pro-
' ceed to the election of a new King, the royal
' house of *Sobieski* was at first preferred to all
' others. But, after the confinement of Prince
' *James*, and the obstinate refusal of Prince
' *Alexander* to accept a Crown, which he thought
' would be of thorns, and might perhaps be
' purchased with the loss of his brothers, many
' foreign Princes were talked of at *Warsaw*, as I
' acquainted you yesterday; but to no purpose;
' the Confederates being resolved to have none
' but a *Piasto*, and having the King to support
' them in it.

' The first of which upon the list was *Opa-
' linski*, on whom they had already cast their
' eyes. He was extremely rich, but, at the
' same time, odious to all the world for his ava-
' rice; over and above which, he died when he
' was talked of most.

' The Cardinal then proposed several other
' *Piastos*; and, in a conversation with General
' *Horn*, particularized Prince *Lubomirski* and the
' Palatine

' Palatine of *Posnania*; of which the General
' having informed his Majesty, he received in-
' structions to support the latter, as the most
' worthy and best inclined. His Eminency af-
' terwards seemed disposed to retract what he
' had said, not denying, 'tis true, that ever he
' named him, but asserting he nominated him as
' the last and youngest of the two. But he was
' given to understand, that he was the most
' agreable to the King, as well for his capacity,
' as for his birth and eminent qualities, and
' likewise that he was favoured by the Deputies
' of *Great Poland*.

' The alliance between the houses of *Radzie-
' owski* and *Lubomirski*, by the marriage of *To-
' wianski* with the daughter of the last, had in-
' duced the Cardinal to espouse the same in-
' terest; and it was even believed, that, if
' his Eminency had succeeded, the office of
' Crown-General had fallen to the share of *To-
' wianski*.

' As to the rest, the election was made *July*
' the 2d; and it was endeavoured even to
' have brought it on sooner, but without effect.
' The Deputies of *Podlachia* only dissented;
' who nevertheless declared openly, they did
' not disapprove the choice of *Stanislaus*, but
' could not agree to an election on that day,
' especially as the Cardinal and several other Se-
' nators had promised to assist at the assembly
' the *Monday* following; maintaining, that, as
' those persons were absent, the action was both
' deprived of its lustre, and was deficient in
' form. Nevertheless, they afterwards came
' over unanimously, and by their solemn acces-
' sion gave as much force to the election, as if
' all those Lords had assisted in person.

After

After all was settled entirely to his Majesty's satisfaction, he took leave of King *Stanislaus*, in the same place where they had their first interview.

July 9. *Charles* decamped from *Blonia*, and gave orders to all his regiments to march towards *Javigost*, where General *Rheinschild* was likewise to post himself the 14th with his army; which set out in the evening from *Bozekow*, and marched through *Bidzini*.

But first General *Rheinschild* detached Lieutenant-Colonel *Zulich* with the cavalry towards *Sendomir*, from whence King *Augustus* had retired so precipitately towards *Jaroslaw*, that he left behind him a magazine well furnished, of which Mr. *de Zulich* rendered himself master.

His Majesty's first day's march was from *Blonia* to *Mezanow* (4 leagues,) where the army rested one day; after which (*June* 11) they proceeded to *Bialla* (2¼ leagues,) the 12th to *Novamiasto* on the river of *Putze* (3 leagues,) where they again rested one day. The 14th they marched on to *Przystik* (4 leagues,) from thence the 15th and 16th through the city of *Radom* to *Cobillani* (4¼ leagues,) the 18th to *Zerwona* (2 leagues,) the 19th to *Borrga* (4 leagues,) then to *Wisnutow* (2 leagues,) and lastly to *Sendomir* the 23d (three leagues,) where his Majesty ordered a bridge to be immediately thrown over the *Vistula*, in order to join the army under General *Rheinschild* at *Javigost*, which had been in that city ever since the 14th, as before mentioned.

During these transactions, our Embassadors at *Warsaw* made the necessary preparations for receiving their publick audience of King *Stanislaus*; and, after all was agreed upon with respect to the ceremonial, which was to be observed on that occasion,

occasion, the 19th of *July* was fixed for the publick entry, which was made in the manner following.

The Embassadors, being repair'd to the cloister of the *Carmelites* in the suburbs of *Leczna*, on the side of the new city, were there received and complimented by three Senators, which were the Palatine of *Siradia*, and the constables of *Inowladislau* and *Plosko*. They were attended thither by the King's equipages, and a great number of the coaches of the Nobility, that were sent to accompany the Embassadors; which last were seated in the King's coach of state, together with the Senators, who sat in the boot: And Mr. *Albedhyl*, Marshal of the Embassy, being mounted on horseback, before the coach, the procession began towards the palace, accompanied by a great number of the Nobility, both in coaches and on horseback. Before the gates of the city, a party of cavalry, belonging to the crown-army, were ranged in one line, and those of the Grand General in another, between which the Embassadors passed to the sound of drums, trumpets, and other martial musick. The streets of the city were lined by the Grand General's infantry. In the outer court of the palace the Cardinal's guard was drawn up. In the inner court 200 *Swedes* appeared under arms; and the balconies of the palace were filled with musicians.

When the Embassadors had quitted the coach, they were complimented at the foot of the great stair-case by Mr. *Poninski*, Master of the Horse and Marshal to his Majesty. The Senators before named waited upon them up stairs, and at the same time gave them the upper hand. At the first entrance above, Prince *Lubomirski*, the Grand

1704. Grand Chamberlain, received them, and conducted them through the Guard-chamber of the *Drabans*, as far as his Majesty's apartment, where the Great-Treasurer of *Lithuania* and Count *Sapicha*, who officiated as Chancellor, received them; and when the King, who was under a canopy of crimson velvet, observed them entering, he advanced some paces towards them, and immediately after returned to his place. The Embassadors then ranged themselves abreast opposite to his Majesty, and put on their hats; after which General *Horn*, the first in the commission, began his speech in *Latin*, and, at the conclusion, presented his letters of credence to his Majesty. Count *Sapieha* replied in *Latin* likewise to the General in behalf of the King.

After the audience was over, the Embassadors repaired, together with the Senators, to the Queen's apartment, to whom Mr. *de Horn* made likewise a compliment in *Latin*, it being the language used in *Poland*, even to their Queens, upon a first audience. At their entrance their Excellencies were covered; but, when the General began his speech, they put off their hats in complaisance to the sex. The suffragan of *Gnesna*, Chancellor to the Queen, returned her Majesty's reply, which was in *Latin*, as well as the former.

The Embassadors then waited on Madam Royal, the mother of the King, but unattended by the Senators, who received them at the entrance of her third apartment, the treasurer *Sapieha* leading her by the hand; they were then conducted to three elbow-chairs, where being seated, they conversed for some time in *French*; and, when they took their leave, were received by the same Senators in the hall, which

which leads to the King's apartment, and conducted to the stair-foot, from whence they returned with the same train as before.

Immediately after this audience the conferences began in the place appointed, and the foundations were laid of a solid and lasting peace and strict alliance between the realms of *Sweden* and *Poland*. The *Polish* Commissaries being the Bishop of *Posnania*, Prince *Lubomirski* Grand-General, the Palatines of *Siradia* and *Podlachia*, the Constable of *Inowladislau*, Mr. *Poninski*, Deputy-Master of the Horse, and several others, who laboured in earnest to put the last hand to the treaty.

It was before remarked, that Major-General *Lowenhaupt* had marched with some thousands of men into *Lithuania* to support the Confederacy, and to render it agreeable to the Nobility, and after what manner he afterwards returned towards the frontiers of *Courland*.

Count *Sapieha*, Grand-General of *Lithuania*, then judged it necessary for his interests, instead of following his Majesty, as he had done till then, to march with his troops into that province, in order to join *Lowenhaupt*. Accordingly he set out, while the King was yet in his winter-quarters at *Heilsberg*, and pass'd through *Prussia* in his way to *Courland*. But Prince *Wisniowiski* had no sooner received intelligence of this motion, but he assembled all his troops to hinder his junction with the *Swedes*; and, marching night and day with all possible diligence through roads little frequented, he came within two leagues of *Sapieha* before he had the least notice of his march.

Notwithstanding which, as Count *Lowenhaupt*, who was well served by his spies, had received information of it time enough to reinforce *Sapieha* with 600 horse, *Wisniowiski*, tho' above 4000 strong, had not courage enough to make the attack, but returned the way he came towards *Birsen*, to be within reach of *Oginski* and the *Muscovites*. By which means Count *Lowenhaupt* had opportunity to join *Sapieha* at his leisure, in a place called *Wobotnicki*; and, having afterwards received a reinforcement of certain infantry from *Riga*, resolved to go in quest of the enemy.

But *Wisniowiski* and *Oginski* apprehending his approach, kept themselves carefully on their guard, and retired into *Lithuania* towards the city of *Cauno*. We pursued them however for several days, tho' to no purpose; except that our fore-runners, now and then, fell in with their rear, of whom they killed several, made 50 or 60 prisoners, and seized certain carriages, in which were some thousands of *Polish* florins, with the Chancery of *Oginski*, by which we discovered his correspondence with the *Muscovites*; as will appear from the following letter, dated at *Poniewies*, from Count *Lowenhaupt* to Secretary *Diepenbroock*, who was then at *Mittau*.

SIR,

'SINCE our march from *Wobotniki*, it has
' been impossible for me to write to you,
' having been ever since in pursuit of the ene-
' my's army, under the command of Messieurs
' *Wisniowiski* and *Oginski*: and never did hare
' make more speed to escape the hounds, than
' these Gentlemen have done, through marshes
' and roads almost impracticable, to avoid being
' forced into an engagement with our troops,
' tho' greatly inferior in number. Certain of our
' fore-runners have nevertheless made above 50
' of

'of them prisoners, together with almost as
'many horses, some carriages, and a sum of
'about 10,000 *Polish* franks in money: Besides
'which, we have seized the papers of *Oginski*,
'among which are some of great consequence,
'especially the copy of a private treaty between
'*Lithuania* and the *Czar* against our Sovereign;
'and certain *Muscovite* letters, of which we un-
'derstand nothing, as having no body here to
'interpret them.

'At present the enemy is near *Birsen*, endea-
'vouring to persuade the *Muscovites*, their only
'hope, to join them, which last were the day
'before yesterday making their terms with
'them, first scrutinizing into the number and
'goodness of *Wisniowiski*'s infantry, and then
'insisting on an oath from all the Generals, Offi-
'cers, and even soldiers of the army, not to
'desert them on any emergency whatever; as
'if fear would not break through all the oaths
'that could be invented, or God had not power
'to render them fruitless. We are obliged to
'wait their resolves; and, if they venture to at-
'tack us, I hope, through the Divine assistance,
'we shall be able to give a good account of
'them. I am, *&c.*

P. S. 'Great numbers of deserters flock to us
'daily; and the last comers give us to under-
'stand, that the enemy expect every hour a new
'reinforcement of *Muscovites*: But that gives
'us no apprehensions; for the good God, in
'whom we confide, will be our safe-guard. If
'Major-General *Schlippenbach* could make a di-
'version in *Livonia*, it would be a very great
'assistance; for then we might be almost cer-
'tain, with the help of Heaven, to master both

'*Wisnia-*

The LIFE *and* HISTORY *of*
' *Wisniowiski* and the *Muscovites* of *Birsen.* You
' would do well in sending a copy of this letter
' to the King's Chancery.

Mr. *de Lowenhaupt,* believing it no longer of any importance to follow an enemy, who fled with such precipitation to avoid the encounter, halted, to see if it would give them spirit to make the attack themselves. But *Oginski* had only made this tour from *Cauno* to *Birsen* to solicite succours from the *Czar.* Provoked at the triumph of the *Sapiehas* his enemies, he never once hesitated to draw into his country, already ruined by his private quarrels, the forces of a Prince, which he would be obliged to subsist; tho' the reflection was so natural, that the province must suffer more from the *Muscovites* than the *Swedes,* because the last were so much fewer in number.

During this interval, Count *Sapieha* convened an assembly of the Nobles at *Poniewies,* to induce them to accept the Confederacy of *Warsaw*; and he had the pleasure to see many of them give their assent accordingly.

Wisniowiski, on the other hand, did the same in one of the cities of *Lithuania,* where he assembled the Nobles to accede to the decree of the Diet of *Lublin*; having it principally in view to enfeeble the first assembly by this division of the Nobility: And his design had such fatal success, that, from this time, their animosities arose even to a dreadful pitch of inhumanity; each party in turn treating the other with all imaginable cruelty, as often as opportunity offer'd, as will appear by the following example.

Count *Zawiska,* Starost of *Minsko,* having been detached by Count *Sapieha* with 900 men, marched

marched about the middle of *June*, with great secrefy, through vaft woods and places little known, towards *Druga* (30 leagues,) to ruin a magazine which the *Mufcovites* had eftablifhed there; which he fucceeded in, and at the fame time furprized 500 Horfe and 200 Dragoons, the greateft part of whom were put to the fword.

Wifniowifki and *Oginfki* had, at laft, finifhed their bargain with the *Mufcovites*, after ufing all manner of expedients to induce them to it; the laft not caring to have any thing to do with a nation, which abandoned its allies in the greateft extremities, nay even in the heat of battle, as was evident from all their paft conduct. The *Lithuanians* therefore were obliged upon oath to combat like men, and truft to their heels for fafety no more.

After having thus united their forces, they refolved to lay fiege to *Seelburg*, an old caftle in the country of *Semigalle*, upon the frontiers of *Courland*, in which was a garrifon of *Swedes*; where being arrived to the number of 14 or 15 thoufand men of both nations, they continued before it ten days, and then prepared for an affault.

In the mean while the Counts *Sapieha* and *Lowenhaupt* advanced to raife the fiege with all their troops; and thofe of *Sapieha* had the good fortune to take 300 carriages on the march, which had been fent under a ftrong efcort from *Birfen* to the *Lithuanian* camp before *Seelburg*; the plunder confifting of an entire fervice of plate, a fum of filver coin, and a large quantity of powder and ball.

The enemies were no fooner advertifed of the approach of our little army, and the advantage which we had obtained upon the road, but they raised the siege, and retired in haste beyond the frontier; insomuch that, when our troops came before the place, they found no signs of them, but the ladders and other necessaries of a siege, which they had left behind. *Sapieha* and *Lowenhaupt* however followed the chace immediately, and, at a place called *Jacobs-stadt*, two leagues from *Seelburg*, obliged them to face about, and come to action.

Mr. *de Lowenhaupt* attacked them first, after having ranged the troops of *Sapieha* behind him to cover his rear; when the *Lithuanians*, without once recollecting their oath, made off instantly with the utmost precipitation, leaving the *Muscovites* to shift for themselves as well as they could; who, having been joined that very day by a considerable reinforcement of Dragoons, and amounting in all to about 5000 men, stood their ground for some time with abundance of obstinacy, but were at last obliged to give way, and abandon the field of battle. The troops of *Sapieha* then did wonders, in slaughtering those who could not defend themselves, which they continued to do till night put a stop to the execution; in which time the enemy lost about 3000 men.

Mr. *de Lowenhaupt* took all their baggage, their cannon, together with their trophies, and a great number of prisoners, among which were several *Swedes*, whom the enemy had carried into slavery, and for some time led about with them. *Oginski*, after this defeat, which he could not recover for a long time, repaired to the *Czar*, who was still wholly taken up with the siege of *Narva*, which advanced every day, tho' the enemy had not yet begun to bombard that city.

In the mean while Vice-Admiral *de Prow*, whose fleet consisted of one ship of the line, five frigates, five brigantines, and a fire-ship, undertook to ruin the works which the enemy had raised in an island called *Rutisari*, situated between *Ingria* and *Finland*, about four leagues from *Petersburg*.

The *Czar*, finding the situation of that island very advantageous for covering his new residence (of which this might be considered as the outwork and barrier, because it lock'd up, as one may say, the entrance of the *Neva*, leaving open but one single passage for ships to the South, that to the North being impracticable for want of depth) had already erected there certain batteries; and, preparing to build, on a bank of sand, separated from the island by the passage above-mentioned, a castle, known since by the name of *Cronslot*, he had posted there all his fleet, consisting of 42 gallies, 7 frigates, and many other vessels, to cover the works as they went on.

Advice of this new enterprize of the *Czar* being soon conveyed to *Sweden*, and it being already foreseen of what dangerous consequence this fortress would prove to us, if an early attempt was not made to take possession both of the streight and the island itself; but, which is hardly to be accounted for, no supply of forces was sent to the Vice-Admiral, to enable him the more effectually to execute a design of such vast importance. This however did not deter him from making the experiment with his little squadron in the month of *June*, but without success, because of the strong batteries which the enemy had raised, and the great fire which was made upon him from all the *Russian* vessels.

Not

Not discouraged with this disappointment, he embark'd on board his ships a thousand men, which were under the command of Lieutenant-General *Maidel* at *Systerbeck*, again set sail, *July* the 15th, towards *Rutisari*; and at his arrival finding but 1500 men left to defend the new works, the castle not yet finished, and the *Russian* fleet absent, landed his troops, and attacked the enemy so briskly, that he first dislodged them, and then routed them entirely, seizing upon all their cannon, and taking prisoners all that had escaped the edge of the sword. The attack was begun by Lieutenant-Colonel *Rose* and Major *Leyon*.

Some time after this, the *Czar* having sent out his parties on the side of *Wiborg* to observe Mr. *de Maidel*, one of them consisting of 2000 Horse and 200 Horse-Granadiers, made an attempt on that General's camp at prayer time, in hope to take his troops unprovided. But they greatly deceived themselves; Mr. *de Maidel* giving them so warm a reception, that, after a short contest, tho' sufficiently bloody, he put them entirely to flight, and held them in chace with the sword over their heads almost as far as *Nyen*; but, before they reached that place, they faced about within a little quarter of a league of a defile, and made a stand to dispute the passage, but were again so vigorously attacked, that they retired in great confusion under the cannon of one of their men of war, which lay near the fortress.

Mr. *de Maidel* then saw himself obliged to give over the pursuit, greatly chagrined that he could make no attempt on the fort of *Nyen*, for want of vessels to pass the river; but, before he returned, set fire to several little magazines, as well

well on the side of *Noteburg*, as on the river towards *Petersburg*.

The city of *Dorpt* now saw itself under a necessity of surrendering to the *Czar*. As the besiegers had kept their cannons and mortars continually in play, both houses and churches were laid in ruins, and two large breaches appeared in the walls. The besieged, on the other hand, had neglected nothing that could preserve the place, and give his Majesty time to send them succours, having even made some sallies, tho' with little success.

July 13th the *Russians* made their assault, and met with a resistance as vigorous as the attack: But, in the end, the besieged being overpowered by numbers, and the enemy lodged under the very gates of the city, the Governor, Colonel *Charles Gustavus Skytte*, was obliged to capitulate, as we shall see more amply in the detail of the siege, written by himself.

April 16th, Commadore *Loscher de Hertzfelt* received orders from Major-General *Schlippenbach* to fit out his squadron, and be ready to enter the *Peipus* to observe the enemy.

May 3. the said Commadore, being now equipt, sailed out of the road of *Dorpt*. The *Russians* were two leagues from the mouth of the river of *Embach*, near an island called *Porkazari*, by which the Commadore was obliged to pass in his way to the lake *Peipus*. As that officer then entertained his friends on board his ship, and at every bumper discharged his cannon, the enemy, who heard the report, advanced to engage him; and he, on the other hand, having been advised of it, made as much haste to meet them; but, being intoxicated with wine, began the action with all the rashness imaginable, in a narrow
part

part of the river, three leagues from *Dorpt*, where the ships could be of no assistance to each other; by which means the enemy, who had lined the high shores on both sides with infantry, made themselves masters of the whole fleet, ship after ship.

The 4th, between six and seven in the morning, the *Russians* had taken 14 vessels; upon which the Commadore, determined not to survive his misfortune, set fire to the powder, and blew himself and his ship up into the air: after which the enemy landed 9000 men three leagues from *Dorpt*.

June 2d, the enemy advanced to *Kirimpal*, where they began to throw a bridge over the river: This I endeavour'd to prevent, by sending thither several detachments to harass them; which not being strong enough to compel them to desist, were obliged to return to the city.

The 5th, the enemy sat down before *Dorpt*, and invested it from the lands of *Kopkoja* to those of *Tannenhof* and *Muhlenhof*, and across the river as far as those of *Hasselau*.

The 6th, the fleet advanced up the *Embach*, and I order'd the suburbs to be burnt.

The 11th, the enemy completed a battery on the other side of the *Embach*, near the gallows, and pushed the trench with vigour.

The 14th, the enemy began, towards the evening, to throw their bombs from a battery of eight mortars, making thirty four single discharges in all.

The 15th, they threw twenty seven bombs, and opened their trenches before the *German* and *Russian* gates.

The 16th, they threw but eighteen bombs.

The

The 17th, a day of fasting and prayer, they threw but few bombs.

The 18th, the like.

The 19th, they began to fire with great violence, throwing no less than 200 bombs, which damaged abundance of houses, and more especially the *Swedish* church.

The same day the enemy finished their bridge over the *Embach*, near *Quistendahl*, and pushed the attack vigorously in several places at once; that is to say, from the camp near *Rathshof* on the road of *Narva*, to the East of the city from the *Embach*, where they carried on their approaches towards that side of the city, which extends from the *Pinotorne* to that of *Russia*, and from thence to the *German* gate; 2. Behind the lands of *Kopkoja*, and on the road to *Riga* to the South of the city from the *Embach*; from whence they drew a line towards a place called *Mistberg*, battering continually the second, third, and fourth bastions, and endeavouring to advance under the new counterscarp; 3. To the North of the city, near the village of *Jehelfer*, proceeding on to the West of the *Embach*, and pushing the trench on the side of the fifth bastion and St. *James*'s gate.

The 20th and 21st, the enemy threw above five hundred bombs.

The 22d, they threw three hundred eighty two more, which damaged the magazine and the *German* church.

From the 23d to the 24th, towards noon, they threw one hundred sixty seven bombs, beside red-hot bullets.

The 24th, they had carried on their approaches from the quarter of *Tekelfer* to within thirty paces of St. *James*'s gate, where they erected a battery.

The 25th, they cannonaded the fifth bastion furiously, and threw eighty four bombs, and the next day two hundred and forty more.

The 27th, we fired with great violence on both sides.

By the 28th we had eighty soldiers and about an hundred burghers and peasants killed, and were almost buried among the ruined houses; which afforded a dreadful spectacle, and became yet more calamitous, as I had no other lodgings ready even for the reception of the poor wounded. This did not however prevent my giving orders for a sally from St. *James*'s gate, which was made at midnight, the 28th or 29th, under the conduct of Lieutenant-Colonel *Brandt*.

We killed at first near 200 of the enemy, and made them give ground; but, as my orders were not punctually obeyed, it was not possible either to dislodge them, or ruin their approaches, as I had imagined. *Brandt* there lost his life, with two Captains, two Captain-Lieutenants, three Ensigns, and thirty Soldiers; and two Captains were taken prisoners.

The 29th, we buried the dead on both sides; but they pour'd in their bombs all night long.

The 30th, they discharged one hundred and seven bombs; but made no great fire the rest of the day.

July the 1st, they threw one hundred and thirty bombs.

The 2d, they threw eighty four.

The 3d, they threw a great number of red-hot balls, which burned several houses.

The 4th, 5th, and 6th, they continued quiet.

The 7th, they began to make a breach with twenty five great pieces of cannon, on the gate of *Russia*, and on the wall which led to *Pinotorn*.

They

They fired likewife with fix more on the gate of
St. *James*, and on the fifth baftion; throwing at
the fame time a great number of bombs, from
fifteen mortars, planted in different places. All
which the enemy continued without intermiffion
till the 13th; and it was my care, in the mean
while, to repair the breaches inceffantly, which
were inceffantly made.

The 12th, the enemy drew out a ditch from
the approaches of *Tekelfer*, as far as the *Embach*,
by the help of which they advanced under a
half moon, which had been raifed before the
gate of *Ruffia*, and which was wholly ruined by
their batteries.

The 13th, they fired with incredible fury, and
threw a great number of bombs. At half an
hour after fix in the evening, I obferved the
enemy prepared to make an affault on the half-
moon, which, as mentioned before, lay in ruins,
and gave proper orders to give them a warm reception. The combat was obftinate and bloody,
and the enemy had already made one entrance
through the palifadoes; but a Lieutenant, who
was pofted there, and who had fcarce any powder left, was fo well feconded by certain infantry which I fent to his affiftance, that the enemy
was repulfed, and thrown beneath the ramparts;
neverthelefs, as they remounted continually with
frefh troops, and continued the affault all night,
till fix o'clock next morning (the 14th) we were
not able to make any farther refiftance, efpecially as we were worn out with fatigue; and confequently they penetrated as far as the gates of the
city, under which they made a lodgment. Finding myfelf then in no condition to hold out any
longer, and ftruck with compaffion for the poor
inhabitants, who had all been put to the fword,

if

1704. if I had perfisted in an obstinacy which would have been deemed unpardonable, I ordered a Drum to beat a parley; but he was killed on the spot, and a second met with the same fate: which obliged me to employ a Trumpet next; on which they forbore firing, and I made use of the opportunity to send a Major to General *Sheremetoff*, who returned me likewise another, with whom I concluded the capitulation following.

1. To march out, drums beating, colours flying, and pieces loaded; with six pieces of brass cannon, and twenty four cartridges for each, with all our arms and baggage, and one month's provisions.

" Granted for three companies only, with
" arms; all the Officers to keep their swords,
" but the rest of the garrison to march out en-
" tirely disarmed.

2. Carriages for the sick and wounded.

" Agreed, for as many as can be procured.

3. To march towards *Reval* by the nearest road.

" Granted.

4. That the Officers shall have leave to sell their goods, or at least to leave them, till they have opportunity to fetch them away.

" Granted.

5. That no soldier of the garrison shall, either by menaces, or any other expedient, be seduced from the service of his Majesty.

" Granted.

6. That all the subjects of his Majesty, of whatever rank, shall have free leave to withdraw themselves and their goods under safe conduct to what other place they please.

" Granted.

7. That

7. That the Clergy and Citizens shall be confirmed in their privileges.

" Granted.

8. That if any of them should incline to retire elsewhere, they shall not be withheld by force.

" Granted.

9. That those who should remove their goods to some other place, might have leave to bring them back without molestation.

" Granted.

10. That the fortress should be restored *in statu quo* to his Majesty.

" R. *Casu existente*.

After all things were thus regulated, I marched out with the garrison: But the capitulation was not observed in all points; they obliged the garrison to divide itself into three parties; one of which repaired to *Riga* with Colonel *Tisenhausen*, the second to *Wiborg*, and the third to *Reval*. They likewise deprived the three companies of their best arms, and distributed others among them that were very indifferent.

As to me, they obliged me to follow the *Czar* to *Narva*.

The 25th, all the *Russian* army decamped from *Dorpt*, and began their march towards that city.

August 7th, they obliged me to appear in the approaches and parly with the besieged.

'Tis reckoned they threw five thousand bombs into the city of *Dorpt* during the siege.

CHARLES GUSTAVUS SKYTTE.

The garrison was conducted under a strong escorte to the places above-mentioned, and were furnished

furnished with horses and carriages necessary for the journey. The *Czar*, who to animate his troops had been present at the assaults, took possession of the gates himself the 15th in the evening, and received the oath of fidelity from the inhabitants; and, to engage that people to submit with a good grace, he sent back to their houses all the peasants who had taken sanctuary in *Dorpt*, allowing them safe-guards, exhorting them to cultivate their grounds as usual, and, by way of encouragement, granting them certain privileges for eight years.

As the greatest part of the inhabitants of the open country had retired to the woods, and were dispersed on all sides, the *Czar* promised one hundred crowns for every Gentleman, fifty for every Priest, and twenty five for every Civil Officer that should be brought in to him; it being his desire to win over a people, whom he flattered himself to have soon under his command: At the same time he published a declaration in favour of the *Livonians*, to whom he promised very great advantages, in case they would submit peaceably to his government.

The End of the FIRST VOLUME.

BOOKS just Published,

Printed for J. HODGES at the *Looking-glass* on *London*-bridge.

1. NATURE DELINEATED: Being Philosophical Conversations; wherein the wonderful Works of Providence in the Animal, Vegetable, and Mineral Creation are laid open; the Solar and Planetary System, and whatever is curious in the Mathematicks, explained. The whole being a complete Course of Natural and Experimental Philosophy; calculated for the Instruction of Youth; in order to prepare them for an early Knowledge of Natural History, and create in their Minds an exalted Idea of the Wisdom of the GREAT CREATOR. Written by way of Dialogue, to render the Conception more familiar and easy. In 4 Vols. 12mo. The 2d Edition, carefully revised and corrected, with large Additions, embellished with great Variety of Copper Plates, representing the principal Subjects treated of; with a Table of Contents, and a complete and copious Index to each Volume. Price bound in Calf, 12 s.

Neatly printed in a Pocket Vol. (Price bound in Calf, 3 s.)

2. The History of the Life and Reign of the Czar PETER the Great, Emperor of all *Russia*, and Father of his Country. Containing, 1. His Travels, Studies, and Personal Fatigues, for the attaining of Knowledge in Civil and Military Affairs, and the Improvement of his Subjects. 2. His Introduction of Arts and Sciences, Naval Force, and Commerce with foreign Nations; also his many Reformations in Church and State, the Army, and the Customs and Manners of his People. 3. His Wars with the *Swedes, Turks, Tartars,* and *Persians*; Victories by Sea and Land; Acquisitions of Territory, and Increase of Power. 4. His Regard to Genius and Merit, with the surprizing Instances of his Favour to General *Le Fort*, Prince *Menzikoff*, and the Empress *Catharine*; and his severe Justice on Offenders, particularly in the Proceedings against the rebellious Czarewitz. By *J. Banks*, Author of *Miscellaneous Works in Verse and Prose*, in two Vols. 8vo; adorned with Sculptures, and illustrated with Notes.

3. A Critical Review of the Politiacl Life of *Oliver Cromwell*, Ld. Protector of the Commonwealth of *England*, *Scotland*, and *Ireland*; containing his Alliances, Advances to Popularity, with a View of the Motives to the Civil War; his Military Exploits both at Home and Abroad; his Management towards the Parliament, Army, and the several Parties he had to deal with; his Behaviour towards foreign Princes and States; with a Summary of his Character, and a Parallel between him and King *Charles* I. as to their Natural Abilities, Penetration, Justice in the Administration of Affairs, &c. By a Gentleman of the *Middle Temple*. Price 4 s.

BOOKS just Publish'd,

Written by CHARLES WHEATLY, M. A. Vicar of Furneux-Pelham in Hartfordshire, and sold by J. NOURSE at the Lamb without Temple-Bar.

1. THE *Nicene* and *Athanasian* Creeds explained and confirmed by Holy Scriptures; in a manner adapted to common Apprehensions. In Eight Sermons, preached in part at the Lady *Moyer*'s Lecture in the Cathedral of St. *Paul, London,* in the Years 1733 and 1734; and since completed; with large Additions, Notes, and References, for the Use of the religious and studious Youth in our two Universities.

2. A Rational Illustration of the Book of Common Prayer, &c. Wherein Liturgies in general are proved lawful and necessary, and an Historical Account is given of our own: The several Tables, Rules, and Kalendar are considered, and the seeming Differences reconciled: All the Rubricks, Prayers, Rites and Ceremonies are explained, and compared with the Liturgies of the Primitive Church: The exact Method and Harmony of every Office is shewed; and all the material Alterations are observed, which have at any time been made since the first Common Prayer Book of King *Edward* VI. with the particular Reasons that occasioned them. The whole being the Substance of every thing Liturgical in Bp. *Sparrow*, Mr. *L'Estrange*, Dr. *Comber*, Dr. *Nichols,* and all former Ritualists, Commentators, or others, upon the same Subject, collected and reduced into one continued and regular Method, and interspersed all along with new Observations. Price in *Folio,* 12 s. in *Octavo,* 6 s.

3. An Historical Vindication of the 55th Canon: Shewing, that the Form of Bidding Prayer, before Sermon, has been prescribed and enjoined ever since the Reformation, and constantly practised by the greatest Divines of our Church; and that it has been lately enforced both by his present Majesty, and our Right Reverend Diocesan the Lord Bishop of *London.* 8vo, 1718. Price 1 s.

4. Christian Exceptions to the Plain Account of the Nature and End of the Sacrament of the Lord's Supper. With a Method proposed for coming at the true and Apostolick Sense of that Holy Sacrament. 8vo. Price 1 s.

5. The Qualifications and Blessings of a good Magistrate: A Sermon preached before the Right Honourable the Lord Mayor, the Worshipful the Aldermen, and the Citizens of *London,* in the Parish-Church of St. *Laurence-Jewry*, on *Thursday* the 29th of *Septemb.* 1737. Before the Election of a Lord Mayor for the Year ensuing. 4to. Price 6 d.

32101 074631332

Check Out More Titles From HardPress Classics Series In this collection we are offering thousands of classic and hard to find books. This series spans a vast array of subjects – so you are bound to find something of interest to enjoy reading and learning about.

Subjects:
Architecture
Art
Biography & Autobiography
Body, Mind &Spirit
Children & Young Adult
Dramas
Education
Fiction
History
Language Arts & Disciplines
Law
Literary Collections
Music
Poetry
Psychology
Science
…and many more.

Visit us at www.hardpress.net

Im The Story
personalised classic books

"Beautiful gift.. lovely finish.
My Niece loves it, so precious!"

Helen R Brumfieldon

★★★★★

JANE IN WONDERLAND

LEWIS CARROLL

UNIQUE GIFT

FOR KIDS, PARTNERS
AND FRIENDS

Timeless books such as:

Kids

Alice in Wonderland · The Jungle Book · The Wonderful Wizard of Oz
Peter and Wendy · Robin Hood · The Prince and The Pauper
The Railway Children · Treasure Island · A Christmas Carol

Adults

Romeo and Juliet · Dracula

- **Highly** Customizable
- **Change** Books Title
- **Replace** Characters Names with yours
- **Upload** Photo for inside page
- **Add** Inscriptions

Visit Im The Story .com
and order yours today!

CPSIA information can be obtained
at www.ICGtesting.com
Printed in the USA
BVHW090054280819
556849BV00017B/2681/P